DATE DUE

Marxism
and Education

Routledge Education Books

Advisory editor: John Eggleston
*Professor of Education
University of Keele*

Marxism
and Education

Madan Sarup

Routledge & Kegan Paul
London, Henley and Boston

First published in 1978
by Routledge & Kegan Paul Ltd
39 Store Street,
London WC1E 7DD,
Broadway House,
Newtown Road,
Henley-on-Thames,
Oxon RG9 1EN and
9 Park Street,
Boston, Mass. 02108, USA
Set by Hope Services, Wantage
and printed in Great Britain by
Lowe & Brydone Ltd
© Madan Sarup 1978

British Library Cataloguing in Publication Data

Sarup, Madan
    Marxism and education.
    1. Educational sociology
    I. Title
    301.5'6   LC191   78-40116

    ISBN 0 7100 8944 9
    ISBN 0 7100 8945 7 Pbk

Contents

Contents

Acknowledgments

This short book is an outcome of studying sociology of education with Michael F.D. Young, and teaching it with my friends, Bob Colquhoun and Ian Hextall. Without their help and encouragement it would not have been possible. I also wish to thank my colleagues in the Sociology Department, and am grateful to many friends, in various study groups of which I am a member, for discussing these ideas with me during the last three years – this book is a product of our *collaboration*. As this book is a result of a course of lectures given to my students at Goldsmiths' College, I owe most to them. They have helped me more than they probably realize. In the final stages I greatly benefited from the comments and criticisms of Barry Cole.

The materialist doctrine that men are the product of circumstances and education, that changed men are therefore the products of other circumstances and of a different education, forgets that circumstances are in fact changed by men and that the educator must himself be educated — Marx, *Theses on Feuerbach*

Introduction

This book is an introduction to some of the recent developments in the sociology of education. So much has happened within the last ten years that the subject has been transformed. It is an exciting area. There have been a succession of new perspectives to understand and learn to use, such as symbolic interactionism, ethnomethodology, and social phenomenology. During the same period there has been an explosion in Marxist theory. Not only new texts, but theorists with new interpretations of Marxism have appeared. Part One of the book is an analysis of the 'interpretive', or phenomenological, perspective as it has been applied to education. After a discussion of its strengths and weaknesses, I discuss in Part Two, some Marxist approaches. I focus on these perspectives because I believe they are important ways of understanding our life-world. They are not mere fashions but are developing traditions with complex inter-relationships that appear antagonistic, overlapping, or necessary to one another to different theorists.

I attempt to explore these relationships not as an eclectic, 'free-floating' intellectual but from a certain position. I have a commitment to radical change in education, and the way that we work and live our lives together. It may well be asked: how can a committed writer be a useful guide to the main controversies in the sociology of education? But I think that commitment need not imply a narrow doctrinaire, static view. Commitment refers to the holding of a moral and political principle, such as the creation of a more acceptable world — but one's analysis of the world, one's understanding of it, can be in flux, and continually developing.

Introduction

You may be surprised to see that the usual chapter headings that appear in traditional textbooks are missing. There are no chapters entitled 'Education and social mobility', or 'Family background, values and achievements'. It is my contention that many of these issues do appear in this book, but are presented in an unusual form. Each perspective has its own vocabulary, its own way of seeing and making sense of the world. The phenomenological perspective postulates that we look at issues as if they were 'anthropologically strange'. I have therefore approached many issues by posing questions that are not usually asked in the 'traditional' sociology of education. And so though the titles 'Stratification and Mobility', 'Social Selection', 'Equality of Educational Opportunity' are not to be found, problems concerning human freedom and equality are discussed first in phenomenological, and then in Marxist, terms. The latter approach is valuable because it insists on grasping the relations within a totality, the relations between schools, the family, work and politics. Moreover, all these relations are grasped within a particular society or social formation. Of course it is conceded that the controversies discussed here have not been resolved; they are not of that nature. The problems of what to do to make our lives happier, and the world better, and how to do it cannot be easily settled. But at least a dialogue can begin.

Theoretical Considerations

As the themes of this book are some of the major controversies in social science, an outline of some of the arguments may be useful. The compression of arguments, however, inevitably leads to dry abstraction and so *some readers may well prefer to pass on to the first chapter and return to this summary later*. The main argument is based on the assumption that it is our task to change the world; to make it better, not just less unacceptable. The focus of the book, therefore, is not on the question of social order but of social change. I attempt to ground my discussion of sociological theory always in a lived world—that of education—which teachers, pupils and others experience every day. Though the discussion of sociological perspectives is interwoven and inseparable from educational issues, for the purpose at hand I will outline the theoretical aspects first. What may appear to be turgid here in this 'abstract' will become clearer in the chapters that follow. Broadly, this book discusses three models of social science: the positivist, the interpretive (or phenomenological), and the Marxist. The principal controversies with which the book deals are the following.

A highly critical stance is taken towards traditional sociology and its positivist approach. I do not deal with it directly in any one specific place; it is rejected throughout the book. Positivism is repudiated because it assumes that reality exists unproblematically; it stresses 'scientific' method and statistical measurement, and separates 'facts' from 'values', 'knowledge' from 'interest'. In short, this view presupposes a passive view of man, and, as its connection with behaviourism shows, it is deterministic. This 'scientific' mode has become dominant; a hierarchy has been created between those who possess such knowledge, the experts, and those who lack it. More and more areas of our life are being defined as 'technical problems', removed from political debate and action, with the expectation that the technical experts can solve them. This view of (manipulative or instrumental) rationality leads to what has been called 'the technological view of politics'.

One of the most trenchant critiques of positivism has come from the interpretive model of social science, or more specifically phenomenological sociology. A sympathetic exposition is given of this stance and its critique of empiricism and scientism, its emphasis on intentionality, and the actor's experience of the world. The phenomenological model of man is explicated by a discussion of Sartre's views on human freedom. I suggest that this approach is adopted by many as a conscious corrective to a traditional sociology which denied the significance of actors' construction of meaning. Phenomenologists assert that our consciousness of the world, our knowledge of it, is through interpretation. I then argue that the phenomenological model with its emphasis on complete freedom, and the ability of consciousness to change the world, has idealist shortcomings. Though it stresses that men act in terms of their interpretations of, and intentions towards, their external conditions, it has difficulties in analysing the particular mechanisms by which a particular social structure constrains its members. It is not able to explain how or why certain repressive features in society continue to exist. I then argue that the phenomenological perspective has other inadequacies. It neglects such issues as ideology and false consciousness. That is to say, it fails to look at how reality may be masked in an important way, particularly by obscuring a situation or rationalizing it. Phenomenological sociology, moreover, has little to say about structural conflict within a society, and nothing about a dialectical understanding of historical change. But the fundamental weakness of this model is that its theory of consciousness is insufficient. It stresses mental de-reification at the expense of other aspects. It tends to ignore the material conditions of existence which, though socially produced, have become objectified and cannot be merely 'thought away'. I suggest that the phenomenological perspective – because its basis is philosophical idealism – encourages people to seek change through the way they *think*, instead of providing them with means by which they can change what they or others are doing. Theoretical de-reification, a possible consequence of this perspective, is not enough. There must be a *practical* de-reification – an actual overthrow of social relations through praxis. It is then argued that such an understanding can be provided by Marxist theory.

After having argued that the phenomenological perspective can result in a theoretical de-reification only and not a practical one, a third model, Marxism, is then proposed, overcoming, transcending the contradictions of the other two. The version of Marxism suggested (owing much to Hegel) is anti-positivist, yet retains some of the features found valuable in the interpretive model. By this I mean, for example, the attempt to understand the intentions and desires of the actors one is observing.

I then argue that Marxism was originally a dialectical method in which critical thought was validated by revolutionary action, but that there have been deterministic tendencies within it which stress a logic of history as a causal process. The latter view is rejected because it leaves little room for the notion that history may be created by human action. The 'scientific', causal view leads to a vulgar Marxism which denies the importance of human action. Several forms of Marxism are discussed. First, in contrast to deterministic Marxism, a humanistic view is presented which explicates Marx's concept of alienation. In the latter part of this book I focus upon those versions of Marxism which represent a move towards an analysis of economic and political structures. One of the main arguments of this book is that though economics and politics can give us understanding of capitalism, praxis is required. That is to say, there should be a unity of theoretical understanding and political practice. But we continuously have to face questions such as the precise relationship between our theory and our practice: How do we define for ourselves the unity of theory and practice? Or, to put it another way, how does one resolve the need for adequate understanding, on the one hand, with the need to translate philosophy into social action, on the other? This is a theme which continually reappears in different forms in the book.

Sociological Perspectives and Education

Throughout this book the epistemological and methodological controversies are seen in the context of *education*. I outline a brief description of the main debates below.

My argument is that 'traditional' sociology of education is positivist. It views knowledge and educational categories consensually, as if they were objective, 'out there' and existed in an unsituated, context-free, manner. Positivist sociology of education believes that its method is neutral, but I want to say that it has certain unexplicated assumptions about the nature of man and society. It is suggested that when positivism is used in the social sciences there are certain logical implications that follow. Positivism is connected with technical rationality, with prediction and *control*. I believe that this method, when applied to education, cannot move beyond a narrow reformist, piecemeal, social engineering.

A group of young sociologists, inspired by the work of Michael F.D. Young, challenged the positivist tradition in the sociology of education. He edited the book *Knowledge and Control: New Directions for the Sociology of Education*. I refer to the approach this book exemplifies as 'New Directions', or the 'new' (as opposed to 'traditional') sociology of education, realizing, of course, the limitations of this shorthand. In

5

opposition to a positivist sociology of education, the group mentioned above adopted a phenomenological stance. As this stance begins by not taking anything for granted, it was useful in that it helped to question ('make problematic') notions such as rationality, childhood, education, etc., which had previously been taken as objective facticities.

One of the features of the 'new' sociology of education is its use of anthropological studies. I show how anthropology has contributed to the examination of our taken-for-granted suppositions; it has shown us that there are alternative ways of ordering not only education but life itself. It is argued that, though there are cultural differences, other cultures are not necessarily deficient. The existence of other adequate logics and rationalities challenge the absoluteness of our own categories. In our schools a particular definition of knowledge has become reified. I argue that the divisions that have been made between school and non-school knowledge, the theoretical and the practical, mental and manual work, are not natural but conventional. These 'splits' are not given and absolute, but produced by men in certain socio-historical periods. Believing, then, that prevailing definitions of education are narrow, hierarchical and repressive, the thrust of the arguments is that if we fully realize that ability, intelligence and other categories are historical, man-made constructs, then we will be prepared to think of alternatives.

Anthropology and phenomenology have this in common: they lead to a questioning of what we normally take for granted and make us aware of other ways of doing things, other forms of life. Though the main phenomenological influences were Schutz (and certain aspects of the work of Merleau-Ponty), I suggest the *spirit* of the 'new' sociology, its excitement and sense of open possibilities, is best understood by studying Sartre's work, with its stress on commitment and man's limitless freedom. This questioning of the dominant conceptions of western 'scientific' rationality, education, the curriculum, and the relativization of knowledge, was seen as a threat by traditionalists. I then discuss the conflict between the 'new' sociologists of education and the 'liberal philosophers' such as Peters and Hirst, whose views are so pervasive. My account of this debate is to be read as (the beginnings of) *a case study of an ideology*. My criticisms are basically directed against a certain tradition (that includes Leavis, Eliot, Bantock, Cox, and others), which propagates a concept of culture which is elitist. There are elements of this tradition within sociology too; I refer to those who emphasize 'cultural transmission' and 'social reproduction' in an undialectical manner. But there is, however, an alternative tradition of education and culture, as Raymond Williams has pointed out, a tradition which attempts to show the historical situatedness of knowledge, and its social character. It is argued that the views of the 'liberal philosophers' lead to reification and alienation and that this has implications that are conservative. Education should not be for 'domestication' but for liberation.

It is then argued that one of the main achievements of the 'new' sociology is that it has shifted attention from the home to the school. This leads to a chapter on classroom studies in which there is a review of the literature that examines class-room practices. I focus on the ways in which teachers classify, 'label' children into hierarchical categories, and suggest that it is *the school* that creates 'failure'.

Though the phenomenological stance has immense de-mystifying potential, there are certain problems which it neglects. After a consideration of these problems, it is suggested that the shift towards the study of what is called 'school-knowledge', using a phenomenological approach, meant that some problems tended to be passed over. The radical pheno-menological stance adopted by some of the writers, such as Michael F.D. Young, Nell Keddie and Geoff Esland in *Knowledge and Control* is seen to have some limitations. It is suggested that their work expresses tendencies towards individualism, ahistoricism, a naively idealist 'social con-struction' thesis, and a cultural and epistemological relativism – all problems arising, basically, from a phenomenological stance. These limitations can be exemplified I think in the argument about 'cultural deprivation', and the debate about whether the practices of other cultures represent a deficit or a difference. An anthropological study such as Thomas Gladwin's *East is a Big Bird: Navigation and Logic on Puluwat Atoll* (1970), though useful in making us question our educational categories and distinctions, also raises many problems. In short, many of the critiques of cultural deprivation were insufficiently critical of their own interpretive (phenomenological) framework. The questioning of assumptions, and the power of consciousness to de-reify, are important factors, but by themselves are not enough. They cannot transform the *status quo* and the coercion and oppression we feel. Nevertheless, the new sociology of education offers a valuable critique of an exclusive and hierarchical view of knowledge and has continually stressed the view that the pupils' world has been predefined for them. I argue in the succeeding sections of the book that the contradictions experienced in our schools and in our everyday lives, such as the alienation that ensues from hierarchical relationships and the separation of theory from practice, are aspects of the deeper contradictions of our society. These may be better understood by a reading of Marx to deepen our analysis. Though some significant books on the sociology of education have appeared in recent years, it is noticeable that in most of them Marx is a missing figure. The few books that do present Marxism at all are usually from a very narrow and limiting viewpoint, closing discussion rather than opening it. In this book (chapters 8 and 9) Marxism is presented in such a way that it is not irreconcilable with some of the insights of phenomenology that are also valued. In my attempt to demonstrate this, I particularly stress the influence of Hegelian thought and Marx's achievement in transforming it. There is an exposition of Marx's conception of reality and his philosophy of internal relations; his views on the dialectic and his conception of human nature and work. In my argument I focus particularly on the concepts alienation and praxis. My intention is to present a Marxism that avoids the dangers of determinism and idealism — a libertarian Marxism.

After outlining 'the general logic of commodity production', I argue that the same process takes place in the case of knowledge. Under the conditions of capitalism, education is conducted under such alienating circumstances that it is a process of de-humanization. This has been accurately depicted in the writings of the 'de-schoolers', but their solution — that each individual is responsible for his own demystification — is an idealist one, because what is necessary to overcome it is not only some form of theoretical self-criticism but social action. Theoretical attempts to solve problems such as alienation through a phenomenological emphasis on the power of consciousness alone, inevitably fail because the problem and its solution involve social practice. Radical change has to manifest itself in praxis.

The second part of this book, then, is concerned largely with the Marxist perspective and education. But as Marxism is not monolithic, I move on to discuss several different versions. These include the contributions of the French theoretician Louis Althusser, and that of selected American historians and political economists of education. These latter theorists, in particular Samuel Bowles and Herbert Gintis, argue that the experiences of the workplace are first formed in the school — that there are linkages between family and school to the occupational structure. This is why any discussion of the nature of schooling and the persistent legitimacy of its methods has to take account of the ways in which they are pervaded by economic structures. Therefore I argue that an understanding of the complex inter-relationships between education and the economy must be based on *an analysis of the nature of work and of monopoly capitalism* in the twentieth century. But our central purpose in understanding these different versions of Marxism, in doing intellectual work, should not be forgotten. We should always be asking: How does this help us to formulate a meaningful sociology of education? If our project is indeed human liberation, what kind of alternative theories of education can we construct — and put into practice? This introduction is becoming lengthy; let's begin. Not that we know the beginning, but that a time comes when we have to begin — somewhere.

Part One

Some Features of the New Sociology of Education

Chapter 1

The Injunctions of the New Approach

A new approach has revolutionized the sociology of education. Its main expression and source of inspiration has been the book edited and introduced by Michael F.D. Young, *Knowledge and Control*. Its contributors have differing perspectives and concerns, but the collection of papers, particularly those by Young, Esland and Keddie, expresses criticism of the traditional sociology of education. This 'new sociology of education' has been described as a fundamental change within the sociology of education.[1] What then were its main criticisms of the traditional sociology of education, and what did the alternative approach suggest we do?

Michael Young begins the 'Introduction' by making two criticisms of the prevailing conception of sociology of education: the absence of theoretical discussion, and the failure to question the assumptions on which much of the 'conventional' work is based. Serious debate had been limited to the 'problem of order' in areas such as stratification, deviance and politics, and discussions of the work of Durkheim, Weber and Marx are rarely included in the traditional textbooks on the sociology of education. By the 'problem of order' I mean the problem of how society manages to cohere. Durkheim, Weber and Marx held differing views about this. The traditional, Durkheimian, view is that individuals cannot create and maintain order, and that constraint, through internalization, is therefore necessary for society to exist. Society must define social meanings *for* individual actors who are merely a reflex of the social system.

The second criticism is that in the past sociologists accepted educational problems, and their own implicit assumptions are

13

'taken for granted'. They raised important issues, but they did not examine or question their basic presuppositions such as, for example, what it was to be educated. By treating 'what it is to be educated' as unproblematic, or consensually agreed, their work could be utilized for the purpose of legitimation of the existing political order.[2] In other words, we should not take for granted existing definitions of education reality but should inquire what implicit assumptions lead to some questions but not others, or some 'answers' but not others, to be accepted as correct or valid. In the eighteenth century feudal and clerical dogmas were taken for granted, and in the nineteenth century it was the assumed absolutism of the market and its laws that were unquestioningly accepted. Today it is the 'scientific' and the 'rational' that are dominant in our lives. Certain social, political and educational beliefs are assumed to follow from the unquestioned acceptance of these legitimizing categories. There should, therefore, be critical questioning of whatever is taken for granted, 'as a matter of course'.

As I cannot hope to provide a comprehensive exposition of Michael Young's writings, what follows is a selective account. His basis thesis of 1971 could perhaps be put in this way: The 'liberal philosophers' like Richard Peters and Paul Hirst start from *a priori* assumptions about the forms of knowledge. They have an absolute conception which justifies what are no more than the socio-historical constructs of a particular time. Their view ignores the point that knowledge is a selection and organization from the available knowledge at a particular time, which involves conscious or unconscious choices. As curricula often come to be defined in terms of the dominant group's ideas of the educated man, we can ask: What model of man is implicit in the views of the 'liberal philosophers'?

Michael Young argues that it is not only people but knowledge that is processed, and, if this is so, we can ask questions about the selection and organization of knowledge. There have been various contributions, of course, to our study of knowledge; the Marxist, Weberian, the Durkheimian traditions, for example, have been valuable, but, till now, *the curriculum* has not been studied.

The most challenging aspect of Young's thesis is the

suggestion that we treat knowledge, or what counts as knowledge, as socially constructed. Discussing this, he notes:[3]

> That knowledge is socially constructed means that the knowledge transmitted in education is neither absolute nor arbitrary but are available 'sets of meanings' which do not 'emerge' but are collectively given. What is regarded as 'logical' or 'valid', is based on various standardized models which are necessarily sets of shared meanings which come to be taken for granted. The 'rules' of the standardized model are negotiated and selected in accordance with the purpose of the discourse, or the intentions of the enquirers. One of the outcomes of this view is that teachers may take these 'rules', these shared, meaningful conventions of what is considered logical, sensible, good reasoning, for granted and then see the failure to comply with the social conventions of teachers as forms of deviance. This does not imply anything about the absolute 'rightness' or 'wrongness' of the teachers' or pupils' statements but does suggest that the interaction involved is in part a product of the dominant defining categories which are taken for granted by the teacher.

And so it follows that we should explore how and why certain dominant categories persist and their possible links with sets of interests and occupational groups. We should also consider the influence of the traditions of a centralized elite which has close links with those holding economic and political power. It should be noted however that neither a mechanistic-deterministic nor a crude conspiracy theory is being referred to here. It is possible that certain educational theories come to be accepted by teachers who begin to act on the basis of these assumptions. Some theories become institutionalized and then are used to legitimate our practices, which, in circular fashion, justify the theories. One of our tasks therefore is to enquire into our institutionalized educational theories and practices and to ask: How has it come about that western academic standards are treated as if they were absolutes?

What Michael Young calls for is a focusing on the relation between social stratification and the stratification of knowledge, that is to say, the social value accorded to different areas and kinds of knowledge. By this means we can raise questions about:

1 The relations between the power structure and curricula.
2 The access to knowledge, and how certain forms of it come to be legitimated as superior to other forms.
3 The relations between knowledge and its functions in different kinds of society.

Then, as if to give us an example, he raises some questions concerning the organization and transmission of knowledge that is accorded 'high status' in our society. He notes that it is taught to the 'ablest' children, usually in homogeneous ability groups, and is then formally assessed. He suggests that academic curricula, high-status knowledge, tends to have 'abstractness', a high level of literacy, minimum relatedness to non-school activities, and a stress on individual performance. These dimensions are social definitions of educational value and they persist because they are the choices which accord with the values and beliefs of dominant groups at a particular time. But these values legitimate the existing organization of knowledge in such a way that even the discussion of alternatives in our society is, for many reasons, difficult. He however does pose the question: Could we not change the criteria of high-class knowledge so that it is concrete rather than abstract, oral rather than literate, related rather than unrelated, and communal rather than individual?

In a later section, where I suggest that one of the important features of the 'new sociology of education' is its use of anthropological studies, I attempt to show by a consideration of Gladwin and other ethnographers that it is possible to conceive of the possibility of the granting of equal status to other sets of cultural choices. That this is possible is because 'education' is – and this is often 'forgotten' – a social construct. There would of course be changes in such labels as 'success' and 'failure', but if many were successful rather than a few, this would entail a parallel redistribution of rewards in terms of wealth, prestige and power.

In brief, this is Michael Young's thesis. Till now, there has been no sociological study of the curriculum, of school knowledge. He proposes that we accept the notion of curricula and forms of assessment as social constructs, that 'knowledge' and education are inventions just like man's other inventions. He then outlines the beginnings of the project and argues that we should adopt a new approach and consider alternatives for a radical, political purpose.

The above is a very schematic outline of just the first six pages of the Introduction to *Knowledge and Control*, but from even such a short section some important features of the reorientation in the sociology of education can be stated in the form of several interlinked propositions. Let us now turn to these 'injunctions', many of which have become the assumptions of most of those who support the 'new' sociology of education.

Some Propositions of 'the New Approach'

1 There should not be an absence of theoretical debate in the sociology of education

It can be convincingly argued that traditional sociology of education was an elaboration of readers' common sense (which is why it is, in some ways, so appealing); till recently, at any rate, it was considered a parasitic discipline. But since the distinction between sociology and sociology of education is breaking down, it is not now possible to say that sociology of education draws on a 'parent' discipline. It is my opinion that the importance of sociology of education, in terms of its general contribution and insights, is increasing. The boundaries between sociological theory, sociology of knowledge and sociology of education are becoming increasingly indistinct. There is a growing awareness that the split between the 'pure' (sociological theory) and the 'applied' (sociology of education) is unproductive.

2 There should be continuous critical questioning of the 'taken for granted'

This proposition, or process rather, is not the exclusive feature or property of any one perspective, but in this context can perhaps be seen as an integral part of a phenomenological

17

approach. This self-awareness, critical self-consciousness, is now one of the meanings of 'reflexivity'.

Phenomenology is a philosophical tradition and a movement with a close connexion with many areas of discourse, and is slowly influencing sociology. Husserl and Schutz, for example, believed that philosophizing must begin by not taking anything for granted. In our everyday experience we do not normally raise fundamental questions; we leave them unexamined. Our consciousness is buried in our concern for the natural, everyday world, and we live in the 'natural attitude'. Phenomenologists say that we must first suspend, or 'put into brackets', the natural attitude. This is the phenomenological 'reduction' or epoché which has been likened to successive peelings off of layers of thought previously taken for granted in order to see what is left, what is presented or construed as essential by thought.

We are urged, then, to make problematic notions such as 'scientific', 'rational', 'childhood', 'the pupil' – and 'education'.[4] Most of the work undertaken in these areas has started from prior assumptions which have been of a limiting and restricting nature. It is for this reason that in the 'new approach' the work of anthropologists is utilized; by looking at other cultures, and then at our own, certain aspects of our own culture which we have always regarded as 'natural', appear in a new light, as anthropologically strange. Anthropology contributes to the examination of our taken for granted suppositions and shows us that there are alternative conceptions of ordering the world.

3 There should be a move towards treating knowledge, or what counts as knowledge, as socially constructed, and a study of the implications that follow from this

This injunction may be seen to contain within it the following overlapping assumptions which are implicit: a rejection of positivism and of objectivist epistemology, and the adoption of the notion that reality is socially constructed. The thesis that knowledge is socially constructed is part of a wider thesis that reality is a social construction. This view is based on the notion that it is not the ontological structure of objects but the *meaning* of our experiences which constitute reality.[5] This means that there is no inherent, intrinsic meaning within objects as if they were 'facts' obvious for all to see. Even so-called 'facts' have to be interpreted, and in this process we give meaning to objects, situations and experiences. The abortion of a child can be a happy occasion for some mothers and a sad loss for others, according to how they choose to see it and how they explain, or make sense, of it to themselves. That is to say, the reality of the social world is constructed by its members in terms of their accounting procedures for explaining it.

If social reality is conceived in this way as socially constituted and not 'out there', existing unproblematically, as is assumed in some versions of the correspondence theory of truth, then a criticism of traditional sociology, with its emphasis on scientific method and measurement, was inevitable. One of phenomenology's strongest contributions to our understanding of the social world is its critique of positivism, and this has influenced some writers to reject any theories of knowledge based on an 'objectivist' epistemology, and treat knowledge as if it was fixed and *not* relative. Many teachers have taken Paul Hirst, for example, to be saying (and acting in the classroom on the supposition) that knowledge is not relative but fixed, and that some types of knowledge, 'the forms', are intrinsically superior to others, 'the fields'. It has already been argued that such a view of knowledge, entailing a passive learner, is fundamentally conservative and elitist. It institutionalizes present practices, legitimizes them; most important, such views of knowledge can be seen as an ideology serving the interests of those who wish to resist radical educational and, therefore, political change. What is being urged by writers sympathetic to the new approach in the sociology of education is that we should not necessarily regard academic curricula as superior; that if we move towards treating knowledge, or what counts as knowledge, as socially constructed, we can recognize such academic curricula as human constructs limiting access to a privileged few — and that this need not be the case.

The rejection of positivism and objectivism, implied by the adoption of a phenomenological perspective, meant that there was a new stress on what can be called, for present purposes, a phenomenological 'model of man'. One of the most important features of such a model is the notion of intentionality, which is used to distinguish human 'action' from 'behaviour'. Phenomenologists hold that all mental activities are always directed towards some object. In brief, intentions determine relevance, and order thought. What is stressed is the individual's own mental ordering processes — that man is a meaning maker. Some sociologists have been excited, 'turned-on' by this way of seeing the world and have emphasized phenomenological sociology as a method of transcending the experienced realities of life day after day. If reality is constructed by our consciousness, our minds, then we are free despite material conditions that may oppress us; by choosing to see them differently we have a way of attaining freedom. These views, usually implicit, are based on a phenomenological model of man and I think can be most clearly explicated by a rendering of Sartre's work which emphasized the notion that man is free, to choose, to transcend oppression.[6] This exposition will be done in a following section, but it is relevant for my present purpose, to point out here that the presuppositions of a phenomenological 'model of man' are linked with a view of knowledge, through such notions as intentionality and meaning. Thus it comes about that the new approach suggests that knowledge is shared; that truth and objectivity are human products, and that knowledge is extricably linked to methods of coming to know. Man is the author of knowledge and reality.

4 There should be a move to accepting members' categories and explanations as valid ways of making sense and giving meaning

This methodological injunction is in marked contrast to the traditional approach which relied almost entirely on the observer's categories and the meanings he inferred; moreover, the observer was presented as having the so-called objective, value-free characteristics of a natural scientist. It is partly for this reason that there are so few accounts in the literature of how patients see medical and psychiatric staff, of how 'deviants' view the police, or of how pupils and teachers feel, think and act. Accepting members' accounts is, of course, not only a feature of the phenomenological method but is adopted, as we shall see, by many anthropologists and ethnographers as well. Charles Frake is an example of an ethnographer who uses natives' accounts, and calls this 'the explicit method'.

These concerns have led to an interest in different types of research. Interactional studies of pupils and teachers have gained impetus from this approach; much of the research focuses on their experience of the classroom, and the learning and teaching of a school subject, the meaning of the curriculum for the participants, or the significance of school-knowledge. Besides this type of research there has also been a development of historical studies dealing with the origins, growth and institutionalization of different subjects such as mathematics, science, history or music. The struggle for different definitions of school-knowledge has made this type of research pertinent to our understanding of competing conceptions of knowledge.

5 *There should be a study of how and why certain defining categories persist, of how and why western academic standards are treated as absolutes*

Because some sociologists of education used relativistic arguments drawn from different sources such as phenomenology and anthropology to criticize narrow and fixed notions of knowledge and education and to suggest other possibilities, alternative versions of the world, they were taken to be implicitly saying that all rationalities, or ways, of looking at the world are equally acceptable; that all propositions are of equal value. This was, I believe, a misunderstanding of the position of the writers who, though they used a phenomenological approach, were also politically committed to changing the prevailing hierarchical conceptions of 'knowledge', 'ability' and, therefore, 'success'. They did, therefore, have 'grounds' and justifications, values and criteria, but they did not make them explicit. Moreover, it must be admitted, there were also ambiguities about the actual methods to be used for challenging and changing those

21

aspects of school-knowledge, like academic standards, that are treated as absolutes.

This section has briefly outlined what I consider to be some of the main propositions, or rather 'injunctions', of the 'new directions' in the sociology of education. The argument that I will develop is that this new approach was a reaction against the 'traditional' sociology of education which was dominant at that time. The new sociology of education rejected the traditional approach which is preoccupied with such concerns as 'education and social mobility', 'the family and educational achievement', 'the school as a formal organization'.

Hostile towards positivism, the new approach rejected empiricist methodology with its emphasis on raw data, statistics, numerical measurement. Positivism, generally speaking, implies an acceptance of the scientists' or observers' categories as valid; as a consequence, this has often meant an imposition of meaning by the (so-called neutral, value-free) scientist – a form of cognitive domination by the 'expert' of the actor. I suggest that moral outrage was certainly an element in the rejection of positivism. The new sociologists of education adopted the 'interpretive' view of social science, which contains many different strands, one of the most influential being social phenomenology. This perspective rejects the belief that the scientific observer is automatically right, and asserts the value of the actor's viewpoint. It is thus (in part) a moral corrective to positivism in that it respects the actors' views of their contexts, their 'rationality', the way they 'see' the world and experience their life-situations. In the attempt to challenge accepted views of education, the writers of the new sociology of education used anthropology as a weapon. In particular, ethnographic studies were used to exemplify their point of view. They wished to question what is usually taken for granted, to suggest that what was often taken as 'natural' was actually 'conventional', and that there were other ways of organizing our learning, other possibilities of living our lives together.

It may have been noticed that some themes continually reappear. I have selected some of them that I hold to be the important features of this approach. In the following four chapters I will present a discussion of the use of anthropological studies, the adoption of a phenomenological model of man (which involves the repudiation of positivism), the rejection of the liberal philosophy of education and the assertion of the importance of studies of the classroom and the curriculum. Let us now turn to the first of these, a discussion of how the work of anthropologists and ethnographers has contributed to our understanding of education.

Chapter 2

The Use of Anthropological Studies

Besides the rejection of the 'culture of positivism' an important feature of the new sociology of education is its increasing use and interest in the work of certain anthropologists, particularly ethnographers. (Ethnographers collect data by observation and fieldwork, and are not necessarily anthropologists.) The section begins with a statement of some of the unexamined presuppositions of nineteenth-century anthropologists and some twentieth-century educators, and a parallelism is noted between, them. Some of the notable methodological contributions of the new ethnography are discussed, in particular the work of Gladwin. In order to pose the question – 'How do we understand logics?' – some work by Conklin and Frake is then reviewed. This leads inevitably to the issue: How do we understand another culture? The section concludes with a return to the topic with which we began: a consideration of the contribution of ethnographers' accounts to our understanding of children's learning. It is argued that it is partly through this new trend that we are increasingly becoming aware that though there are cultural differences in thought, other cultures are not necessarily deficient. In fact, the existence of other adequate logics and rationalities challenges the absoluteness of our own. Let us now look at some of the questions raised by anthropological materials.

I propose in this section then to argue that similarities can be seen between the assumptions of many nineteenth-century anthropologists and the presuppositions of many twentieth-century educators. In the course of the discussion I will also try and consider the question: What contribution have ethnographers' accounts of non-western cultures made to our understanding of 'cultural deprivation'?

Let us look first at some of the assumptions of nineteenth-century anthropologists: post-Darwinian social scientists believed that human society evolved in a continuum from the primitive to civilized society – like the technological states of the western Europe. This was related to their view that the young of the species recapitulate the history of the species. It was also held that the primitive adult was equivalent to the civilized child. Lévy-Bruhl called primitive mentality 'pre-logical': 'the collective representations of the European are exclusively intellectual and distinct from emotional realms, in the primitive person these basic beliefs are fused with emotional components'. Primitive culture, then, implied primitive thought, it was mystical and pre-logical. The prevailing view was that the observed differences in thinking were interpreted as reflecting differing capabilities. Boas was amongst the first to reject this idea – that differences in culture imply differences in thought – and argued that previous observers had failed to understand the people they were describing; they mistook their own lack of understanding as evidence of their informants' stupidity.

Now, in some ways, the assumptions of many contemporary educators as regards working-class children are very similar. This view stems partly from the way 'the problem', with all its consequences, has been conceptualized: Why do children from the poorer groups in our society fail to do as well at school as they should? The main assumption concerns school-knowledge; like 'primitives', working-class children are thought not to have the conceptual tools for comprehending the forms of knowledge which have historically come to count as school-knowledge. Maxine Greene has written of the reification of knowledge that occurs; this view of knowledge sees the curriculum as 'a structure of socially-prescribed knowledge, external to the knower, there to be mastered, learned'. A consequence of treating knowledge as a 'facticity' is that the notion of the learner as an existing person mainly concerned with making sense of his 'life-world' is ignored. My point is that such a view in education is equivalent to the ethnocentricism of early anthropologists. Just as the native is made to feel ashamed of his world and is prescribed a new way of seeing the world by the western

The Use of Anthropological Studies

anthropologist, so children are prescribed reified forms of knowledge which produce a view of social reality that is mechanistic and deterministic.

Especially prevalent in our society is an ability theory which states that different groups or individuals develop better, more generalized, intellectual abilities than others. This can be seen in the work of many educational psychologists who emphasize measures of ability such as 'IQ' on the basis of the assumption that a given task will evoke the same kind of behaviour, regardless of who performs the task. Cognitive development is thus seen as the acquisition of more powerful higher order structures. A popular application of this principle is the current approach to the 'culturally deprived' child, who is seen rather like a primitive native without conceptual tools.

To the great advances made by anthropologists, ethno-scientists and linguistic anthropologists have in particular made a considerable contribution. They have stressed two important points; first, they have maintained that ethno-graphic description should be according to the principles of classification of the people they are studying. Second, that cultural differences in thought processes are reducible to differences in classification.[1]

Though there has been much work on different cultures, there has been little work on logical processes, that is to say the cognitive strategies used in solving problems. Why is it that poor people tend to do badly in school and in intelligence tests? It is suggested that the research that there is emphasizes contrasts with middle-class thinking — it quantifies divergences from middle-class culture, and accepts the qualities to be measured as a given. All this sort of work is, however, largely psychological and tells us nothing about reasoning processes. Cognition is not just a psychological factor, it is also a culturally-influenced process.

Now a reason why some sociologists of education are increasingly realizing the importance of ethnographers' accounts is that many of them demonstrate that though there are cultural differences in thought, other cultures are not necessarily deficient.[2] In fact the existence of other adequate logics and rationalities challenges the absoluteness of our own. Their work supports C. Wright Mills's contention

26

that there are different logics; they are socially constructed, and socially situated among the group to whom they are the logical ways of thinking and doing. In our culture many assume that formal logic is absolute, and that only through 'the forms of knowledge' can there be the development of rationality and mind.

But we know that definitions of knowledge vary in different cultures; that it is man made; and if in our schools it has become not only institutionalized and objectified but reified and alienating, we know that the divisions we have made between school and non-school knowledge, intellectual and manual, theoretical and practical, liberal and vocational, are not necessary, and can be changed. I suggest that the more there is the realization that our notions of say 'ability', 'intelligence', 'teacher', 'pupil', are historical man-made constructs, the more readily we will be prepared to think of alternatives if we find prevailing definitions narrow, limiting, hierarchical and, therefore, coercive.

But how has our understanding of learning in schools been enriched by ethnographers' accounts? I believe that they have made the following contributions: first, they maintain that *categories should not be imposed*. An ethnographer does not attempt to impose his views and categories of experience on the phenomena he studies. This is a view shared by phenomenological sociologists, who hold that one has to take the role of the actor, see the world from his standpoint. In so many aspects of education, however, imposition still takes place, the values of the 'middle class' are thought of as being the 'mainstream' ones and imposed on others through the selection, 'pacing' and assessment of school-knowledge. It is then argued that the cognitive development of poorer groups is stunted or, as Arthur Jensen would say, lacking in Type 2 conceptual learning.

Second, ethnographers maintain that *cognition is related to cultural context*. They emphasize that cognition cannot be studied as an activity isolated from its cultural context. To study cognition is to study cognitive behaviour in a particular situation, and the relation of this behaviour to other aspects of the culture. Again, this is similar to the views of those who have adopted what has been called the 'interpretive paradigm', some of whom have been influenced by phenomenological theorizing. They emphasize, too, that actions are always dependent on their situational context. Not only actions, but words, language itself, meanings should always be studied in relation to their context. (This is a meaning of indexicality.) That is to say, actions should be seen in terms of the meaning of the context, and the context in turn is understood to be what it is through the same actions. And yet, if this is so, why is it that in an educational context learning in schools is still often regarded as an activity isolated from the home culture? Why is the value of the life-experience that the child brings to school still not recognized? The learning of any logic is a highly-situated activity which cannot be treated as if it were context free if it is to become part of the life-world of the learner.

Third, ethnographers maintain that *people are good at doing what is important to them*. They have shown us that societies vary in the kinds of tasks they pose for their members. It follows that people will be good at doing the things that are important to them and that they have occasion to do often. Thus the Kpelle in Nigeria are good at estimating rice, the Subanun of the Philippines at diagnosing diseases and the Puluwat Islanders of the Pacific at navigation.

I want now to focus on one of these examples, that of the Puluwat Islanders, and in particular to the contribution of Thomas Gladwin to educational debate. *East is a Big Bird* is a study of the Puluwatans who live on a small atoll in Micronesia.[3] He describes the principles incorporated in the design of their sailing canoes, and the astounding navigational skills which they learn through oral tradition. Each journey is pre-planned and rests on a specified body of knowledge which is practical and useful. Ignoring the passenger-carrying ships that are available, they pilot their canoes, without a compass, across thousands of miles in the open Pacific. Their navigation depends upon features of sea and sky and is founded on a system of logic so complex that westerners cannot duplicate it without the use of advanced instruments. Thus what is learnt as 'practical' on Puluwat would be categorized as highly 'theoretical', 'abstract', in one of our naval colleges. Ironically, when a Puluwat navigator is given one of our 'intelligence tests', it indicates that his level of mental achievement is low! Such tests are largely inadequate because they violate the principles I outlined earlier: that categories should not be imposed, cognition is related to cultural context, and the appreciation of the fact that people are good at doing what is important to them. Gladwin argues that tests are just as inappropriate for poor peoples in our own societies; just as different societies have different styles of thinking, the difference in cognition between middle-class and working-class children in our schools may be in the style of thinking, in the strategies. He then comments that it is possible that we make a false dichotomy in our schools between abstract and concrete thinking. The abstract and the concrete can intimately coexist in the working mind of the navigator and, say, an urban taxi-driver. Therefore we need not always associate middle-class thinking with 'abstraction', and lower-class thinking with 'concreteness'. We should perhaps remind ourselves here that Robin Horton too has cast doubt on most of the well-worn dichotomies: causally oriented – supernaturally oriented, national – mystical, etc. Gladwin, furthermore, reminds us that 'abstract' thinking should not always be related to innovative thinking. Puluwat navigation contains abstractions of a high order, but within the system there is little room or need for innovation. In modern societies, abstract thinking and innovative problem-solving are linked to superior intelligence. All three qualities are often attributed to 'middle-class intelligence' and said to be lacking in the 'concrete' style of thinking of poorly educated lower-class persons. Puluwat navigation, though intelligent and 'abstract', is *not* innovative. For many people there is a lack of necessity for making innovations, but this does not mean that they cannot innovate – merely that they have very little practice in using heuristics, experimental devices to solve new problems. Gladwin's own view is that to get qualifications, to do well at school, to do intelligence tests, one has to use heuristics, and we may be being unfair to poor children who do not see the need for heuristics and yet are capable of 'abstract' (if one has to use the word) thinking. For me, the most valuable contribution of Gladwin's work is that it raises such fundamental questions as: What is 'abstract', what is 'theory'? It calls into question certain ways of thinking, 'universalistic rationality', and suggests that notions like 'abstract' are problematic. There is no universalistic type of thinking, or logic; they are not absolutes but are situationally specific. This is to argue, as the work of Robin Horton,[4] Michael Cole and Thomas Gladwin shows, that what is considered 'abstract', is culturally situated. That this is a 'relativistic' view of knowledge is not denied – but it is not a form of relativism where 'anything goes'. This relativistic assumption is grounded in a theoretical interest: the view that knowledge should not be regarded as a body of knowledge but as a human activity. Knowledge is not absolute and 'given', but is relative and 'produced' by men. The new sociology of education is a fundamental critique of any hierarchical and exclusive view of knowledge.

If ways of thinking and logic are situationally specific, as I have attempted to argue here, a question that arises is: How do we understand them, these 'logics'? To highlight this problem I am going to refer first to a field study by Conklin, and then to one by Frake.[5] Colour, in the western technical sense, is not a universal concept and in many languages there is no unitary terminological equivalent. In his fieldwork in the Philippines, studying the Hanunoo colour system, Harold Conklin found many inconsistencies; but after some time he realized that the apparent complexity of the colour system could be reduced, at the most generalized level, to four basic terms: lightness/darkness, wetness/dryness. At first he had failed to distinguish sharply between sensory reception, on the one hand, and perceptual categorization, on the other. And so he learnt that what appeared to be colour confusion resulted from his own inadequate knowledge of the internal structure of the colour system.

Anthropologists have to learn, besides such internal structures, not only a substantive vocabulary but also its 'rules in use' which arise from the social context and cannot be context free. From a work such as 'The Diagnosis of Disease among the Subanun of Mindanao' we can learn how Charles Frake had to grapple with problems similar to children trying to learn school-knowledge. Frake found that he could not do his fieldwork without first finding out the folk rules and schemes of knowledge used by members to perceive, classify and explain social reality. How could he come to know the rules of interpretation being used by the natives? The discussion of disease is a very important matter to the

30

Subanun, and so Frake focuses on the problem of how natives do the label-assigning work of disease diagnosis. He suggests three methods which seem to me to be important in any study which tries to identify an underlying pattern behind a series of appearances; the analytic, the perceptual and the explicit.

The analytic method makes use of the outsider's means of coding. In practice this would mean the outside observer's method of categorization, the observer diagnosing an illness in western terms, and then comparing it with the diagnosis of the native. This method, however, is not helpful in that western conceptions are too different to allow any meaningful comparison. Second, there is *the perceptual method*; this is when a disease is named by a native and the observer tries to note the physical symptoms that the native is perceiving. The difficulty with this method is that one does not know what precisely the native is perceiving, and so mistakes can be made. Third, there is *the explicit method*, which involves asking the native. It is found that informants rarely disagree about the term itself, but nevertheless there was frequent disagreement about its application to a particular case. This is one of the disadvantages of this method, in that it gives knowledge of the meaning of terms 'in principle' but not of their application in socially defined situations. In other words, knowing an abstract rule is not enough; we have to know 'the rule in use', when and how it is applied in a particular context or on a particular occasion. Yet, an advantage of this method is that there is built-in validation: when the natives agree about a diagnosis, the observer can accept it as being right. The use of this method means that an observer's propositions can be supported to the extent that his descriptions of native imputations allow an outsider 'to pass' among the natives as if he were one of them. This has been stated by Goodenough in the following way: 'To know a culture is to have learnt whatever it is one has to know or believe in order to operate in a manner acceptable to its members and to do so in any role that they accept for anyone of themselves.[6]

It has been a recurrent theme of this book that 'knowledge' is taken for granted, it is viewed consensually and as if it were objective, 'out there', and unsituated or context free.

There has been little research on the experience of alienation and other consequences of such a view, but the work of some anthropologists has certainly stimulated sociologists of education to raise questions that we often did not recognize before. Frake's paper, for example, can help to remind us of some problems about learning in schools; children trying to learn school-knowledge are faced with the same sorts of difficulties and problems that anthropologists are confronted with when they are trying to understand a different culture. But how is school-knowledge made available? How do we expect children to set about trying to acquire the rules of knowledge in use?

Ethnographers have raised other important and even wider questions for us. The problem of how we come to understand 'logics' was mentioned earlier, but this is part of the basic question: How do we get to 'know' another culture at all? How do we understand another culture?

At this stage, I want to allude briefly to some issues arising from the Peter Winch's views in *The Idea of a Social Science.*[7] We have been warned by Winch of the danger of committing category mistakes. (This often occurs as a consequence of what Frake calls the analytic method.) Concisely, his argument is that there are different realms of discourse and that each realm (or culture) has its own logic and sense of consistency, and must be understood from within its own conventions, its own criteria of rationality. If we do not do this we make category mistakes. Though I agree with Winch that actions must necessarily be identified with actor's concepts, I disagree with his view that cultures are noncomparable. The thrust of Winch's argument, and this is the reason why he has been included in this discussion, is that the use of ethnographic material to apply to our own culture, for the purpose of raising questions about alternatives in education (as we have been suggesting), would be seen as invalid.

But it should be pointed out that by Winch's argument sociology would be culture bound — it would be impossible for a primitive to understand statements about civilized societies and equally impossible for a civilized man to understand statements about primitive societies. There is no space here for this controversy, the reader being advised to consult the references, but perhaps it could be said that Winch is telling us merely that certain anthropologists did their work badly. If Winch is wrong and we *can* utilize the contributions of the ethnographers, this raises yet another problem. Then the sociologists of education have to inform us of the criteria of logic and rationality by which they select one ethnography rather than another and tell us the use to which these materials can be put. To put it simply, if it is claimed that ethnographic studies provide grounds (good reasons) for relativism, if all knowledge is related to the context of its production, then relativists cannot claim to be superior to those who hold 'absolutist' views. Relativists thus become caught in their own trap. They can make no value-judgments. And if no such judgements can be made, such a viewpoint can have no relevance for emancipatory political action. The problem is this: after having rejected the 'culture of positivism', the new sociologists of education cannot claim to ground their accounts in an objectively available social world – for that world would itself be a feature of their method. What, then, is the justification of their own theorizing and how do they ground their accounts? What are 'the auspices' of their theorizing and on what grounds is their own enquiry better or more adequate? Some of these issues will be taken up in later sections, where it will be argued that many of the accounts by writers, influenced by the new orientation in the sociology of education, are grounded in a particular interest, a political egalitarianism.

In conclusion, I have suggested in this section some reasons why the 'new' sociology of education utilized anthropological and ethnographic studies. It was, of course, a way of questioning our assumptions, our habitual ways of thinking and accepting existing educational 'norms'. But it was more than this; it was a way of intervening in the deficit/difference debate, it was a moral act based on the recognition that some cultures are oppressed – as the usual term for this topic shows and yet, at the same time, disguises: cultural deprivation. Inevitably ethnographies of different cultures raised questions about the nature of research and rationality; that is to say, how do we, any of us, make sense of other people, and what do we think of those with a different form of life from our own? I have also hinted at the looming issue of relativism, which is a problem to some and a solution for others — but I will have more to say about this in later sections.

Nevertheless a valuable contribution of ethnographers' accounts, it seems to me, is that in studying how we understand another culture we are forced to try and understand how our children understand school-knowledge. In recognizing this we are led to ask other questions: To what extent does the school-knowledge transmitted to pupils remain objectified and external? To what extent does it prescribe for them a way of seeing the world? And if the world is pre-defined as subject centred, hierarchical and elitist, we can reasonably say that school-knowledge is a feature of Man's alienation.

We know that understanding a culture is very difficult, but only now are we realizing that we know so little about the learning processes of the strangers in the schools. Little is known of how children give meaning to their educational experience, how they adapt, interpret, make sense of it. That children can do this, and can do no other, is an expression of a certain view, and I would want to argue that many statements like this in the 'new sociology of education' point to a phenomenological model of man. For many, the adoption of such a model, in contrast to the dominant positivist and deterministic model, was an exciting and liberating experience. I will attempt to describe some features of a phenomenological 'model of man' by considering some of the views of Jean-Paul Sartre. This is not because the 'new sociology of education' has been specifically influenced by him, but because his work is accessible, and can be used to serve as an introduction to some aspects of the phenomenology of Husserl, Heiddegger, Merleau-Ponty and others. But before we turn our attention to Sartre, let us look at some of the issues underlying one of phenomenology's outstanding achievements — its critique of positivism and science.

Chapter 3

The Adoption of a Phenomenological Model of Man

Phenomenology and Positivism

There is a vast literature on the nature of science, the philosophy and sociology of science. There are also many critiques, but most of these discussions are usually staged within the accepted framework or paradigm – they are not critiques which begin by rejecting the basic presuppositions of science. One of the most important features of phenomenology is that it is a rejection of science from without. Writers such as Husserl, Heidegger and Merleau-Ponty have played an important part in this movement, and I will now try to isolate some important features of their work so as to provide a base from which I can outline a model of man which is used in some of the recent work in sociology of education.

Writers in the phenomenological tradition have wanted to free people from the illusion of objectivity, and the tendency to generalize, predict and explain. They regard objectivity, the acceptance of the views of the observer, as an obstacle to understanding, and have admired the method of Socratic enquiry which shatters accepted presuppositions. This of course often produces confusion and bewilderment – it means forgoing the myth that there are hard identifiable facts in the world about which hard definite statements can be made to correspond. Generally speaking, most phenomenologists believe that there is no such thing as an absolute objective truth in science, but Edmund Husserl was an interesting exception to this rule in that he believed phenomenology was a scientific method. His belief in scientific exactitude was only in his early period, however, and he later came to accept the notion that objects are constituted as objects for us by virtue of their significance for us. That is to say, our consciousness of the world, and our knowledge of it, is through interpretation. He came to believe that before experience can be analysed by phenomenologists, a kind of preliminary reduction or epoché, a suspension of science, was necessary so that the presuppositions of science could be exposed. A phenomenologist concentrates as far as he can upon the pure experience as he has it, without presuppositions or concepts derived from elsewhere than the experience itself. The phenomenologist sets aside his normal standpoint, or performs an epoché. He puts into brackets, disregards, the causes of his experience. He performs a phenomenological reduction to the facts themselves. This view – that experience should be examined as it is internally presented to one – is the method of Husserl, Heidegger, Merleau-Ponty and Sartre.[1]

An anti-scientific approach to the world can be seen in the work of Maurice Merleau-Ponty, for whom scientific language always sticks to what is perceived and does not go beyond what is actually given. He believed that there was a great danger in the scientific assumption that the world consists of objects which are completely and totally distinct from the observing subject. He stated that as long as science insists upon an absolute distinction between the perceiving subject and the object perceived we will not be able to understand perception. Moreover, there cannot be a causal connexion between my actions and the world. In a causal judgment there are two separable elements: the burning match, for example, causes a factory fire. But Merleau-Ponty argues that my action cannot be caused by the physical world, since It and I are one; we are not two separable elements. And if my actions are not caused by the world, they are free.

Phenomenologists such as Husserl and Merleau-Ponty are saying that science fails to understand its nature as it attempts to stand outside the 'life-world'. But how has it happened that natural science has come to claim that it exclusively embodies the European tradition of rational thinking?

According to one view, to understand this we have to look to Greek thought, particularly Plato. For the Greeks, the ideal man was the man of reason, like Plato, who stressed the universal, abstract and timeless essences of forms and ideas. Plato emphasized, as against the insecurities of flux, the 'really real' objects in the universe, the universals, or 'ideas'. The ideal attitude for the Greeks was one not of commitment but of detachment, as exemplified in mathematics, logic, science. This can be viewed as the victory of reason over the poetic, mythic functions of theorizing. Philosophers dealt with the super-sensible world of abstractions, the ideas, but poets and artists were condemned to the world of the senses, to the constant flux of becoming. Science is a peculiarly western product and became possible only because the Greeks differentiated reason from feeling and intuition. The highest embodiment of the view that 'one's rational self is one's real self' came to be the rational philosopher and the theoretical scientist. For an account which attempts to describe this more precisely, one has to look at Heidegger's view that the Greeks detached the 'figure' from the 'ground'.[2]

The object which has been detached from the enveloping ground of Being can be measured and calculated, but the essence of the object, the thing-in-itself, becomes more and more remote from Man. In other words, the figure has come into sharper focus, but the ground has become detached. This act of detachment was accompanied by a momentous shift in the meaning of truth. The Greeks adopted truth as the correctness of an intellectual judgment. By adopting this meaning of truth, by differentiating reason from feeling and intuition, they were able to develop science, a uniquely western product. Thus, according to this story, western and eastern Man parted ways because each had made a different decision as to what truth was. But we cannot define ourselves without negating the alternatives that we do not become. The scientistic pre-definition of reality meant inevitably that the wholeness of Man was lost – this was the fall of Being. Heidegger's central theme can thus be seen as the estrangement of Man from his own being and Being itself. He believed that from the beginning the thought of western Man had been bound to things, to objects, and that Reason made thinking about Being difficult. Being is not an empty abstraction, it is something in which all of us are immersed. Heidegger's work, then, is an attempt to describe what human existence is, its general traits, and to clarify what truth is. For Heidegger, what Man becomes – in his history as well as in his thinking – turns upon the decision he makes as to what truth is.

I should now like to indicate briefly what I mean by the term 'positivism'. The tenets of positivism are usually held to be:

First, that there is no dichotomy between the physical world and the human world.

Second, that the types of explanation and description in the natural sciences are not different from those in the social world.

Third, that all the concepts in social science can be 'reduced' or translated into the language of natural science. In other words, by positivism I am referring to the view that conceives of knowledge as a neutral picturing of fact. Positivism assumes that Nature or an external reality is the author of truth. It believes that valid knowledge is detached from particular knowing subjects; we have already criticized this feature, the separation of the subject from the object of his knowledge. It is partly because of this detached quality that knowledge is seen as inherently neutral. The positivist view has been most influential in science, where it is often argued that there is a unitary scientific method and that, by its use, knowledge is verifiable. It is usually argued by positivists that natural science is rooted in intersubjectively evident observations, experimentation that is reproducible, and that it accepts explanations only when they predict outcomes which are publically verifiable. Scientific study can give us truly objective knowledge and be value free. Social science, therefore, should have the same epistemology and methodology as those employed in the natural sciences.

I believe that the 'culture of positivism' has become pervasive in our society. The standard of certainty and exactness has come to be regarded as the only explanatory model for social knowledge. The presumption is always that science provides *the* paradigm of 'correct' thinking, of rationality. And so scientific methods are being increasingly applied. Note how often we are told that scientists can tell us the most efficient means to the achievement of ends. It is argued that questions of means are resolvable into questions of fact. If political problems can be made technical, experts can solve them. More and more areas of our life are being defined as 'technical' problems and are removed from political debate. This line of argument – how positivism has certain implications for political practice, how positivism in science has become an ideology in advanced capitalist society – is a view advanced by many Marxists.[3] But, as we have seen, phenomenologists such as Husserl and Heidegger have also made invaluable critiques of positivism in science. This is one sense, and there are many, in which Marxism and phenomenology share a common project. A writer who closely studied German phenomenology is Jean-Paul Sartre, whose book *Being and Nothingness* develops many of the notions of Husserl and Heidegger, and whose later work, *Search for a Method* is an attempt to integrate phenomenology with a humanistic Marxism.

Sartre's 'Model of Man'

For Sartre, we cannot doubt our consciousness, for to doubt is to be conscious. He denies altogether the existence of an unconscious mind. Consciousness and freedom are given together. The essence of Man lies in the liberty of Man's existence by which he chooses himself, and so makes himself what he is. A man is his life. I wish to suggest that this view of the actor – it could be called 'a model of Man' – seems to have been adopted to varying degrees (implicitly or explicitly) by some sociologists working with the new approaches in the sociology of education, who have argued, to put it tersely, that what is taken for granted about the world is the product of human choice, and that if 'realities' are socially produced it follows that they can be transformed – the world could be changed if we could see it differently. I wish to suggest that such a view is based on a 'model of Man' which finds its clearest expression in Sartre's work, and believe that it is important to study his views for the following reasons. If in some sense we are all concerned with 'order' and 'control', with how problems of constraint and coercion are manifest in all societies (whether through consciousness or reified 'social structure'), then it is important to know what existentialists have to say about the problem of freedom. Their work is a description of the interaction between Man and the world, and they see the problem of freedom as a practical problem. They want YOU to experience it and practice it. Second, one can see in his work the hostility to the 'objectivity' of science. The natural scientist in accepting the role of the observer discovers general laws. Thus the uniqueness of Man is undermined, subjectivity is made harder to achieve. In a sense, then, causation is an illusion; the world of explanations and reasons is not the world of existence. Third, many of his concepts have sociological parallels; for example, bad faith is closely related to reification. His notions about time, the inter-relationship of the past and the future to the present, his views on motives, are enlightening for us in our attempt to study meaning in human interaction. Fourth, Sartre's late work raises critical issues about phenomenology and Marxism; there are irreconcilable differences between them – can they be integrated? Can such a grafting, in the future, solve the twin problems of imposition on the one hand and relativism on the other? For me, Sartre embodies the contradictions and anguish of our times and, through his life and work, poses questions about *our* praxis, the kinds of action that we can engage in. These themes will be discussed in my final chapter, but now let us turn our attention to his work.

Sartre's early work owes a great deal to Husserl, whose writings he introduced to France, and Heidegger. These writings were mainly on the imagination and the emotions: for Sartre, perception and imagination are two modes of consciousness. Man's ability to imagine things, to project what is not the case, is connected with the concept of freedom, the ability to choose. In other worlds, Man's capacity both to perceive the world and to act upon it is dependent on his freedom, and this freedom expresses itself in his ability to see what things are not, to envisage possibilities, and to accept or reject what has been envisaged. Sartre believes that the emotions, like all other mental events, are intentional. Emotion means something being directed towards some object, and can be explained only in terms of this object. Emotion is a way of apprehending the world. 'When we cannot see our way, we can no longer put up with so exacting and difficult a world. . .All ways are barred and nevertheless we must act. So then we try to change the world, to live in it as though the relations between things were not governed by deterministic processes but by magic.' Emotion is magic, a transformation of the world. Imagination and emotion, then, are two essential modes of awareness of the world. The central doctrine is that men are nothing but what they choose to become, their essence consists in what they choose to do, how they choose to see the world. Emotion arises when men choose to see the world in a certain way; they are also committed to imagining and they are actively free, to act, to judge, to comprehend, to create. Sartre's philosophy rests on the twin pillars of human powers of self-analysis and human freedom. We are free not only to do as we choose, but to feel as we choose, to *be* whatever we choose.

In *Being and Nothingness* Sartre argues that we must distinguish between three modes of being, between Being-in-itself, Being-for-others, and Being-for-itself. Being-in-itself is when an individual protects himself against the recognition of his own freedom, when he pretends to be inert, managed by people, and therefore having no choice, a thing. Sartre illustrates this with the story of a girl who goes out with a man for the first time. After the 'preliminaries', her companion takes her hand. She knows that leaving her hand in his amounts to committing herself to an affair. The woman then leaves her hand where it is, but does not notice that she has left it there. Her hand is a thing and cannot be held responsible for what happens to it because it is regarded as being quite separate from herself. This is one pattern of Bad Faith, the self-deception when we pretend that we have to do things (which in fact we are plainly choosing to do because we want to).

A Being-for-others is the individual that pretends to be nothing except what others want him to be. He acts out the role as if determined by how he is meant to be. To illustrate this, Sartre gives the example of someone playing at being a waiter, a person who pretends to be nothing but what people think him, a waiter and nothing more. This second mode of existence is also a pattern of Bad Faith, which is the evasion of our responsibilities when we treat ourselves as wholly determined in our behaviour by the view which others take of us.

In contrast, Being-for-itself is the desirable mode of existence, and is identical with conscious being. At the centre of the 'For-itself' there is a lack, a gap, which is perhaps to do with the striving of individuals towards their possibilities, and it must remain unsatisfied as long as a being is conscious. Conscious beings, Beings-for-themselves, have no fixed 'essences' which determine how they shall behave. They create their essences as they go along, by constantly choosing to fill up the gap between themselves and their futures. Consciousness, then, having no essence, is empty, and constructed out of nothing except plans and projects. As Sartre points out:

> The difference between doing things and having things happen to one, is a manifest difference, which can be experienced all the time. There are some things which we physically cannot do, yet we are still free to live with these restrictions in *one way* rather than another. . .a way of denying freedom is to regard oneself as bound by given purposes. I have undeniable power to choose in what way I live my circumstances – to manage them and even to react to them as I choose.

Bad Faith, or *mauvaise foi*, is the attempt to escape from the anguish which men suffer when they are brought face to face with their own freedom. We are responsible not only for what we do, but for what we feel. When this responsibility is more than we can bear, we develop tricks and devices for evading it (like irony). We pretend things are inevitable when they are not.

Sartre thus totally rejects the view that we have to conform to roles, or indeed any form of determinism. (We may be forced by circumstances to live *in* a certain situation, but *how* we live there is how we choose.) This is why Sartre utterly rejects Freud; his objections are these: First, in Freud's view it is external circumstances and the history of the subject which determine whether this or that shall be acted upon. Second, the agent acts as he does because of the factors in his history which determine him to do so, and he is not able himself to tell what the meaning of his acts is until they are afterwards interpreted *for* him by his analyst. Third, human reality is always interpreted solely by a return to the past from the standpoint of the present. (The dimension of the future does not exist in Freudian psychology.) Sartre argues against these views and states that human beings must, by their very nature, strive to overcome their lack of essence by filling up the void within themselves by plans and projects. Even if our choices are entirely restricted — even if we are in prison, for instance — we must choose how to evaluate it, how to conceive the possibility of escape or release. If people were not free, they could not be as we in fact know that they are — capable of initiating things and also of pretending and evading things.

In this rendering of Sartre's thought I have excluded certain features of his work; that is to say, I have elected to say little about his belief that we experience a sense of the absurd, a feeling of nausea and anguish, and have highlighted his views on human action, how whatever we choose makes us what we are. Human action, then, as opposed to mere happening, entails intention. Consciousness must always be consciousness of the world from the point of view of a potential agent. Freedom is thus built into the concept of action, and is a necessary part of the concept of consciousness as well. Without consciousness as consciousness of something to be done, there would be no action. We look at things in one way rather than another. We could look at things differently, we could even decide to do so. It is from our way of looking at things that our motives and actions arise; our actions both arise from and reveal our motives. The past in itself cannot force a man to act; it is the situation regarded as unbearable which causes it. In other words, a state of affairs cannot be a motive; only the awareness of a state of affairs as something to be changed can be. What constitutes a motive for acting is an apprehension of the situation as something to be overcome, as something which we can change. Sartre, then, is telling us that we confer certain values upon things, thus making them into motives, that we may not know what we value until we are called on to prove it in action.

The most important feature of Sartre's position outlined above is his radical view of human freedom, and his rejection of any view that would reduce Man to his biology, or history to the functioning of natural or economic laws. He has always felt that the logical forms and the language in which our thought is expressed are appropriate only for the objects of science and not for the free process which is Man. In *Being and Nothingness* Sartre had written about freedom both as if it is a fact and as an object of an imperative. Gradually Sartre came to realize that 'psychological' freedom and political freedom are inextricable even though they are not identical. That is to say, there was a shift in his interest from the psychological freedom, which most people ignore or seek to evade, to the practical freedom people experience. Man's possession of psychological freedom was largely an abstraction, of little value in producing a satisfying life to the individual person. Sartre came to believe that men cannot fight for their political freedom unless they are free and recognize that this is so; it is because men are existentially free that he came to demand for them a political and practical freedom.

Sartre's Phenomenological Marxism

These changes were gradually discernible in Sartre's thinking after 1946, and then in 1957 he argued, in *Search for a Method*, that Marxism was the leading philosophy of our time and that existentialism was a contributory ideology within its framework.[4] The importance of this essay, originally called *Existentialism and Marxism*, lies partly in his refusal to identify Marxism with Russian communism. For Sartre, deterministic Marxists hold that we are economically and culturally conditioned, and so leave no place for freedom. Sartre, then, wished to remedy the *a priori* and dogmatic features of 'Stalinist' Marxism, and emphasize the human project, the notion that Man makes his being. In the early work *Being and Nothingness*, consciousness which *is* freedom recognizes itself in *anguish*; perhaps, even more basically, it experiences itself as desire. But in *Search for A Method* Sartre says that the fundamental existential feature is *need*. While desire suggests change and freedom, need is related to scarcity — there is simply not enough of the most immediate things necessary to stay alive and of those things which make life satisfying. This material fact of scarcity is there at the start, but human action makes out of the material fact a specific social pattern. It is Sartre's belief that transformed social relations and technical progress must free humanity from the yoke of scarcity. He defines Man as the being who possesses the possibility of making history, and emphasizes 'the human project', the notion that man makes his being by launching himself towards the future. In his later work Sartre accepts completely Marx's notion that 'men make their history upon the basis of prior conditions'. Some 'deterministic' Marxists have interpreted this statement as though it said that men are conditioned. Sartre, however, never denies the existence of the conditions, but he insists that it is still men who make history. The most fundamental characteristic of Man as consciousness is his ability to go beyond the situation. He is never identical with it but rather exists as a relation to it. Thus he determines how he will live it and what its meaning is to be. But at the same time he cannot exist except in a situation, and the process of continual surpassing (which is history) must include the particular conditions which go to make up the situation. Human freedom, Sartre asserted, must now be understood in the context of history, which was largely the history of class struggle. In short, Sartre adopted the Marxist view that the mode of men's lives is directly determined by the mode and relations of production. Moreover, the dominant ideas and values of a period are the ideas and values of the dominant class. And that history is in large part the history of the class struggle, and men will have freedom only when class is abolished. But in becoming a Marxist, Sartre suggests that we should search for a method whereby a phenomenological Marxism can hope to understand both individual persons and history: 'a Marxism which has been de-Stalinized, which recognizes that it is still in its infancy, a Marxism which reinstates the individual and his praxis at the very heart of history' — this seems to Sartre the proper place of an existentialist freedom to commit itself.

The change in Sartre's views from *Being and Nothingness* to *Search for a Method* which I have briefly described can be interpreted as a change from idealism to Marxism. Marx himself had been aware of the dangers of idealism and had criticized the Young Hegelians for it. Those features of life which may be regarded as dehumanizing were seen by Marx as neither necessary features of the human condition for all time, nor as arbitrarily legitimated ways of seeing. They resulted at any given point in historical time from real social relationships grounded in the relations of production – the dialectical relationship between material production and consciousness. And so, for Marx, the solution to man's dehumanization and the alienation of knowledge, lay not merely in mental criticism. He criticized the Young Hegelians for believing that men and their relationships are the products of consciousness and all that is needed is that we interpret what exists in a different way. Marx strongly opposed this and agreed that mental criticism, theoretical de-reification, was not enough; there must be a practical de-reification, and actual overthrow of social relations. I have stressed this point for several reasons: first, this particular criticism of the idealist position has been made of the Young Hegelians, and indeed of Marx's own early views. Second, this criticism of the idealist position can also be levelled at Sartre's views at the time he wrote *Being and Nothingness*. One of the interesting features of Sartre's radical conversion for me are the questions it raises about a phenomenological approach, questions with which Sartre must have constantly wrestled. What are the weaknesses of most phenomenological theorizing? What are the topics which phenomenological writers tend to neglect or misunderstand? I shall argue in chapter 6 that they are the neglect of the dialectic between consciousness and social being, and that of praxis. Questions concerning ideology and false consciousness are often underemphasized, as are certain issues connected with social structure, accounting procedures and power relations. It will be argued that problems concerned with the validity of accounts and dilemmas of imposition are often sidestepped, and that the stress of many phenomenologists on mental or theoretical de-reification is of only limited value.

Two Versions of Phenomenology: the Analytic and the Possibilitarian

I want now to relate the above depiction of a 'phenomenological model of Man' to the new sociology of education. A brief introduction to some aspect of *one* form of phenomenology has been given because it seems to me to be the best expression of the *spirit* of the new sociology of education.

Another way of saying this is that the roots of this approach to education lie in the interpretive (as opposed to the positivist or normative) tradition of social science.[5] Interpretive sociologists have often conceived of themselves as belonging to a tradition that confronts the institutionalized orthodoxy of academicism. Within the interpretive tradition, however, there are theorists as different as Husserl, Heidegger, Schutz, Berger and Luckmann, Mead, Merleau-Ponty or Sartre. Not only are there many interpretations of each writer, but most of them have different phases or periods within their work. I am suggesting that 'interpretive sociology' is such an ambiguous category that it is unhelpful. Nor can one talk of 'phenomenological sociology' usefully, as such a broad term disguises real differences. This is not to make the charge that the 'new' sociology of education is eclectic; in a sense its project of educational change has always remained consistent. But since the interpretive tradition includes within its aegis such a wide variety of different stances there are inevitably many ambiguities in the 'new' sociology of education. There is the irony that though the new approach has a radical political purpose, phenomenology has often been acknowledged as being apolitical, or even reactionary.[6] Within the interpretive tradition, a valuable distinction has been made between two positions which may help to illustrate this.[7] Though both 'the analytic' and 'the possibilitarian' positions are grounded in phenomenology, their differences are very marked; they have different conceptions of doing sociology and of its purpose.

The analytic position has been influenced by Heidegger (and, to some extent, Wittgenstein), and is exemplified in the work of Alan Blum and Peter McHugh. Analysts such as Blum and McHugh are very critical of all forms of scientific thinking, positivism. Not only do they reject the Popperian version of science, but also that version of positive speaking embodied in ethnomethodology. Both forms of positivism are committed to 'what is the case'. But Blum and McHugh are not interested in what is the case, but what it shows. They stress speech as a showing. The basis of their work is the recognition that what is spoken is less significant than what its speaking covers over. As they want to exemplify 'analysis', not membership, they have no respect for member's usage. In other words, they attempt to go beyond considerations about the mundane world and the rules of 'a language game', to 'the form of life' that makes that game playable. As Blum and McHugh write: 'Analysis is the concern not with anything said or written but with the grounds of whatever is said — the foundations that make what is said possible, sensible, conceivable.'[8] They consider, then, the possible community (and communities can be constructed in texts) that different theorists belong to. In this way, it could be said that they are reminding sociologists of the philosophical traditions in which they work. My own view is that this form of 'reflexive sociology' is very much absorbed in the meaning and nature of 'theorizing' and in epistemological problems. In a recent work they show how they continually responded to each other's papers, exploring the grounds of each other's formulations. As they themselves say, in being done, this work always makes available for analysis a new problem, namely how *it* is possible. I feel that this kind of work has little bearing on the struggle to make a better world. The 'new' sociology of education has no sympathy with this type of apolitical theorizing. It is felt that more is needed than merely 'showing' the form of life, and that, if possible, it should be challenged.

The other wing of the interpretive social science 'movement' whose primary concern is education emphasizes different features of phenomenological sociology. These, the 'possibilitarians' stress the modes, the possibilities, of transcending the experienced realities of everyday life. Writers on education such as Maxine Greene have been particularly influenced by the existentialism of Sartre and his model of Man.[9] Her main themes are authenticity, choice, the vast potential for change. The new sociologists of education often quote her writings.

> The phenomenologist would say that the self-aware teacher, functioning in situations known to be dehumanizing can give his students a sense of their possibilities to themselves.
>
> What is the teacher to do when he is asked to teach poor children . . .? If he supposes that a student's environment has been sterile and restrictive must he conclude that the student is for ever fated to a type of retardation? . . . As a teacher, however, he is committed to open possibilities.

No matter how pessimistic the predictions, no matter how appalling the test scores, he must act *as if* his students are free agents, responsible for choosing themselves.

It is because of these (naive?) optimistic beliefs that educational change can be brought about through the consciousness of teachers, completely disregarding structural constraints, that these views have been termed 'possibilitarian'. Much of this early work within the 'new' sociology of education radiates optimism and confidence; it stresses the power of consciousness to de-reify and change one's experience of reality. 'Possibilitarians' appealed to being authentic, the 'recovery of being'. The existentialist vocabulary points to the fact that the assumptions, the model of Man, held by these writers had certain similarities to that held by Sartre in his early work, where the undue emphasis placed on intentionality, choice of interpretation, psychological freedom suggested that one could overcome alienation by some sort of subjective conversion. In his later work, however, Sartre came to believe, as we have seen, that such an idealist notion ignored 'the power of circumstances'. In a similar way, some of the earlier work within the sociology of education stressed the possibilitarian view and had little to say about the lived experience of those to whom they most wanted to speak — the teachers who experience constraint in the classroom every day of their lives. Many of these teachers are aware of the theoretical possibilities of actually shaping their world but still feel coerced and oppressed by it. There is now an increasing recognition that mere questioning of assumptions cannot by itself transform the *status quo* and our lived realities. It is partly for this reason that some of the early work is seen as naively utopian.

In this chapter I have given a brief introduction to some aspects of phenomenology because the 'new' sociology of education explicitly adopted this stance. I have suggested that this approach was a conscious corrective to traditional positivist sociology which denied the significance of intentionality and freedom in the expression of human action. Second, I have focused on Sartre's early thought.[10] Within his philosophy I have stressed the power of consciousness, choice, and man's freedom to show that certain parallels can be drawn with the idealist views of the sociologists associated with 'new directions' in education, who were interested in similar notions. Though the distinction between 'the analytic' and 'the possibilitarian' positions may seem schematic, it is stated primarily to make the point that it is the Sartrean 'possibilitarian' stance that has fired the imagination of sociologists working within the 'new approach'. They quickly recognized aspects of 'possibilitarianism' in the work of Maxine Greene, Paulo Freire, Ivan Illich and others, and utilized them. Third, I have stated that in Sartre's work there was a reorientation from a phenomenological to a humanist-Marxist framework. This too was to be the experience of most of the new sociologists who gradually realized the limitations of mental de-reification at the expense of other elements. That is to say, material conditions of existence, though socially produced, have become objectified, and cannot be merely thought away. As with Sartre's early work, the emphasis on theoretical de-reification meant that there was a neglect of the economic constraints that arise from the mode of production in our society.

My argument, so far, may be summarized as follows. Rejecting positivism, and its association with an exploitative culture, the new sociology of education utilized some of the tenets and materials of anthropology and ethnography to attempt to bring about change. They were in opposition to structural functionalism and its reifications and wished to replace it with an interpretive model of social science. There was, perhaps, a tension between their adoption of social phenomenology, which can be seen as an apolitical stance, and their egalitarian aims. Political and moral principles, however vague and inexplicit, were involved because they did see themselves as struggling against the dominant pattern of power and privilege. Their critiques of hierarchy and elitism in the practice of education inevitably led to a polemic with certain philosophers of education. It is this issue that will be the main topic of the next chapter.

Chapter 4

The Rejection of the Liberal Philosophy of Education

I have argued in previous chapters that the main project of the 'new' sociology of education is the attempt to make the world better, the realization of a free and equal society in which dialogue would be the ideal form of relationship. Grounded in a vision of a just society, this view entails de-reification of the world of education. Things long unchanged appear unchangeable. By de-reification, I mean the conscious realization that though the world appears 'natural' and inevitable, really it is produced and controlled by us.

My primary concern in this chapter is to outline and discuss the main issues of the bitter debate between some philosophers of education and the 'new' sociologists of education. As I will be discussing the same issues: the relationships between pupils and teachers, teaching, the forms of knowledge, the curriculum, from differing perspectives, some repetition is unavoidable. The chapter consists of three sections.

The first deals with the *philosophers* of education; some criticisms are made of Peters and Hirst and their views. This section should enable us to understand some of the reasons why the philosophy of education that is dominant in this country was rejected by the sociologists of whom I am writing.

The second section focuses on the *sociologists* associated with the phenomenological approach, as manifested in *Knowledge and Control*. They wished to repudiate traditional, hierarchical givens. 'Labelling', and the artificial segmentation of different areas of discourse was also rejected. I suggest that the 'new' sociology of education was deeply influenced

51

by Paulo Freire's criticisms of the 'banking' model of education, and by Maxine Greene's critique of the 'Anglo-American' tradition of philosophy. Greene stresses the point that the curriculum should not be seen as something objective, pre-structured, external to the knower. It must be made meaningful by consciousness. This section, then, is a phenomenological critique of prevailing definitions.

In the third section of this chapter I suggest that it may also be useful to study knowledge from a Marxist perspective. From this viewpoint it is possible to see philosophy of education as an ideology that supports existing political and economic hierarchies. It is my contention that the liberal philosophers' view of 'education as initiation' legitimates an inequitable set of social arrangements.

Some Criticisms of Peters and Hirst

The views of philosophers of education, like those of Richard Peters and Paul Hirst, have attained a dominant status in most colleges of education.[1] They believe education to be an initiation into worth-while activities; 'the initiation into forms of knowledge and public traditions enshrined in a public language'. In their view education is the transmission of modes of thought and conduct which have standards written into them, by reference to which it is possible to act, think and feel with varying degrees of skill, relevance and taste. Thus described, education can have no ends beyond itself, and its values derive from principles and standards implicit in it.[2] Paul Hirst has argued that historically the concept of liberal education was known to the Greeks, who based it on the forms of knowledge they had achieved. He states that the definition and justification of liberal education since then has often been based on the nature and significance of the forms of knowledge. This seems to him a more objective and constant ground than when there have been the vested interests of political, religious and utilitarian pressure groups to contend with. For these philosophers, then, education must be worked out in terms of the 'forms of knowledge' which are publicly specifiable. Education is determined in scope and content by knowledge itself and is thereby concerned with the development of mind.[3] It is a necessary feature of knowledge as such that there be public criteria which give objectivity to knowledge, and this in turn gives objectivity to the concept of liberal education.

Rather than attempt a detailed critique of the work of Peters and Hirst I shall limit my discussion to a few issues directly linked to the *sociological* concerns of this book, and to outline the main areas of confrontation between the 'new' sociologists of education and the philosophers of education. (I will refer to Peters and Hirst as the 'liberal philosophers', but later in this chapter will use this term in a political sense.) However, besides making criticisms of the liberal philosophers, I hope also to point out *alternative conceptions* that derive from the work of anthropologists and social phenomenologists. First, let us briefly consider the views of the 'liberal philosophers' on the relationship between pupils, teachers and knowledge.

My first contention is that these philosophers' model of education implies an asymmetric relationship – it presumes a superiority of the teacher. By saying that they have an asymmetric bias, I mean that there is an over-emphasis on the way social meanings are imposed on children. There is a parallel here between these philosophers and some positivist sociologists who also believe that meanings are the same for everyone, shared universally. That is to say, both the liberal philosophers and the positivistic sociologists of education do not consider sufficiently the construction of meaning by pupils and others.[4] The liberal philosophers have a 'deficit' view of pupils. Thus the teacher has a corpus of knowledge to be transmitted, and the pupil has a deficit until he has been brought 'up' to it; in a word, initiated. This has been called the 'banking' model of education. The teacher's view or definition may be imposed on a child for whom it has very little meaning. The imposition lies in the fact that the liberal philosophers have a pre-defined notion of rationality. It means that the theorizing of children, working with different notions of logic and rationality, is often denied. The Kantian notion of respect for persons is often alluded to, but does not the taken-for-granted superiority of the knowledge of the teacher imply a lack of respect for the other ways of theorizing?

I want now, briefly, to comment on the liberal philosophers' view of knowledge. Paul Hirst, particularly, has argued that there is a division of knowledge into seven 'forms'. He claims that these divisions are not arbitrary but unavoidable, and that therefore thinking must submit to impersonal standards. He has written that the forms of knowledge, mathematics, the sciences, knowledge of other minds (history), religion, philosophy, ethics and the arts have the following characteristics. Each form contains key concepts which belong to it alone. Second, each form of knowledge has a distinctive logical structure and the concepts of one form cannot be used in discussing another form which has its own relevant concepts. Third, each form of knowledge, with its own concepts, logical structure and particular techniques, had distinctive expressions that are testable against experience. Each form may have distinctive types of questions and the expressions are testable by the particular criteria that are peculiar to the form.[5] The liberal philosphers gloss over many of the difficulties concerning the procedures and tests of validity.

There is, for example, the question of different interpretations of phenomena and events in history. In ethics and philosophy there is little agreement as to the principles on which to base human action. Among artists there is disagreement about what is or is not an art object. There are, moreover, conflicts amongst practitioners about the nature of their own discipline; in such cases the criteria of validity of one perspective cannot be applied even to the work of those who hold a different perspective. The notion of epistemic community can hardly apply here. It is for reasons such as these that the assertion that the forms of knowledge have distinctive procedures and tests of validity is in need of further explanation and justification. Moreover, Hirst deals chiefly with propositional knowledge and his work appears to exclude two other kinds of knowledge: knowing how, or skills, and knowledge by acquaintance. Propositional knowledge remains abstract unless linked with these. This emphasis on the propositional is not found in the new sociologists of education, who always stress the notion that experiences are meaningless unless they are made meaningful by understanding.

The liberal philosophers have asserted that there must be independent criteria, standards of validity, to which all should defer. It is said these factors arise from the structure of knowledge that is above bargaining.[6] Knowledge is not open to any set of definitions – after all, for communication to take place, there must be agreement about definitions, agreements about judgments. I concede that at a very simple level there may be common-sense knowledge that is socially agreed, and which is non-ideological. But even in philosophy there are competing rationalist, empiricist and pragmatic traditions in discussing knowledge. But most philosophers, and I am generalizing here, have tended to treat knowledge as a truth, an absolute. I impute to most English philosophers of education the belief that knowledge is absolute, that it is fixed and unchanging, that it has independent criteria and is therefore above bargaining. Knowledge, for them, is seen as a set of unsituated, uncontexted meanings. For example, they claim that they possess the criteria for knowing what knowledge is worth while; knowledge being thought of as if it was context free, universalistic. But, of course, what the liberal philosophers of education say is related to the *way* they do philosophy. This is my next point.

It is from Wittgenstein that linguistic analysis, or 'ordinary-use' philosophy, is derived, and much of the work of most philosophers of education in this country is based on the analysis of concepts and their use in language. Contrary to what many critics believe, ordinary language philosophy is concerned not merely with words but also with the world, and can enrich our understanding of politics, society and human thought.[7] But the liberal philosophers have adopted a particular reading of Wittgenstein which conveys the intent that ordinary language philosophy is merely verbal. Their method makes use of 'central' or 'paradigm' cases, and of their analysis of concepts we can always ask: Whose 'normal' use is it? That normal usage may vary according to different groups is not considered. Moreover, they sharpen the concept and stipulate its use, ignoring the fact that others may have different, unshared meanings. In other words, through their method they prescribe for us a way of seeing. Few challenge this way of doing philosophy. Some philosophers, of course, do show that perhaps Peters's usage of a word is not central as he claims (or that others use it differently with equal, or greater, significance), but in doing this they accept Peters's mode of philosophizing, his version of 'rational' argument. It seems to me that even those philosophers of education who are critical of the dominant mode share too many of its assumptions to be useful to us who wish to challenge prevailing coercive attitudes and structures, and formulate alternatives. In brief, I have suggested that the 'method' of the liberal philosophers has usually been taken for granted; they themselves have thought of it as objective, context free, consensual, rather in the same way as many sociologists of education regarded their own subject. An important feature of the method of the liberal philosophers consists of seeing knowledge as independent and 'out there' and conceiving of themselves as 'messengers', as if it is through them that knowledge speaks. They do not conceive that it is they who take it upon themselves to give a version of knowledge, 'rationality' and 'education', and so realize and maintain it.[8]

The Undermining of Traditional Hierarchies

As the new sociology was against inequality, it rejected many traditional hierarchies as being oppressive. 'Labelling', too, was repudiated. I use this term, from symbolic interactionist theory, to refer to the process where a weak or deviant group is categorized invidiously. Pupils, for example, are 'labelled' as being of less ability by being placed in certain streams, or they are thought of as being 'culturally deprived'. The rejection of labels is based on a desire to prevent the painful effect of this process which often results in treating others as other than they may be. Some sort of process by which we categorize the world may be inevitable, but this particular form, labelling, implies imposition; it is a form of social control. Labels, moreover, ensure closure in one's thoughts. (This is precisely the danger of diagrammatic 'maps' of intellectual positions presented to students; rather than clarify, they often close discussion). This does not mean of course that categorizations are never made; that, in the infinite regress of relativism, 'anything goes'. The changes wanted lie in a certain direction.

The refusal of the new sociologists to make traditional hierarchical distinctions applies to several areas. But, perhaps,

I should put this less strongly; rather than a refusal there is a *reluctance* to make hierarchical distinctions. This often leads in practice to the adoption of the inverse of the usual, 'taken-for-granted' view. It is held, for example that:

> Pupils can contribute as much to learning as teachers.
> Teachers' research is as useful as that of sociologists.
> Actors' categories are more adequate than those of scientific observers.
> Lay theorizing is as meaningful as professional.

The above statements seem to me to be some of the key presuppositions of the new sociology, and derive, in part, from the phenomenological writings of Schutz on actors' categories, Merleau-Ponty on childhood and Garfinkel on common-sense theorizing.

In evaluating the views of the new sociologists of education I think it is helpful to be aware of these presuppositions – that which is the basis of our belief, but is usually not stated, and which, even if uncovered, always needs further explication. The important point is that the new sociologists believed that their project could begin by *stressing similarities rather than differences* between children and adults, lay and professional, pupils and teachers, common-sense theorizing. *This may be seen as a possible programme of acts undermining the traditional hierarchical 'givens'.* But these are not only political acts but moral ones, because they involve the returning of respect to those whom it has been previously denied. If these presuppositions seem 'to turn the world upside down', it is because they are about relationships of dominance and subordinancy; though they derive from social phenomenology, they have a moral and *political* dimension.

Sociology, then, is seen as a moral pursuit. But an apparent contradiction could be pointed out to us: How can we be committed to sociology as a moral pursuit, if ethics is possible only on the basis of a suspended commitment? Such a question is based on the view that there is a logical distinction which can be made between facts and values; it is founded on the belief that it is possible to conceive of one without the other. This is a belief I would want to deny; there is nothing that we know, towards which we do not have attitudes, and that in knowing something we already esteem or condemn it.

Likewise, our values are attached to what we take to be the 'facts'. Each includes the other. In other words, judgments can never be severed from their contexts.

With 'context' we face again familiar questions: What is the context, and how close or far should we draw it? What is relevant within it? How and why do we perceive and demarcate it in a certain place? There are also other difficulties: on the one hand we have spoken of the reluctance to make distinctions, and yet I have suggested above that in knowing something we already esteem or condemn it. Perhaps the former is a theoretical point – what we would like to believe – and the latter, a practical one – what we actually do? This may be another of those issues that are successfully resolved by people in their daily practice.

That there are difficulties with the position is obvious.[9] It is difficult not to make hierarchical distinctions. Of course, the above presuppositions need explication; 'as useful', 'as meaningful', to whom and for what? Such a relativistic approach, when applied to the practical problems of everyday living, leads to many ambiguities and problems, which will be discussed in chapters 6 and 7. But now let us turn to the pupil-teacher relationship, and note how the views of the new sociologists of education contrast with those of the liberal philosophers.

I believe that the thinking of the 'new' sociologists about teaching has been deeply influenced by Paulo Freire. It is, perhaps, through the study of his work that the reader would gain most insight into alternative conceptions of education.[10] In brief, Freire argues that in most institutions today the teacher-student relationship has fundamentally a narrative character; the narrating subject is the teacher, and the patient listening objects are the students, who are treated as containers or receptacles. In the 'banking' concept of education the scope of action allowed to students extends only so far as receiving, filing and storing the deposits. The teacher makes deposits which the students patiently receive, memorize and repeat. The banking concept of education has the following practices: the teacher teaches and the students are taught. The teacher knows everything and students know nothing. The teacher chooses and the student complies. The teacher is the subject, the pupils mere objects. This seems to sum up so much of the teaching that goes on in our schools.

Freire believes that this 'deposit-making' education should be replaced with problem-posing education in which students become critical co-investigators in dialogue with the teacher. For the dialogical teacher-student the content of education is a 're-presentation' to individuals of the things about which they want to know more. The content of education includes generative themes which are obtained from the students, but of course the teacher also has a right to suggest themes. Freire stresses that there must be a concern for the links between themes, a concern to pose these themes as problems, and a concern for their historical-cultural context. The task of the dialogical teacher, who is in an interdisciplinary team, is to 'represent' these themes to the individuals from whom he received them, not as a lecture but as problems. In other words, the themes which come from the students return to them not as contents to be deposited but as problems to be solved. In short, teachers and students are both subjects in the task of unveiling reality and re-creating knowledge through common reflection and action; thus, teachers and students discover themselves as its permanent re-creators. Freire's writings, it seems to me, are a continual reminder of how some formerly passive students can turn against their domestication when they come to perceive that reality is really a process undergoing transformation. Freire believes in praxis, the action of men in order to change reality for the purposes of human liberation.

It is also important to look at the work of Maxine Greene, as she has written a phenomenological critique of the liberal philosophers of education, and their views on the curriculum and knowledge. She argues that their way of seeing, their understanding of the alternative conceptions of philosophy, is limited. The work of Peters, Hirst and P.H. Phenix is part of what has been called 'the Anglo-American tradition'. This way of doing philosophy has persistently ignored or at best has been dismissive of another conception of philosophy, the European phenomenological tradition which has its roots in the work of Hegel, Husserl and Heidegger, and is represented today by the work of Sartre, Merleau-Ponty and others.

Maxine Greene, who has made this distinction between the traditions, has used literature as an example to show the difference.[11] She points out that in Britain and America the autonomy and impersonality of art is stressed – it is seen as a self-enclosed, isolated structure. But the phenomenological tradition believes that a literary work – or a curriculum – cannot be divorced from experience. In this tradition each work is treated as a manifestation of an individual writer's experience – a conscious effort on the part of an artist to understand his own lived-world. A reader must then re-create it in terms of his consciousness. There must be continual reconstructions if a work is to be meaningful. The reader does not merely regenerate; he creates a new totality. She finds these views suggestive for 'a conception of the learner who is"open to the world", eager indeed condemned to give meaning to it – and in the process of doing so recreating or generating the materials of a curriculum in terms of his consciousness'. To make sense is to liberate oneself. Maxine Greene is critical of Peters who is, *par excellence*, an exponent of an objective pre-structured approach to the curriculum where the disciplines are objective, existent, external to the knower, there to be discovered, mastered, learned. She argues that parents, teachers, policemen, psychiatrists – and curriculum designers – are enforcers of reality, and that if the curriculum is seen as something external to the search for meaning it becomes an alienating edifice.The curriculum requires a subject if it is to be disclosed, and it can be disclosed only if the learner, himself engaged in generating the structures, lends the curriculum his life. Only when a student is committed to act upon the world will learning occur. We should, therefore, present a curriculum in such a way that it does not impose or enforce. To the philosophers of education in the Anglo-American tradition, the curriculum and its relation to a concept of knowledge is very different. They support the view that there is some knowledge that is 'abstract' and therefore superior. Knowledge that is 'practical' is regarded as having low status. And so 'abstract' theorizing becomes possible only for the initiated, privileged few.

But, in opposition to the liberal philosophers, the 'new' sociologists of education wish to maintain that we are all theorists. We are not simply passive agents who adjust to external stimuli but are active agents who organize and make sense of our worlds. It is crucial to point out that these definitions are not god-given, or in the nature of things, but are social constructions, and if a definition of 'abstract' limits and constricts us, and if we realize this, then we can change this hierarchical view of knowledge. This point, that knowledge and what is regarded as abstract thought should not be treated as a 'given', as something objective, context free or universal, and consensual, can be illustrated by examples from the work of anthropologists such as John Gay and Michael Cole, Robin Horton and Thomas Gladwin, among others, which shows that what is considered 'abstract' is socially and culturally situated. Both anthropologists and the 'new sociologists or education' stress, then, the contextual and situated character of knowledge.[12] They emphasize that notions like 'ability', 'childhood', 'knowledge', and so forth are socially constructed. Knowledge, like language, is not independent of its use, and should be understood in its social and historical context.

Liberal Philosophy of Education as an Ideology

Many English philosophers of education, like Peters and Hirst, have ignored the question of ideology. They have not seen their own work as ideological. It could be argued that such is the range of knowledge, and what is seen as provisionally 'successful', 'useful' and 'adequate', that many philosophers have ignored questions such as: How is knowledge selected and maintained? In what ways is knowledge distributed and legitimated? Sociologists of knowledge have been increasingly influential as they have focused their attention on trying to account for different bodies of knowledge and epistemologies in different societies, in different times, and their growth and change. Because thought is not independent of an historical- and socially-determined set of meanings, sociologists have tried to relate thought to social positions, to occupational, political and other interest groups. Their view is that knowledge is neither absolute nor autonomous. It is not value free but is grounded in the actions and interests of men.

Knowledge can be described and accounted for differently by various approaches. A Durkheimian, for instance, might stress the reproduction of knowledge rather than its production. A phenomenologist, on the other hand, might focus on *how* knowledge is constructed rather than why it is made real in certain ways. But one of the problems with the phenomenological approach is its injunction always to accept the viewpoint of the actor, and the rationality of others in different forms of life. This can lead to many difficulties, as it is not possible to know which view is right or wrong. What do we believe, how do we act, if different views contradict one another? If all must be accepted – then we are faced with relativism. In other words, the relativism of phenomenologically-inspired sociology of education may not have any way of criticizing different varieties of knowledge. Some other perspective – such as a Marxian one – may therefore be a necessity. These problems will be fully discussed in chapter 6. In chapter 7 I will argue for the necessity of an integration of phenomenology and Marxism. But, to continue with the task at hand, I suggest that we take a preliminary look at some aspects of knowledge from a Marxist perspective. This will allow us to study the influential 'mainstream' philosophy of education that is taught in this country as a liberal ideology.

A reading of Marx may provide a model of Man as a producer; a creature of need, who in order to obtain satisfaction of his needs, created tools and invented work. Through his own work Man controls Nature and appropriates it in part. Work then modifies nature, externally and internally, and itself becomes a need. And then needs change, as work modifies them by producing new goods. Man, then, is linked with Nature, and has a dialectical relationship with it, transforms it to appropriate it, both around and inside himself. Social existence determines consciousness. In this view, knowledge or ideas are never free from the interests of the actors involved in their production. It may be remembered that Marx argued that 'the ideas of the ruling class are in every epoch the ruling ideas . . . they regulate the production and distribution of the ideas of their age'.[13] But in what ways are the ideas of the ruling class ideologies? What are their constituent features and what purposes do they serve?

For Marx an ideology was a distorted account, and these accounts had themselves to be accounted for (by the mode of production). Ideologies deal with segments of human weakness and are sometimes used to account for and justify inexplicable or absurd actions. The importance of ideologies lies in the fact that they are ways of interpretation which limit possibilities, or conceiving of alternatives. I now suggest that the following characteristics are the necessary conditions of an ideology. Ideologies start as a partial view of the world and remain unaware of their presuppositions. Second, they refract reality via pre-existing categories selected by dominant groups and acceptable to them. Third, they generate special and limited interests. Fourth, they have a significant part in maintaining order without force by securing the assent of the oppressed and exploited to their own situation. They do this by creating images for the dominant class or group.[14]

If we begin with the presupposition that there is no inherent, intrinsic meaning to objects, and that perception is relative, it could be said that the world does not consist of objects which are completely and totally distinct from the observing subject. All knowledge is grounded in perception, but all perception is from a certain spatial point and refers to other points in space. In the same way, perception is also necessarily perception at a particular time and it refers to time past and time to come. Perception and therefore knowledge, being relative and emergent, certain rules and criteria are agreed and defined by groups. A particular view is agreed upon by a group for many reasons such as biographical, historical, economic ones. A group then attempts to maintain and tries to legitimate a way of seeing and understanding which becomes *the* way. *Bodies of shared meanings held by groups such as teachers or psychiatrists can be viewed as ideologies.* In other words, ideas and beliefs of practitioners such as managers or politicians can be located historically and in their institutional context. There can also be observed the tendency of groups to make the knowledge from their point of view appear *absolute*.

It will have been noticed that a persistent theme of the new sociology of education is that knowledge is inevitably selected — but how and by whom? And why is one particular selection regarded as superior to another? This process of selection is not usually discussed, and many philosophers of education treat knowledge as if it were independent of Man and the methods of its production. The liberal philosophers seem to give to the forms of knowledge a kind of *a priori*, unexaminable, unchangeable status. They are unwilling to admit that the forms of knowledge are no more than the historical constructs of a particular time. What they emphasize is that knowledge is 'objective', that knowledge is external to the individual and imposed on him. This separates the knower from the known; it separates knowledge from the context of its use. To put it in another way, the liberal philosophers make knowledge the subject and men the predicate. These questions, however, are not only about 'knowledge', but about *men* who have concepts of knowledge and action. By not fully appreciating the constructive nature of human consciousness, the philosophers' view removes responsibility from men for the world. The new sociology of education emphasizes the human character of what we know; that knowing cannot be detached from what it is to know. Knowledge is the relation between knower and known.

There is then a growing questioning of education as initiation into the forms of knowledge and 'worth-while' activities. We should perhaps judge the liberal philosophers not only by what they advocate in educational theory but what they support in practice. If they see themselves as manning the gates to the public traditions, does their conservatism fulfil a reactionary purpose?

Let me try and sum all this up. It has been suggested that the liberal philosophers' model of education as initiation presumes a superiority of the teacher. There is a common assumption that the greater the age or experience of the teacher the more valid their prescriptions for the young. Those still at school are still defined as 'incapable', needing remedying. The prevalent notion is that because they are young they are in some sense 'deficient'. In this process children are sifted so that only a few are allowed to 'the top of the pyramid'. Examinations are the mechanism by which this is done and are demonstrations by the examiners of what constitutes valid knowledge. The ability of some students to pass these examinations can be looked at as no more than having learnt the examiner's rules. Both teachers and students can thus be seen as acting in a form of bad faith, where both treat knowledge purely instrumentally. My argument is not merely that examinations are part of the increasing bureaucratization of knowledge, but that there is a much more serious consequence if one regards knowledge as a facticity. If the disciplines are seen as objectively existent, external to the knower, as so many philosophers of education see them, then there is real danger; if the curriculum is seen as something external to the search for meaning, it may become an alienating edifice. It is possible that much of the alienation that is felt in the schools is one of the many unintended consequences of the teachings of the liberal philosophers.

In contrast to this view of knowledge it is suggested that different areas be looked at not as 'bodies of knowledge' but as human activities. This implies that the emphasis would be not on 'purity' but on relevance to everyday life. The adoption of such an approach would entail an end to the present hierarchical subject-defined view of the world. Knowledge would cease to be exclusive to a narrow professional group but would be thought of in terms of interest and understanding reaching all people.

In short, it is my contention that the liberal philosophers treat education as if it was the transmission of worth-while activities in schools, which are themselves regarded as if they were neutral institutions. The worth-whileness of the activities, the contents of the curriculum, are rarely questioned; the nature of education and knowledge is taken for granted, fixed. Their model of education is based on hierarchical views of knowledge, and its differentiation into 'abstract' and 'practical' is then related to their treatment of learners. Their conception of the nature of philosophy is narrow but even their own method contains many limitations. The problematic nature of the 'forms of knowledge' thesis is not recognized and the belief in the externality of knowledge leads to its reification. By the reification of knowledge I am referring to the notion that 'knowledge' is variable and changes historically, but that it is legitimized and we are brought to think of it as a natural and necessary *fact*. One of the unintended consequences for many individuals of these views is that, among other factors, the reification of knowledge leads to alienation – a process that refers to manipulation by hostile forces in which there is separation from, and loss of control over, one's immediate environment. It can be said, then, that the liberal philosophers are ethnocentric, remaining unconscious of the normative nature of their presuppositions, and on the basis of these presuppositions they are both evaluative and prescriptive. And, as all theoretical positions have implications for political practice, we can therefore ask: What are the implications of their stance?

Through the form and content of their philosophy of education, the liberal philosophers prescribe for us a restricted way of seeing the world. These philosophers have a particular view of the nature of Man, rationality, society, but they seem to be unaware of the presuppositions of their own inquiries. Moreover, they have not recognized the inescapable social character of philosophy. For them social reality lies outside the individuals who make up society, and in this process they come to treat knowledge as if it were something other than a human product, a manifestation of divine will or a fact of nature; they reify knowledge. Inevitably the combination of their particular view of the nature of man, of knowledge, of society, produces a view of social life that is hierarchical, elitist and oppressive. This view of social reality, the outcome of their assumptions and method, is then prescribed for us as *the* way of seeing and talking about the world. There are of course many versions of liberal theory, but, broadly speaking, I mean by it the view that there should be a gradual improvement of existing social arrangements. Liberals desire social amelioration but without conflict, and their work tends to legitimize an inequitable set of social arrangements. The philosophers discussed above not only believe in liberal education – they wish to preserve the *status quo* through a doctrine as to what counts as knowledge – but are liberal in *politics*. Being reformist, their work supports the existing power structure.

I have argued in this chapter that this particular philosophy, 'education as initiation', stresses the superiority of the teacher, and a curriculum that is based on a hierarchical view of knowledge. In such a view knowledge comes to be reified. Alienation is one consequence. Gradually this group of writers have come to dominate the teaching of the philosophy of education in this country. This should be a matter of serious concern because this particular view of education is inextricably linked with persuasive definitions of authority, freedom, democracy. That is to say, their philosophy of education is based on certain assumptions about the interrelationship between education and society which are characteristic of liberal politics. Reform may be urged — but only on the margins. The philosophy of education propagated by Peters and Hirst is an ideology that supports the existing pattern of power and privilege.

Chapter 5

The Importance of Classroom Studies

In the last three chapters I have attempted to show how the 'new' sociology of education challenged those aspects of the prevailing conception of education which it regarded as oppressive. This chapter consists of six sections. I begin by recalling the key features of 'traditional' sociology of education. This is counterposed with the radically different conceptions of the 'new' approach concerning the nature of Man and knowledge. It will be argued that one of the achievements of this approach is that it shifted attention from the home to what happens in the classroom.

After this introductory section, a few selected classroom studies – those of Becker, Rist, Hargreaves and Werthman – are utilized to focus upon the implicit assumptions of teachers, and how these affect the organization of the material, and the treatment of pupils. The third section continues the main theme: the defining processes that occur within the school itself; how teachers observe, classify and react to class-type differences in the behaviour of children. In other words, how, through the process of teachers' classification, the 'labelling' of pupils into different categories, the school creates failure. In the fourth section some limitations of the 'labelling' approach are discussed. The study 'Classroom Knowledge' by Keddie is examined in the fifth section. In contrast, the chapter concludes with an assessment of a study which is explicitly critical of the phenomenological approach in sociology. The authors of this study, Sharp and Green, regard 'progressivism' in education as utopian, a mode of social control, an ideology.

Differing Approaches in the Sociology of Education: the Structural-Functionalist and the Interpretive

One of the most persistent questions in education has been: Why do working-class children fail? The explanation usually given by traditional sociology was in terms of antecedent factors such as the social class to which the children belonged, or the kind of family upbringing they had received. In most discussions of cultural deprivation similar arguments (drawn from social pathology) were used; children being seen as coming from deficient backgrounds, being inadequately socialized, or culturally deprived, and therefore needing enrichment, compensatory education. Much of the research was concerned with social stratification and the ways in which social class was made significant in the school. But many of the 'traditional' sociologists who gave such explanations were liberal rather than radical. The notion of stratification, for example, was not questioned; it was as if social justice was obtained if and when intelligent working-class children were mobile enough to enter the middle class. Other assumptions in their work are those of the dominant sociological paradigm of the period. There was an espousal of structural functionalism; of positivist methodology such as statistics; a stress on consensus, and a belief in a passive model of Man. Individuals were seen as inactive, their responses being pre-determined, their identities being fixed by early childhood experiences. A study of some of the papers in Halsey, Floud and Anderson's sociology of education reader *Education, Economy and Society* illustrates well what I mean, particularly Talcott Parsons's 'The School Class as a Social System' (see chapter 1, n. 2). Parsons sees a school class from a functional point of view; it is an agency of socialization, the internalization of values and norms that a child could not learn from his family alone. The school class is a place where children are trained to have commitments to certain shared values and technical capacities required by society. The stress is on the specific *role* of the individual. Skill, for example, is thought of in terms of tasks involved in a role. According to this view, teachers are merely agents of the community's school system, and are involved in a process by which children are selected and allocated differential status.

Work in this tradition is common; studies continue to appear where educational failure is explained in terms of faulty socialization, or deficiencies in the home. Certain behaviours or conditions are observed at school and the causes are sought in the child's pre-school life. The new 'interpretive' sociology of education rejected structural-functionalism; the latter, it was argued, ignored the *social* character of classrooms, places where reality is constructed and negotiated. The 'new' sociology shifted our attention from the home to the classroom. By popularizing American research and producing significant work of its own, it focused attention on a topic which previously had been neglected in the sociology of education in Britain: the study of classrooms. In our everyday lives we usually take the qualities and charac-teristics of children, or pupil-learners, for granted, our con-ceptions being those of our culture and our time. The 'new' sociology made available a radically different approach – it questioned what was taken to be 'natural' or 'obvious'.[1] This was, in part, the attraction of work that dealt with con-ceptions of childhood in other times, or of learners in other cultures, which made conventional, accepted, views prob-lematic. If one examines traditional textbooks, it can be seen that pupils are viewed as passive learners who have to be socialized into the cultural norms, the central value system of 'society'. In such a sociology, because of a positivist view of language, there was no possibility of interpretation. Nor was negotiation possible.

Against these views, the 'new' sociology advanced different notions of the nature of Man and of knowledge. It argued that because the focus had been on equality of opportunity, school organization and selection, *knowledge*, particularly its social organization and distribution, had been overlooked. The traditional view of knowledge that prevails is that real worth-while knowledge is theoretical, verbal, abstract (that is to say, unrelated to everyday life). Its main qualities are seen to be absolute and objective. This is denied by the 'new' sociologists of education, who stress the social origin and relativity of knowledge, and argue that truth and objectivity are social products.

An important feature of many of the classroom studies that I will be considering is that they pose questions about knowledge: What are the different models of mind that teachers implicitly have, and what importance does it have for the way they teach, the way the material is organized and the way the pupil is treated? Most of the classroom studies are based on the symbolic interactionism of George Herbert Mead; their appeal was immediate. Dealing with the micro-level of society, this stance was so obviously human and humane that it was seen as challenging and abstract and deterministic structural-functionalism dominant in sociology. Interactionism postulates the view that people (and objects) have no inherent characteristics, no intrinsic qualities; these are constructed through mutual definition, negotiation.[2] Some of the studies also draw on the social phenomenology of Alfred Schutz.[3] This perspective stresses that the world is created by consciousness; reality is socially constructed. Reality is a situated, on-going and negotiable process, and language is a filter system for the construction of meaning. While in traditional sociology education was seen mainly as an agent of socialization, in this view socialization itself is seen as a reciprocal relationship. The pupil is an active learner and it places on him responsibility for his own learning, and 'authoring the world'. This phenomenological view of the learner is also expressed clearly in the writings of Paulo Freire. The 'new' sociologists of education found much in common with Freire's work, which contains both phenomeno-logical and Marxist elements. His work provided inspiration: 'All educational practice implies a theoretical stance on the educator's part. This stance implies an interpretation of man and his world'. To think of pupils as empty vessels to be filled is wrong, according to Freire, who suggests that pupils and teachers should collaborate and construct the world together in a dialogical relationship.

Some Classroom Studies

My aim in this chapter is not to give systematic expositions of classroom studies, which are well known.[4] In this inter-pretive exploration of a few selected studies my intention is to focus on some of the questions they raise, problems that are difficult to solve. One of the key studies that illustrate the process whereby teachers classify pupils, and the consequences that follow from this, was made by H.S. Becker.[5] He suggests that workers in the service occupations, waitresses, mechanics – and teachers – have an image of their 'ideal client'. It is in terms of *this fiction* that they fashion their conception of how their work ought to be performed, and their actual work techniques. He found, for example, that differences in ability to do school work, as perceived by teachers, leads to differences in actual teaching techniques. Less is expected of those teachers whose subjects are more difficult to teach; and the problem becomes more aggravated in each grade. These are, of course, themes developed by other sociologists. Becker argues that schools favour middle-class values such as material success, individual striving, thrift and social mobility. Many teachers cannot comprehend the behaviour of poor children who fail to display these virtues. Indeed, their values are so different that they deeply offend the middle-class teachers' sensibilities; the pupils' values are unacceptable. The dilemma is that professionals depend on society to provide them with 'ideal' clients, but many factors, such as social class, operate to produce clients who fail to have these specifications.

This theme, how teachers classify, is also the subject of R.C. Rist's research which was done in a black primary school.[6] A teacher who differentiated children in the reception class based her classification on physical appearance, ease of interaction, the quality and quantity of English and a sketchy knowledge of home background. At the table nearest to her she placed the fast learners, the 'Tigers'. The others, the 'Cardinals' and the 'Clowns', were placed at tables further away from her. They, of course, received some teaching, but they made fewer attempts to interact with their teacher, and were given less opportunity to show their knowledge. This study, one of many, illustrates how the process of teachers' classification contributes to pupils' failure.

That teachers create pupil failure is also shown by works such as David Hargreaves' *Social Relations in a Secondary School*.[7] It is a study of teacher classification, of streaming; how pupils, in response to being labelled, develop certain behaviour patterns. Like Becker, he argues that the school is founded on, fosters and perpetuates middle-class values; the higher the stream the greater the degree of conformity to middle-class values. The higher the stream the greater is the pupil-commitment to school, satisfaction with school life and conformity to the expectations of teachers. The teacher tends to categorize pupils on the basis of stream. He expects certain behaviour, and he may in his own behaviour emit expectations to which the pupil will conform – an example of a self-fulfilling prophecy. The values held by the low-stream pupils are the opposite of those held by their peers in the high streams. Those in the low streams have a sense of failure. The school accentuates this by reducing their occupational aspirations. The allocation and attitudes of teachers increase this divergence between upper and lower streams. Streaming is thus self-validating in that it *manufactures* the differences on which it is justified. The new sociologists of education had a similar analysis. It is through processes such as these that success is guaranteed for some, whereas there is the institutionalization of failure for others. And the pressure on teachers to make these hierarchical classifications, different ways of grading and marking students, *which parallels the division of labour*, is increasing.

'Labelling' and Negotiation

My argument, so far, is that one of the consequences of the shift of attention from the home to the classroom was that the blame for failure was removed from the child and family. The *school* was the definer of failure – but how? This is where the question of classification is vital; it is through this process that teachers place pupils in certain categories and define for them their identities. 'Labelling' imposes an identity on a pupil by organizing the *expectations* of teachers, parents and others, in their interactions with the child. It sharply reduces alternative ways for the pupil to relate to it. Classification then forecloses alternative interpretations of an individual or situation. It is a mode of control.[8] After all, it is not the student's own classification that is used, but of those who have power to 'label', the 'reality-definers'. Through classification of pupils into different categories teachers and administrators define 'success' and 'failure'. Once given, the labels tend to remain fixed and lead to differential treatment, as so many of these studies show. If a teacher has to complete a large number of reports and record cards, and time is short, then he is likely, in Cicourel's words 'to routinize the character of the cases he handles and view them as falling within some general (but not explicit) principles about human nature, youth, delinquency'.[9]

Once written, objectified, the reports represent the truth; they influence not only teachers' perceptions of pupils, but also pupils' perception of themselves. There is then a close connection between educators' categories and pupils' careers, because, ultimately, labelling affects pupils' life chances. Writing about institutions where students are regularly assigned to counsellors, Kitsuse and Cicourel remark: 'What is even more disturbing is the prospect that this solicitous treatment will produce a new generation of youth socialized to the practice of easy confessions and receptive to 'professional' explanations of who they are and what they aspire to become.'[10]

Streaming is a metaphor, if you like, of the type of hierarchical distinctions that the 'new' sociology of education is against. Many teachers and administrators locate problems in the pupils who are perceived as 'failures' or 'troublemakers'. But, as many of the new writers pointed out, if attention was focused on the meaning of classroom situations from the viewpoint of the pupils (whom teachers regarded as 'problems', 'thick', 'yobbos', 'ineducable'), we might discover quite different explanations for educational success or failure. Carl Werthman's study, it seems to me, conforms to such a 'programme', in that it deals with the meaning of classroom interaction in a way that makes the behaviour of apparently difficult students sensible and rational.[11] It is different from many other studies in that it focuses not only on the teacher's system of classification, but on his awareness that students have certain expectations and (implicit) rules. Werthman shows that students, too, are involved in the process of classification and negotiation. He describes how if the teacher's actions are seen as fair, the student accepted the teacher's definition of the situation. Students considered it important that they be given explanations and reasons by teachers. Conflict and behaviour problems arose only in those classes where teachers infringed students' rules — where, for example, some teachers attempted to command attention and exercize authority without politeness and respect; or commented on matters such as race, appearance and intelligence; or again, whose grading was manifestly unfair. A theme of the study then is that learning is a social matter; it is not an arbitrary imposition of will, but a continuous process of negotiation.

In the classroom, where teachers and pupils are continuously involved in interpreting the on-going situation, and negotiating reality, by shaping each other's responses, the role of language is clearly very important. The relationships between teachers' knowledge and pupils' interpretations and understanding is discussed in Barnes's work.[12] He particularly stresses that teachers think and talk in a technical language and that this acts as a barrier to children's learning. Their pupils' understanding, however, is based on everyday experience. In classroom discussions there is often a tension between the teacher who is stressing so-called 'theoretical knowledge', and the pupil who is using 'common-sense' knowledge of the home. This work raises not only questions about the possible advantages or disadvantages of specialist languages, but also wider issues about communication and the nature of language, which cannot be dealt with adequately here.

Some Limitations of the 'Labelling' Approach

In the studies mentioned so far I have underlined the following points. The first is classification. All human beings have to classify to make sense and order the world; we have to categorize in order to know what action to do next, to do science, to decide whom to help or to spend our time with. Briefly, it seems sensible to classify according to one's needs or principles. But classifications, 'bright', 'stupid', 'beautiful', 'ugly', 'interesting', 'boring', inevitably hurt people. Not only the context but the *purpose* for which the classification is made is important. The 'new' sociologists of education focused upon the form of classification that makes invidious hierarchic distinctions. The ability to make these consequential classifications is related to questions of power. It was just not conceived, in traditional sociology, that children, pupils, prisoners or patients could have influence. The interpretive sociologists were the first to suggest that in interaction people did actually bargain. So the asymmetry was corrected; it came to be recognized that even such people are not passive. 'Making out' is a form of negotiation.[13] But it needs to be pointed out that the power of the sub-group can easily be over-exaggerated — particularly if 'power' is conceived in a subjectivist or mentalistic way. If patients had as much power as psychiatrists, they would not be in asylums. Teachers and pupils do negotiate over rules, but it must be conceded that, as things are, teachers are more powerful. I make this obvious point because in the wish to emphasize individual free will, the negotiation and construction of reality, phenomenological (or interpretive) sociologists are often one sided and deny any form of social necessity or determinism whatsoever.

As I stated earlier, much of the work on classrooms utilized an interactionist perspective, in particular what is called 'labelling' theory — the basis of which is the notion that 'we become what we are called'. Now, there is an irony in that symbolic interactionism is often understood as a humanizing alternative to the Parsonian 'systems' approach; but labelling theory, which is a part of the interactionist perspective, by stressing the power of the definer who labels, is another form of determinism.[14] Moreover, if a strong labelling argument is used about the power of teachers' classifications and the consequences that follow, there must be an assumption that though pupils may, in some senses, be able to influence negotiation, teachers ultimately have more power. But, sometimes, there has also been a wish to stress negotiation, symmetry of relations, and both the 'labelling' and the 'negotiation' arguments have been used together. The two positions are, in their extreme forms, contradictory and should not be conflated.

Classroom Knowledge

Keddie's study has become a classic in the study of the defining processes that occur within the school itself.[15] Every issue mentioned in this chapter can be found in it somewhere; thus underlining the point that classroom studies cannot limit themselves to a narrow focus but inevitably involve topics such as teachers' classifications, expectations and the differential treatment, as in streaming, that is one of the consequences of it; the use of language: the organization of the curriculum; in short, everything we call 'school-knowledge'.

In the humanities department of the school where she did her research she noted that the teachers had a very progressive set of ideas. For example they believed *in theory* that:

1 Intelligence is not determined by heredity (differential educational performance being due to differences in motivation).
2 Streaming maintains social divisions as it favours middle-class children. It fixes the expectations of teachers and pupils and is likely to lower motivation. (Besides, the criteria of stream allocation have been discredited anyway.)
3 A differentiated curriculum divided pupils, and so the school should try to unite them. The ideas were believed in what Keddie calls 'the educationalist context', but when the teachers were in the classroom ('the teacher context'), they behaved very differently. The teachers organized their activities in the classroom around values which, as educators, they denied. To put it simply, there was a discrepancy between their 'words' and their 'deeds'. The teachers operated in such a way that they actually sustained what (theoretically, in the educationalist context) they disapproved of.

But the knowledge of what pupils are like is at odds with the image of pupils that the same teachers hold as educationists, since it derives from streaming whose validity the educator denies. (In the educationist context there seems to be more of a concern not with things as they are, but how things ought to be.)

The important points to register are these:

1 As stated above, there is a tendency to attribute to pupils the normal characteristics of their ability band – but what constitutes ability is not made explicit. As Keddie remarks, 'Ability is an organizing and unexamined concept for teachers whose categorization of pupils on the grounds of ability derives largely from social class judgements of

pupils' social moral, and intellectual behaviour'.[16]

2 Though, as educationists, the teachers constructed courses to limit their own didactic authority, in the teacher context enquiry was, in fact, still heavily teacher directed.

3 A- and C-stream pupils approach classroom knowledge from different positions and different expectations. A-stream pupils seem to have a willingness to wait for the teacher's definition, and to accept the categories offered.

4 It is assumed that C-stream pupils cannot master subjects, that they need stories, not abstractions, real things, not intellectual things. One of the teachers comments:[17]

> I can, I hope, do things which are very useful and valuable to the C child which I don't feel are as necessary for the A child. But they're all doing economics . . . Well, that leads on to a special study of labour for the Cs. Rewards for labour — wages. Wages can then be considered for girls in terms of why they're paid often lower than men's pay and what sorts of factors determine the different wages rates for different sorts of employment. . .taxation and the practical elements of how to fill in tax forms and what you get relief for, whereas . . . I'd be much more concerned with how the different types of taxation work, with the higher ability child . . . the effects that different forms of taxation have on the rates of economic growth — the more sophisticated elements which the lower-ability child, it may not be possible for him to grasp the ideas that are part of that type of study. . .

This illustrates how one consequence of differential treatment is the way categories of analysis are made available to or withheld from pupils.

5 It is suggested by Keddie that teachers have 'a relevance structure' which derives from their notion of what counts as knowledge within a given subject. Teachers consider whether a pupil's comment or question has meaning within the relevance structure. But this depends on the imputed ability and status of the pupil; that is to say, when similar questions are asked by A- and C-stream children they are categorized differently by the teacher. A searching question asked by a C-stream pupil is often

interpreted as being inappropriate, asked in order to make trouble or 'for a laugh'.

Keddie also considers the social organization of curriculum knowledge and suggests that it may be remoteness from everyday life that is an important element in legitimating academic knowledge in schools. It is the failure of high ability pupils to question what they are taught that may contribute to their educational achievement. Those who master subjects are successful. Schools thus maintain social order through the taken-for-granted categories; they process pupils and knowledge in mutually confirming ways. Her conclusion is that it seems likely that the hierarchical categories of ability and knowledge may persist in unstreamed classes, and lead to the differentiation of undifferentiated curricula because teachers differentiate in selection of content and in pedagogy between pupils perceived as of high and low ability. She warns us that school innovation will not be radical unless the categories teachers use to organize what they know about pupils, and to determine what counts as knowledge, undergo a fundamental change.

The theme of many classroom studies, then, is that people's behaviour varies according to their perceptions of ability, intelligence, class. The categories that may affect our behaviour include colour, sex, occupation, and there are many others – according to our notions of relevance. The 'new' sociology of education stressed one aspect of this problem; they made us much more aware how, by classification, teachers contribute to, indeed create, failure. One of the purposes of this work was that teachers should become aware of the processes involved, and the consequences of making hierarchical distinctions. But we need to know more about these matters: If, and when, teachers do become aware of the presuppositions on which their classifications of people and knowledge are based and their possible consequences, to what extent do they change?

I have always found Keddie's concluding exhortation a problem. Supposing that teachers did change the categories they used to organize what they know about pupils, to determine what counts as knowledge, what would these categories be? An existential difficulty is that all categories seem to be double edged; categorization involves snubs, being excluded. There is a political difficulty also: living in the sort of society that we do, we are all influenced by its vocabulary, and it is difficult for us to conceive of categories outside of our time. And even when they are conceived there may always be problems in their application. In this sense Keddie's paper can be seen as dealing with some aspects of problems of *theory and practice* that we all face.

Ideology in the Classroom: Progressivism

Most of the studies discussed above have been based on 'interpretive' sociological perspectives. (It should not be forgotten, however, that there are important differences between the interactionist and the phenomenological approaches.) Our final classroom study is explicitly anti-phenomenological. Rachel Sharp and Anthony Green have published their research in a book entitled *Education and Social Control*.[18] Its two main themes are progressivism as an educational ideology, and social phenomenology, or more precisely, the 'new' phenomenological sociology, of education. They are highly critical both of so-called 'progressivism' and of phenomenology. I will outline their views on child-centred education here and postpone discussion of the criticisms of phenomenology to chapter 7.

Sharp and Green did their research on the progressive, child-centred approach in three classrooms in the infant department of a school. They state that the child-centred teachers saw themselves as opposing the authoritarian assumptions of the formal traditional approaches. But it was noticed that the effects produced by the teachers were very similar to the hierarchical differentiations of pupils characteristic of formal methods. The authors point to the contradiction within progressive education: though it claims to foster the development of autonomy and the self, what it actually provides is a more efficient *socializing* environment. It is suggested that the child-centred teacher with his 'individualistic, voluntarist and psychologistic solution to the problem of freedom fails to appreciate the ways in which, even in his own practice, the effects of a complex stratified industrial society penetrate the school'. Sharp and Green, then, want to focus upon, and study, the ways in which the wider social structural forces impinge upon or influence what goes on in the school classroom. They write that the following processes are at work. Social control is maintained through schools; pupils, teachers and parents are initiated into appropriate attitudes that maintain the *status quo*. The processing of pupils' identities is seen as the beginnings of social selection for the stratification system. In advanced industrial societies, education has become increasingly involved in selection for a stratified, hierarchical society. Progressivism receives support because it is a very effective means of social control. Not only does it have certain therapeutic features which are useful for 'cooling people out', but it allows for a wider range of children's attributes to be evaluated. In these ways educational institutions are playing a crucial role in the reproduction of the socio-economic system. The writers argue that child-centred educators, like the de-schoolers, are involved in an 'emotional turning away from society and an attempt within the confines of education to bring about [the] transformation of individual consciousness'.[19] But they state that this is romantic conservatism. Progressive education is utopian; the failure to consider the social parameter reduces 'the progressive educator to little more than an unwilling apologist of the system'. In my view, the book has several weaknesses which arise from a disjunction between the authors' theory and their practice. Though the authors' aim is to make a critique of idealism, the approach they use, symbolic interactionism, is a form of it. In spite of their criticisms of micro-sociology, the discussion in their book remains within the problematic of the individual subject. Their own position, Marxism, remains vague, unformulated and unsatisfactory. To give an example, they remark how circumstances influence consciousness and then they state that they do not have a theory of the relationship between existence and consciousness; 'there is as yet no satisfactory theory of ideology which clearly articulates the mediation of ideas and the social context in which they arise'. There is, then, a lack of fit between their theoretical considerations and their methodological practice, which is basically interactionist. Lacking a consistent view and vocabulary, they are eclectic. And though they accept the macro–micro distinction, they never explicate their own view of society, nor is the 'school–society' relationship examined. Now, of course, there are some similarities in the analysis of Keddie and that of Sharp and Green. In both we find sponsorship of certain children by teachers, and selective organization of the *content* of education. What Sharp and Green really want to stress are the shortcomings, the inadequacy, of the new sociology of education, but this is an issue that they do not explicitly tackle. Of course, ultimately, all our theories and practices have to be appraised. How are we to assess the contribution of the 'new' sociology of education in focusing our attention on what goes on in classrooms? First, I will outline what I consider to be its genuine achievements, and then suggest some of the serious limitations of the approach.

The renewal of interest in studies of the classroom brought about by the new sociology of education was a vindication of humanity against system. After the abstract functionalist theorizing about 'the educational system', the focus on classrooms reminded sociologists of education where the action was. It reminds me of students who told me of what they felt when, after recondite discussions about the law, they actually visited the courts and studied how judges acted and the assumptions they held. In sociology, classrooms have now come to be considered worth-while arenas of study.[20] The new approach corrected the previously asymmetrical view and has given a new sense of respect to the actors involved – the pupils and teachers. And as all teaching involves a view of learning, these studies brought together, in a new way, a sense of the whole, the inter-relatedness of teacher, pupil (and the mediation between) knowledge. The 'new' sociology is interested in the relationship between the distribution of power and the distribution of knowledge, and it is in its classroom studies that the discussion of these problems is situated in a concrete manner.[21] Most valuably the classroom studies have made us realize that schools are oppressive because they categorize and rank children, who come to accept hierarchies. (Incidentally, this is also one of Illich's arguments for de-schooling.) Classroom studies have made us more mindful of our taken-for-granted *processes* of classification and question the categories that we use. The hope is that if, in examining our assumptions, the consequences are coercive, we can change them. These studies, in pointing to the schools for institutionalizing failure, helped us to formulate important questions such as: What counts as success and failure in our society? How are these definitions constructed, by whom, and in whose interest? In the sociology of education these were original questions. It could be said, however, that the *processes* by which these definitions were constructed were often treated as if they were of more importance than the practical aspects, which somehow became submerged in epistemological debates. Though the achievements of the 'new' sociology of education in bringing the classroom and the actors within it to the centre of our interest should not be underestimated, attention must also be drawn towards its limitations. I state them briefly here, as some of the criticisms will be discussed in more detail in the following chapters.

Though the 'new' sociology of education was fundamentally egalitarian and desired radical social change, it was in a sense not *explicitly* political. It was the relativist phenomenological aspects of its critique that came to be highlighted. Consider knowledge – in the debate about whether it should be conceived of as being 'theoretical' or 'common-sense', the new writers argued that theoretical knowledge was that which had been so defined by 'the experts' for the purpose of legitimating themselves; knowledge was reified to mystify others. 'Theoretical' knowledge was, then, rather like an ideology – for the interests of ruling groups. In opposition to the established view, the 'new' sociology of education supported the importance of 'common-sense' knowledge. Confirmation for such a view was found in phenomenological theorizing, which had a trenchant critique of positivism and stressed the value of individual intuition. But it was insufficiently understood that though common sense can be a basis, a starting-point, because it usually contains many ideas that are fragmentary and incoherent, it must be transcended.

At first social phenomenology, combined with symbolic interaction, was very fruitful, and there was a considerable increase in classroom research. Nell Keddie, John Beck, Chris Jenks, for example, asked some original questions: What are teachers' explanations of what they are doing?

What are the accounting procedures they use? What are their rules in use? As the sociology of education became more theoretical and philosophical, researchers became more reflexive and self-questioning. How should we interpret classroom interaction? What are the grounds of our research procedures? For some of us these epistemological problems made research increasingly difficult.[22] These problems, it was realized, stem from 'interpretive' sociology. In the next chapter I will argue that though the phenomenological perspective has an immense demystifying potential, it also entails certain problems which it neglects or evades.

Chapter 6

Some Problems in Phenomenological Sociology

Introduction

I will begin this chapter with some general remarks about the difficulties encountered in doing sociological work. After these introductory reflections I focus upon phenomenological sociology to draw attention to the fact that this approach neglects or evades certain problems. If, for example, all accounts are valid, there is the problem of relativism, which leaves us impotent to make any act or decision. (On the other hand, if they are not equally valid, are we then entitled to impose our views on others? Can we be sure? History is littered with the corpses of those killed for what we would now call false beliefs.) I have selected three issues that I consider particularly important for discussion:

First, a question which is not usually examined within phenomenology, that of ideology and false-consciousness.

Second, the question of mentalism. This is concerned with the issue whether the world exists apart from our conscious-ness of it, or, as idealists and many phenomenologists believe, is it constructed entirely by the mind? What, then, are 'social structures'? For example, does 'class' exist or is it merely a reification? And what is the relationship between social structure, accounting procedures (the processes by which we make the world 'real') and power relations?

Third, the problem of relativism. If there are no checks for truth and validity, by what criteria does one act con-sistently and rationally? And is there not the danger that those who have power then define the 'truth'?

Of the three interlinking problems, relativism is seen to be the most crucial. In conclusion, it is argued that relativism is nihilism. Though both Marxism and phenomenology have a common aim, de-reification, there is a vital distinction between them. While phenomenologists stress the power of consciousness to de-reify, the aim of Marxists is practical de-reification – change that takes place not only in the minds of individuals but in the real world also. But both forms of de-reification can begin only with understanding. When we begin the work of sociological understanding, what are the 'troubles' we have had to overcome?

A convincing account often requires the observation of actual behaviour by the researcher, but many interactional situations such as cabinet meetings, selection boards, family quarrels, are often private. And yet when access is possible, participant observation inevitably leads to some distortion and we are often faced with moral questions as well. When we come to classify material there is the problem of typicality; that is the question of what is to be taken as data, the units of comparison. In making comparisons of like with like we have to consider how the data are organized, in relation to what, and with what degree of comparability. If we use quantification some important qualifications, and questions of meaning, are ignored; even the concepts we use make 'objectivity' difficult in that they all carry evaluations. The hypotheses we make may be self-justifying or self-falsifying; the hypothesis having an influence on the actual research. There are many problems also regarding the nature of causal explanation: how are the relevant factors to be selected from a vast constellation? How far back does one go? And, anyway, does the notion of causality strictly apply only to the physical world?

One of the main difficulties is that in these matters we are dealing with a multiplicity of sentient purposive beings; human beings, in a context, interacting with each other. We are therefore largely dealing with interpretations of inter-pretations. The difficulties enumerated above can and should be themselves legitimate subjects of study and research.[1] All these problems can occur within one another, but imagine now the difficulties in cross-cultural, or comparative, socio-logical and anthropological work.[2] We are then again faced with fundamental questions, such as: Are there criteria for

the accuracy, 'objectivity', 'truth' or 'adequacy' of our interpretations and accounts, and if so, how do they come about?
There are also several other fundamental questions concerning
knowledge which should be mentioned: these relate to
ideology and false-consciousness, 'objectivism' and 'subjectivism', the relativization of knowledge and power, and it
is to a discussion of these issues to which we now turn.

The Validity of Accounts and the Dilemma of Imposition

The first question that I wish to point to concerns the contradiction between the Marxist notions of ideology and false-
consciousness and the phenomenological injunction to derive
concepts only from the actor. A Marxist may want to say
that human action can be understood neither independently
of the meaning nor simply identified with his own interpretation. It is agreed that human beings can act only on the
basis of some understanding, but it does not follow from
this that their activity, or the world, possesses the character
which they understand it to have. For example, human
beings may act under the belief that they are free and equal
when the opposite is the case. In such a situation, defining
their activity as they comprehend it will lead us to mis-
construe their act – the sort of mystification that is the
purpose of ideology![3]

But if one believes that the other has been 'taken in' by
ideology, that another's knowledge is merely false-consciousness, then one implication is that one's sociological
work should be corrective and revelatory. On the other
hand many phenomenologists dissolve the concept of ideology,
dispense with 'false-consciousness' – they are not terms in
their vocabulary. But in everyday life we are often in situations
where we have to act and make decisions; we say that one
version is better than another. Then one's acts involve intervention, imposition of our views on 'children', the 'culturally
deprived', the 'mentally ill' and the 'deviant', 'savages', others.
What are our grounds? And if we do act in this way, are not
truth criteria presupposed? The awareness of the problem
outlined above has culminated in many phenomenological
theorists continually impaling themselves on two apparently

87

irresolvable problems: the validity of accounts, and the dilemmas of imposition. A phenomenological position implies that accounts are not placed in a hierarchy of 'adequacy' but are recognized as equally valid versions of the world that are offered by sociologists and others alike.[4] This view leads to the problems of relativism, and we then have to answer the question: Is one way of seeing the world better than another? If this is *not* the case, then those who seem to accept what we might call poverty, hunger, disease, superstition, death at an early age, can be left, without us feeling responsibility or guilt, in their own versions of 'reality' and rationality. But if we believe that some ways of being in the world are better than others, do we then intervene, and impose our views? If we are convinced of our own rightness and regard others as mistaken or wrong, is intervention justified? The phenomenological perspective requires the viewpoint of the actor being taken seriously. Indeed, acceptance of the actors' viewpoint entails a non-interventionist stance. Such a stance is premised on the notion that the actors' view must be right. And if there are many groups of actors, many different ways of living, then, within their own social context, they are all equally valid. From a phenomenological perspective, it is because of this relativism that intervention is not necessary. But from a Marxist perspective it can be argued that actors' ways of thinking may be incorrect. Some actors may be deliberately misled, so that they do not see what is in their class interest. In other words, there may be macro-features which have an independent reality of which actors or participants are not aware. There may be forces that influence, or determine, the thoughts and actions of participants, and produce consequences which they did not intend. Indeed it has been argued that the construction of realities may be more influenced by power relations, socialization processes and class structures.[5] That the norms of social interaction are crystallizations of power- and work-relations, and if they are, they cannot be the result of accounting procedures. According to this view, ethnomethodology is reductionist, and the phenomenological method of bracketing blinds us to the growing danger that all our interpretive potentialities may be strangled by the growing dominance of a scientistic pre-definition of reality.

We are faced with the following problem: Is it not impossible to transcend certain limitations in the understanding of 'human reality' without transcending at the same time the framework of capitalist society? Do these views point to some of the limitations of phenomenology or is this yet an example of the reification of structure?

The Problem of Mentalism

The second question I would like to raise is that of the problem of mentalism. It has been maintained by some phenomenological sociologists that the social order has no existence at all independent of the members' accounting and describing practices.[6] They consider it necessary to suspend all notions of social order so as to concentrate on the study of reality construction procedures. That is to say, some phenomenologists and ethnomethodologists often write as if the physical, natural, world is 'out there' and real, and the world of mental states is 'in here' and real, but that the social world has no such autonomous existence. Social phenomena are real only in so far as the individual's actions and interpretations routinely confirm them as such. In other words, the idea of an independent social reality is suspended or abandoned. Let me try and clarify this. Generally speaking, phenomenologists believe that phenomena do not 'speak for themselves', but have to be *given* a character. They are produced by our consciousness. It is argued that in describing phenomena we constitute them. Social life, then, is a construction of, and constituted by, the activities of people's minds. One strand of phenomenology regards this construction of reality, through theorizing, to be circular in the following way. Theorists negotiate methods which provide for explaining the social world. The explanation is a rendering of the world, a description of the phenomena within it, by the method. Now, theorists also negotiate canons or standards of explanation which relate to the method. Each form of theorizing, then, has its own version of description, method, evaluation, which interlock. Thus, Durkheimians, Weberians, Marxians, have their own methods and canons, and are non-comparable. In this view, as the methods and canons are negotiated, so the versions they provide are irremediably authoritative versions of that world. Their 'rightness' or 'wrongness' is simply a matter of negotiated consciousness. Positivism, interpretive social science, critical theory, all having their own methods and criteria, form separate, self-validating, 'circles'. There are therefore no independent yardsticks for each view of the world. Many phenomenological sociologists admit that *language* externalizes and objectifies actors' explanations, definitions and perceptions, and in this way constitutes the social world. But if society — as many of them suggest — is 'entirely in the mind', a strictly mentalistic view is being adopted. This, an extreme version of philosophical idealism, insists that consciousness produces the world. There are several responses to this argument. J.H. Goldthorpe, for example, has argued that rules, laws, etiquette, are not just symbolic expressions of people's mental states.[7] They are more than mentalistic constructs and do in some sense exist independently of situations of their use. In arguing that conventions do exist independently of particular occasions of use, he resorts to Popperian notions of objective knowledge.[8]

Popper has asserted that there are what he calls three 'Worlds'. The first is of physical states (World 1). The second world consists of the private states of mind of individuals, subjective experiences (World 2). There is also the public domain, of objective ideas (World 3). All the libraries and museums of the world consists of World 3 material — that which is on paper, and not in the head. He suggests that they are different worlds of reality; 2 interacts directly with both 1 and 3, and 1 and 3 interact indirectly via 2. Popper's third world is the objective content of thought, theories, works of art; he calls this world 'intelligibilia', and, for him, the objective content of ideas exists quite independently of anyone actually knowing it (for example, an unread book). And in so far as they are externalized in symbolic or linguistic form, they can live on autonomously. A law, a customary practice, can exist as an intelligible even when it is in no one's mind. It is there to be possibly invoked and appealed to even if variously construed. For Popper, then, knowledge in the objective sense is knowledge without a knower. It is knowledge without a knowing subject. It is this that phenomenologists deny.

Relativism

My third question concerns relativism. Let us begin with C. Wright Mills, who made some significant points about knowledge. He stated that what we call 'reasoning', being logical, or validating the truth of an assertion, all involve reference to various standardized models. Rules of logic, he said, are conventional and are shaped and selected in accordance with the purpose of the discourse, or the intentions of the enquirers.[9] Mills's main point seems to be that logics, truth criteria, rules of proof, are all grounded in common cultures — not in anything external to those who use such rules. Thus what is logical is a question of how in a particular context a particular rule is used. For Mills, then, rules are viewed as members' categories and members call on other's knowledge of a common culture of logic which provides them with criteria (the implications of treating knowledge, or 'what counts as knowledge', as 'socially constructed' are immense and will be discussed elsewhere). If knowledge is totally relativized, it cannot be objective in an absolute sense.

Now there are many versions of relativism; it can arise from many sources. There is, for example, the relativism that is an outcome of phenomenological theorizing, having its basis in idealist assumptions. C. Wright Mills's version seems to be akin to the relativism advocated by Peter Winch in *The Idea of a Social Science*. I briefly referred to this particular view of relativism in our discussion of anthropological studies.[10] Winch's argument, in brief, is that forms of life (what Mills calls 'common cultures') cannot be criticized from some external viewpoint, because there is no such external and independent standard. I want to suggest that just as relativism can arise from philosophical, anthropological, phenomenological and other sources, it can also be criticized from different perspectives or points of view. If one conceives of perspectives in the deeper sense of justifications, fundamental presuppositions, grounds, it is possible to say that we can be critical from different 'bases' of rationality. I want now to outline briefly one such argument against 'form of life' relativism based on 'scientific rationality'.

A well-known opponent of (Winch's) relativism is Ernest Gellner.[11] Gellner states that while Wittgenstein taught philosophers not to ask for the meaning but the use, Winch advises us not to look for the cause, but the meaning. Winch believes that within a society or culture all concepts are shared, and quotes Wittgenstein: 'What has to be accepted, the given, is – as one could say – forms of life'. One of Winch's first problems is that Wittgenstein's notion of a form of life is an abstract model and that he gave no example of it. So does it mean all those who speak, for example, English, or does it include sub-cultures as well? And if it includes sub-cultures, how many individuals constitute 'a form of life'? Second, forms of life are numerous, diverse, they overlap and undergo change. Which of them is to be accepted? That is to say that sometimes these forms do not accept themselves as given, as something to be accepted. If a society rejects its own past practice as irrational or wrong, then it implies that *some* principle of selection has been employed. Winch is committed to excluding the possibility of a whole society being wrong in its belief, but Gellner asserts that whole societies have, in fact, come to believe that what they believed in the past was absurd. This is how societies that became Christian thought of their previous paganism. When Winch is faced with the fact that cultures themselves indulge in self-correction and self-condemnation, he asserts that the corrections emanate from *inside*; but Gellner argues that this again is not so, as the diffusion of industrial-scientific society throughout the world shows. Also, it is interesting to note that Winch's principle of universal sympathy, or benevolent interpretation, does exclude the social use of ambiguity and absurdity; it excludes the possibility of false-consciousness. Moreover, Winch does not realize that 'forms of life' are related to *history*. (Both of these points would be important features in a Marxist account.) There are other, fundamental, questions to be asked: To be able to make his point, where does Winch stand? It appears that Winch's account assumes a philosophical vantage-point outside and above all societies, and yet it should be noted that he gives us no warrant to apply his relativism to his own arguments. Does not his relativism lead to a paradox when applied to itself? Relativists forget that the world we live in is one of countless over-lapping traditions, and that these overlapping cultures, civilizations, have extremely unequal *technical and cognitive power.* Gellner's arguments are based on his belief in the effectiveness of scientific industrial civilization — that science brings about the possibility of a certain material 'liberation'. (The basis of Gellner's rationality is, then, universal science, which remains for him an unquestioned assumption. Questions such as the use of science as a form of domination and exploitation do not occur to him.)

Thus it seems, that when we are faced with different views of the world, we have at least the following choices: 'Absolutist' imposition, which entails the denial of realities of others. A characteristic of this positivist stance is the 'labelling' of others as 'inferior', 'deprived', 'schizophrenic', 'stupid', 'wrong'. Such hierarchization justifies our own beliefs and actions, and legitimates the exploitation of others. The up-surge of a phenomenological sociology of education was a reaction against this and other aspects of positivism in the social sciences: structural functionalism and empiricism in sociology, logical positivism in philosophy, and behaviourism in psychology.[12]

The acceptance of phenomenology, however, leads to another problem, relativism. But perhaps this is possible only when we are theorizing. When we have to act, if we believe that different accounts are equally valid, we have no basis for making a choice. Our choice, then, is without *reason*, it might as well be random. This is absurd. Relativism, then, is nihilism. Nietzsche defined nihilism as the situation in which everything is permitted. If this is the case, it makes no difference what we do. And so nothing is worth anything. It has been argued that there is an actual pervasive presence of nihilism today. This is the contemporary crisis of reason.[13] However, one way of overcoming, transcending, the problems of both positivism and phenomenology may be a commit-ment to some notion of human liberation exemplified in, say, Marxist theory and practice.[14] But, then, how does one reconcile a phenomenological commitment to the actor-member's versions of the world with a Marxist commitment to struggle against exploitation? How is it possible to have dialogical relationships and yet believe in revolution?

I suggest that one way of making a reconciliation (or is it a break?) between the two paradigms is by seeing the similarities and the differences in their view of (de)reification.[15]

It could be said that many radical sociologists, those working with some variety of phenomenological and/or Marxist perspectives, are involved in kinds of action aimed at de-reification. Reification has been described as 'that historical and political process wherein the products of human practice, the objectified expressions of man's interaction with other men and nature, become alienated from the actual producers and thus appear in consciousness as independent and autonomous things'. Discussing these aspects of reification, John Horton points out that in political terms 'to reify' means to legitimize an exploitative practice on the grounds that it is a factual and unvarying standard for human adjustment.[16] Reified thinking never grasps the practical, managed character of reality. Reification is of course implied in the concept of alienation and is an integral part of any criticism of capitalism. Those inclined towards 'social realism', the structural-functionalists, find dehumanized and transcendental metaphors of system and structure to explain the manipulation of men. On the other hand, the 'nominalists' — action theorists and phenomenologists — refuse to take the order metaphors for granted but end up describing how and not why men construct orderly accounts of their world. For Horton, then, all concepts are politically intended accounts; reification is a political strategy. What happens in reification is that a historical and variable condition is legitimized as a natural and necessary fact. It is readily admitted that phenomenologists have a theoretical understanding of reification. They are having an important de-reifying effect because they are saying that the reified and objective character of social reality are human accomplishments yet to be described. The understanding of some phenomenological sociologists is uncritical and they themselves sometimes reify an abstract ahistorical consciousness. A crucial question seems to be that if, and when, one decides which basic conceptual structure one is going to choose to work within, to what degree is one supporting or subverting existing power arrangements? Reified thinking about social practice factualizes ruling realities. But, perhaps, this sort of phenomenological de-reification is of little use, because it sidesteps the basic role of interest in the construction of knowledge and the problem of why (rather than how) certain stable accounts emerge from practice. As Horton has suggested, it is not enough to know that the objective appearance of reality is managed: 'we want to know also why that objectivity is so oppressive and how it can be overcome.' In brief, reification is the ploy of ruling interests and is the false-consciousness of alienated labour. Phenomenology de-reifies, but to think radically is to *practice* de-reification.

To summarize: I have suggested that some phenomenological approaches have neglected questions concerning ideology and false-consciousness, the relationship between social structure, accounting procedures and power relations. Moreover, some versions of phenomenology have glossed over problems such as the validity of accounts, the dilemmas of imposition and the vital distinction between theoretical and practical de-reification. But what is the relationship to education? It is this: the 'new sociology of education', which is an emergent approach questioning prevailing conceptions of school knowledge and is concerned with the possibilities of change, adopted a phenomenological stance. I have argued in this chapter that the phenomenological approach tends to neglect, misunderstand or evade such problems as relativism and the concepts of ideology and false-consciousness. The same problems existed in the 'new' sociology of education and, for a time, these also tended to be passed over. In the next chapter I shall consider how these problems of phenomenological sociology re-surfaced in the field of education, and how the recognition of the limitations of phenomenology led to a change within the new sociology of education.

Chapter 7

Towards a Radical Reappraisal

In earlier chapters I have argued that writers of the 'new' sociology of education, Michael F.D. Young, Geoff Esland and others, were deeply critical of positivism and felt 'liberated' by the phenomenological perspective. They questioned traditional hierarchies such as the accepted notions that 'theory' was superior to 'common sense', or that a 'pure' subject was superior to an 'applied' one. Their views were an expression of their beliefs in 'man's right to author his world'. For example, they argued that categories such as 'rationality' were not natural like the colour of one's eyes, or the shape of one's nose, but were man made, socially produced. 'Deprivation', to take another example, was the outcome of the activities of particular people with certain assumptions and practices. If social and educational reality was not based on natural immutable laws but was socially produced, then if it were experienced as oppressive it could be changed. It was hoped that teachers and others, on becoming aware of the presuppositions they were working with, might then see the world differently, and change it. It was gradually realized, however, that this notion of change had been conceived too narrowly; it had some of the limitations of a phenomenological sociology of education.

Following on from the last chapter, where I indicated some of the problems that are implied in the adoption of a phenomenological approach, I now want to examine these problems in the context of education. I will begin by looking at some of the questions raised by the 'new' sociology of education, and continue the discussion of some of the issues introduced in the last chapter such as the ambiguities of the philosophically idealist position, and the relativization of knowledge. The chapter concludes with the discussion of the difficulties of educational change in our society, and the growing recognition that a critical theory needs to be developed that may enable us to re-formulate the relationship between the individual, education and society (in a way that transcends both positivist and idealist limitations) for the purpose of human liberation.

The realization that educational change was more difficult to bring about than we had hoped was a gradual one. There was 'a change from within'; a questioning of our own assumptions, hopes, actions. My first point is that the writers representing the new sociology of education, though committed to a rejection of positivism, did not fully appreciate its strength. It is stronger than many of us had supposed, and it is difficult successfully to challenge it. It is wrong to think of positivism as a neutral, independent, tool for capturing the world. It is a mathematical view of the world and claims to satisfy man's material needs.[1] But what was not sufficiently recognized was that positivism is an *ideology* involving hidden forms of domination and repression. Positivism is deeply entrenched in our society, but we know little about how it works. Of course, a little work has been done; it has been shown that there is a connection between positivist theory and a liberal-reformist conception of political practice. It can be demonstrated that there is an inter-relationship between positivist scientific explanation and prediction. The implication is that, with the manipulation of certain variables, a state of affairs can be brought about or prevented. Scientific knowledge comes to be thought of in terms of technical control. Indeed, it is because of the connection with the idea of control that a positivist social science has institutional backing. What happens is this: social, or policy, scientists may think they are giving neutral, merely technical, advice, but they may be mis-characterizing their activity. To say that political decisions are only technical may serve to hide evaluative elements by removing them from public discussion. Thus a viewpoint that claims to be a nonpolitical method becomes an ideology. Positivist social science necessarily *reifies*. Reification means taking conventional activities and treating them as natural entities which have a separate existence and operate independently of the wishes of social actors. Now a policy scientist necessarily treats some aspects of a particular social institution as simply given, beyond political evaluation and control, because it is in terms of these that the scientist is able to make his calculations. Thus policy science accepts some social arrangements as *necessarily* the way they are. By treating society as governed by natural laws, the impression is given that some features of society are unalterable. Thus reification limits the horizons of possible political action by circumscribing the area within which one can act politically. It is *assumed* that only a scientific approach in political life can ensure a rational solution to political problems. It is taken for granted that questions of *means* are amenable to a scientific solution. The impression is thus given that the ends of political life are undebatable in a rational manner – not worthy of discussion. Imaginative discussion of alternative worlds is 'mere subjectivism'. Such a science inevitably supports those who are dominant. The tendencies towards reification, and towards buttressing the hold of dominant groups, jointly repress political discussion – which in turn reinforces the hold of dominant groups.[2]

I stressed in the last chapter that the 'new' sociology of education adopted a phenomenological model of social science but without realizing the full implications of the relativism inherent in that position. Relativism, which seemed at first to be an answer, became more of a problem.[3] So, apart from underestimating the power of positivism, there were also issues to be confronted from the relativization of knowledge. Writers on the new sociology of education stressed knowledge as a human construction, and the notion that man gives meaning to his world. Combined with a rejection of the academic curriculum as being hierarchical, this led to the relativization of knowledge. But the 'relativization of knowledge' has had little effect in transforming consciousness and overthrowing prevailing hierarchies; this much is admitted. The notion that theoretical (or mental) de-reification of an objectivist view of knowledge is a humanizing, radical, act is questionable because it is only mental – it is basically an idealist position. In the classroom a few teachers became genuinely confused; they did not want to conceive of learning as a 'commodity' to be consumed, or as something to be 'banked'. Some of them had a fear of putting forward any viewpoint or mode of thinking at all upon pupils in case it was interpreted as undialogical or impositional. Let me give an example of the sort of dilemma that many teachers experienced. I remember on one teaching practice visiting a student-teacher who had studied phenomenology on her sociology course. She believed that the teaching of her colleagues was impositional, and felt that she did not want to teach like they did. There are, no doubt, some teachers who believe in phenomenology theoretically but, in practice, manage to set it aside when in the classroom. My student, however, wished to practice, live, her phenomenological beliefs. All her lessons seemed to me to consist only of 'chats', and I suggested to her that she was not 'teaching'. Does not teaching imply a difference between pupil and learner, a difference between what is known and what can be known? Teaching seems inevitably to involve intervention – but how can we prevent it from being seen as impositional? This is a problem not only for some phenomenologists who are teachers but also for sociologists who are phenomenologists. I think I would want to say that because of her (misguided) respect for pupils' ways of constructing reality, the student-teacher actually prevented them from gaining the knowledge that might give them the power to create a less oppressive world. Many teachers were like this. They had no clear idea of how to proceed. And the writers of new approach were unable to formulate concrete alternative proposals and procedures. Educational change has been difficult to bring about not only because of the implicit idealism, and problems of relativism in knowledge, but because there is a lack of clear alternative re-definitions of education that teachers could adopt. But, then, is this not a problem all of us face? How is it possible to be programmatic, to give directives, without being seen by others as impositional and coercive? Third, it was conceded that there had been a naive idealism which had led to a neglect of the material aspects of existence. In other words, phenomenological sociology had made us aware of forms of consciousness, but we had neglected to relate this to social structure – to the market, the property and power relationships which define the capitalist system.[4]

Towards a Radical Reappraisal

This is the main thrust of Rachel Sharp and Anthony Green's book, *Education and Social Control.*[5] In chapter 5 I commented briefly on one of its main themes, progressivism as an educational ideology. I now want to turn to their critique of the 'new' sociology of education. They see the possibility of this approach developing into a new orthodoxy, and becoming the dominant perspective. It is important to point out, however, that this book was published after the writers of the new sociology of education themselves came to realize the main weakness of the phenomenological approach. Sharp and Green begin their criticisms by suggesting that phenomenological sociology is primarily concerned with social psychology rather than sociology, and that these different levels of analysis should not be confused. Social phenomenologists are idealists in that they see the external social world as a mere subjective construction of the 'constituting consciousness'. This idealist stance leads to relativism, since there are no means for distinguishing between things seeming to be the case to the actor, and things being the case. Moreover, the phenomenological perspective does not enable us to pose the question why it is that certain meanings emerge rather than others. Society ceases to be the external force that can condition people's actions and guide them with its apparatus of control and culture. Phenomenologists are so preoccupied with the problem of meaning that they neglect man's relationship to the material world. In short, Sharp and Green's book is a critique of philosophical idealism and of methodological individualism.

The authors do not agree that the starting-point for sociological inquiry should be the subjective categories of social actors, because to remain at the level of consciousness may mask the extent to which such consciousness may conceal and distort the underlying structure of relationships. They believe, rather, that there are basic societal structures which impose constraints, irrespective of how actors define it. In other words, the systems of meanings of the acting subject are limited and shaped by the structural arrangements in which the individual is located.

Many phenomenologists stress negotiation; it is assumed in some classroom studies, for example, that interaction occurs on a basis of democratic negotiation between interested parties who are political equals. But this is just not the case; certain things are non-negotiable. The terms of the debate, its very form, and even the procedures which determine the solution, are often determined by others with more power. There is an unequal distribution of power in what Sharp and Green call the 'macro-structure'. Idealist notions reduce power to the ability to define reality for others – as if it were merely some conceptual or linguistic matter. Phenomenologists with their ahistorical categories too often stress man's freedom and do not see themselves as social products of particular kinds of circumstances. Power implies bringing sanctions to bear against others, irrespective of their definition of reality. Phenomenologists too often over-emphasize the rule-governed nature of life, the underlying taken-for-granted rules which regulate and define social interaction; but order, it must be remembered, also comes about through the use of power and constraint. Moreover, phenomenologists focus on the micro-levels of interaction, and do not realize that it is the macro-structure that shapes the distribution of resources and power and may materially affect the interactions of individuals at the micro-level. There is, then, a need to integrate micro-research with a more macro-approach. What we should do is to consider knowledge and interests. Interests, as Habermas has suggested, are socially structured around men's relationship to the material world. For Sharp and Green, 'the social world is structured not merely by language and meaning but by the modes and forces of material production and the system of domination which is related in some way to material reality and its control'.

They propose therefore a Marxist perspective which retains the model of man as an active being with intentionality, but also locates him with a context which may resist, block or distort his projects. It should be noted that Sharp and Green (unlike phenomenologists) employ the concept of false-consciousness, the notion that the actors' consciousness may be incorrect.

While I agree with the above criticisms of phenomenology – after all, I have made them myself, often using the same sources and similar arguments – I do have a number of reservations. I think that their criticisms of phenomenology cannot be applied without qualification to the 'new' sociology of education. For example, Sharp and Green place both social phenomenologists and child-centred educationists in the liberal tradition which generally supports the *status quo*. They suggest that phenomenologists may even be performing an idealist function in the sense that they mask the oppressive face of social reality. Now this *may* be true of some schools of phenomenology (and would have to be demonstrated), but it is untrue to say this of the 'new' sociology of education, because, as I have argued throughout this book, this approach has an egalitarian purpose; it attempts to unmask oppression (even if its analysis of it is found wanting); it always stresses the historical nature of our constructs and the need for radical change. It is obvious that I value the achievements of the 'new' sociology of education (and in earlier chapters of this book have attempted to make this work more available) and that Sharp and Green are hostile towards it. But nowhere do they appraise it. I believe that perception is irreversible and regard the phenomenological approach as being valuable in many ways. (On this issue I refer readers to chapter 12.)

To conclude this chapter, let me summarize some of my main points. The 'new' sociology of education 'changed from within' and conceded that it had underestimated the power of positivism, the problems of relativism and the implications of a naive idealism. The phenomenological thesis of the construction of reality laid such a stress on consciousness that it became detached from its products; there was a tendency to detach man from the world.[6] Another way of putting it would be that in this idealist position there was a tendency to disregard the material aspects of existence, which though socially produced cannot merely be thought away. An extreme form of this idealism was expressed by Hegel: 'Theoretical work, as I convince myself more every day, accomplishes more in the world than practical work, when the empire of the mind is revolutionized, then reality must follow'.[7] One can be aware of the theoretical possibility of changing the world but still feel shaped and oppressed by it. Consider, for a moment, the examination system – or one of the dominant educational theories concerning socialization, language or thought – these may all be experienced as social facts, as if they were objects in the world. Their social nature is masked, and we often forget that they are the outcome of activities by people in the world. But remembering this is obviously not enough. Theoretical de-reification (the belief that the questioning and criticism of assumptions, changes in consciousness can change reality) is not enough because it does not solve the problem of overcoming these constraints. We still have to analyse how and why social and educational reality come to be constructed in particular ways. The problem that remains is that even when we come to understand *how* we see the world we still have to know how to transcend it. What should we do about it? Faced with these dilemmas, sociology of education developed a new orientation as it came to be increasingly understood that the contradictions experienced in our schools and in our every-day lives — such as the alienation that ensues from hierarchical relationships, and the separation of theory from practice — were aspects of the deeper contradictions of our society.[8] In this context there came about a new awareness of the importance of Marx as a social theorist, and how a re-reading of Marx might enable us to be more precise in our criticisms and, second, help us to develop a strategy for revolutionary change.

Part Two

Marxism
and Education

Chapter 8

An Introduction to Marxism

The Necessity for a Marxist Sociology of Education

I suggested in the last chapter that one of the negative features of the phenomenological stance of the 'new' sociology of education was that the theory of education, and the schools themselves, were not placed sufficiently in their *social and economic context*. Phenomenologists, in stressing that categories are constructed rather than 'given', recommend the critical unmasking of assumptions. But, I would argue, that as this is only a mental activity, it is not going to change the situation. The 'new' sociology of education, I now believe, had an inadequate notion of how institutional change could come about. It was teachers who, through a change of their classroom practices, were to be the motors of educational change. But they could hardly do this by themselves. Fundamentally, what was lacking was the realization that the struggle to liberate education and the struggle to democratize economic life are inextricably linked. There was a need for teachers and pupils, schools and education, to be re-conceived in relation to other elements of the social whole, the totality.

It was in this context that, among sociologists connected with the phenomenological approach to educational change, there was a new awareness of Marx as a social theorist, and a felt need to study Marxism seriously. Because of this re-orientation in the sociology of education, it may be useful at this point to have an introduction to Marx and Marxism, so that later discussions of education, work and alienation are grounded in an understanding of this world-view. In this chapter I propose first to describe Marx's own theoretical

107

beginnings; how his achievement in social and political thought was based on his synthesis and transformation of two philosophical traditions. Marx utilized certain elements of the politics and philosophy of the idealism of Hegel and the materialism of Feuerbach. But he also rejected certain elements of both these thinkers. I focus particularly on Hegel, because Marx's criticism of Hegel is partly a re-statement of his general critique of philosophical idealism. This is of particular interest to us, as the new sociology of education also held an idealist position, which stressed the primacy of thought and neglected the existence of material factors such as the economy.

The second section of this chapter examines two important Marxist concepts, two contradictory ideas that exist side by side: alienation, the notion that Man is impotent to act, and praxis, the notion that Man's world *is* his activity. The evolution and meaning of these terms is traced from their Hegelian background, the themes being discussed in more detail in later sections of this book. The concern with alienation, then, leads to questions of practical emancipation. I argue that attempts to solve problems such as alienation theoretically inevitably fail because the problem and its solution involve social practice. After a brief exposition of Marx's theory of social change, the chapter concludes with an account of how, after Marx's death, orthodox Marxism became increasingly scientistic and positivist and it is suggested that such 'vulgar', deterministic Marxism denies the scope and significance of human action, of praxis, to transform the world.

Marx's Theoretical Beginnings

Durkheim, Merton and Parsons represent a tradition in which the underlying topic is order and stability, and the explanation of it. To generalize, one could say that most of these early classical sociologists believed that society was a reality greater than the individuals who compose it. This is 'sociological realism', the view that society is not a simple aggregate of individuals but a reality *sui generis*. In this view, society is composed of relationships and institutions, society creates individuals who can conform only to certain roles. 'Social facts' are stressed as 'real', external, independent and coercive. Often a biological analogy is used and society is seen as a system of independent parts or structures which serve the needs of the system. The implication of this viewpoint is that social laws are seen as dominating men with absolute necessity and all that they can do is to submit; in this tradition the individual is passive, adapting to the environment.[1] In many ways this is an inadequate account of Man. Many functionalists, for example, because they are mainly interested in the patterned recurrence of typicalities, treat man only as a unit. The methodological implication of this view is that data are primarily demographic rates and are measured as indices of function or malfunction. The model is that of positivism, of natural science, and the emphasis is on measurement.

Marx breaks with this tradition; he differs from most of the sociologists of the classical tradition because of his belief in the active model of Man. He believed that Man was infinitely perfectable and condemned the capitalist system for debasing and deforming him. Man had become increasingly alienated, a creature of the very social conditions he himself had created; but he did not have to remain a prisoner of those conditions. Communism was not an end, but a means to Man's greater humanity; he proposed the view, therefore, that Man and society have to be reconciled in such a way that Man does not suffer. It has been said that Marx's work provoked a response that accounts in large measure for the character of western sociology. Marx's social thought can be seen as an intellectual watershed in that he revived and synthesized critical, revolutionary and scientific tendencies. Irving Zeitlin's argument is that Durkheim, Weber, Vilfredo Pareto and Gaetano Mosca were provoked to a response, which has been called 'the debate with Marx's ghost'.[2] Many of these writers emphasized the problem of order in a deliberate attempt to avoid the spectre of disorder, change, revolution. Marxism, then, is of fundamental importance not only for the seminal ideas but for the critical intellectual response these ideas provoked. So, in a sense, the importance of Marx and his critics lies not in whether their specific theories were right or wrong but in the models they provide for theorizing. (Without this debate between Marx and his critics, what would the discipline of sociology look like?)

Let us begin by a brief examination of the views of Hegel and Feuerbach, the materials out of which Marx synthesized his thought.

Hegelian Idealism: the Dialectic and Negative Thinking

Marx's achievement in social and political thought was based on a transformation and synthesis of two traditions: German idealism as exemplified in the work of Hegel, and philosophical radicalism as expressed in the materialism of Feuerbach. First let me sketch two of Hegel's notions: the dialectic and negative thinking.

Hegel was an 'idealist' — one who believes that explanation must be in terms of mental causes, that ideas rather than objects are of greater importance: in other words, that thought is reality. One of his central notions was that of the dialectic: a statement or condition is produced and is opposed by the antithesis. The contradiction or conflict then produces a synthesis which itself becomes a new synthesis at a more advanced level. Hegel asserted that it is according to this process that all change, history, the development of nations, could be understood. This process, moreover, is leading to perfection as each stage in the world's development is the expression of the inner struggle of the 'Absolute Mind' to achieve self-realization. The Absolute was constantly striving to overcome contradictions by rendering itself intelligible and consistent, through the world which was its expression. The Objective or Absolute Mind is portrayed as striving constantly to overcome or resolve this dialectic of thesis and antithesis by higher syntheses until the Absolute reaches completion. The cosmos will then be a completely coherent entity which can be entirely understood. Thus for Hegel the dialectic is fundamentally a religious or metaphysical process; for him only mind is real and only mental actions and effects can form a basis for accounting for the world of our experience.[3]

An important feature of dialectical thinking is that it suggests that the form in which a thing immediately appears is not yet its true form and that what one sees is a negative condition and not the real potentiality.[4]

For Hegel there is in the last analysis no distinction between mind and its object. Both have a common denominator, which Hegel calls Reason and which appears under the guise of Spirit in the historical world. Spirit is both subjective and objective, and its 'internal contradictions' are resolved in the dialectical process, whereby the potentialities of all things unfold in a pattern of self-transcendence to a higher unity.

This is obviously a break with formal logic and 'scientific' modes of theorizing. Positivism, for example, treats facts in their immediately given form as truth, and excludes knowledge of everything that may not yet be a fact. The dialectical method is thus opposed to positivism. Though Marx was greatly influenced by Hegel's dialectical method and negative mode of thinking he also drew upon some of Feuerbach's criticisms of Hegel to constitute his own thought.

Feuerbach's Materialism and his Transformative Method

The aspects of the Hegelian system that aroused the most controversy at that time in Germany were those dealing with theology. A group called the Young Hegelians rejected these aspects and attempted to place Man again in the centre of the universe. The leading critic of the religious aspects of Hegelianism was Feuerbach, to whom we now turn.

Feuerbach argued that Hegel supposed thought to be subject, and existence to be the mere object or predicate. Hegel's subject was seen to exist outside of space and time and his whole philosophy was recognized as having conservative and quietistic implications. Feuerbach therefore set out to develop his own materialistic philosophy, an inversion of Hegelianism. This 'transformative method' is based on turning Hegelian idealism upside down; in other words, he transformed the traditional subject of idealist philosophy into a predicate, and the traditional predicate, Man, into a subject. If one started with Man, the concrete Man could be liberated from the subservience imposed on him by Hegelian metaphysics. This method made the starting-point of all social and philosophical discussion not thought, mind, consciousness or spirit – but Man.

Marx's Critique of Hegel and Feuerbach

Feuerbach's materialist writings were a criticism of the abstractions of idealist metaphysics, and a defence of the senses and natural existence. Thus they offered to Marx the necessary corrective to Hegel's system; moreover, by using Feuerbach's 'transformative method', Marx was enabled to get rid of Hegel's neo-platonic idealism.

Marx's first systematic work in which he used this method was 'The Critique of Hegel's Philosophy of Right'. Here both Marx's indebtedness and his struggle against the Hegelian system became evident; it has been put nicely by Lefebvre: 'Throughout his life Marx renewed assaults on the fortress (perhaps a better metaphor would be Kafka's Castle) of Hegelianism'. Marx was drawn to Hegel's philosophy because he saw in it a powerful instrument for changing reality.

Let us consider now how Marx synthesized certain elements of Feuerbach and Hegel, using as illustrative examples Marx's views on the State and civil society, and then on property.

Hegel had depicted civil society as a clash of social forces to be transcended by the universality of the State. The State was for him a separate distinct entity which had an existence of its own and was more important than any individual. In Marx's view, however, the State's claim to appear as the general interest could be shown to be a cloak for class interests. The modern State, as Hegel conceived it, was an exemplification of alienation, where the political had become separate from the social. Since the modern Hegelian State had been defined as an inverted reality, reality must be inverted once more by the transformative method, and man be made again a subject.

Marx also uses Feuerbach's method to show that property itself inverts the relations between the human subject and the world of objects. He argues that in Hegelianism property is transformed from an object of the will into a master. When one says that a person is determined by one's class position, one is really saying that a man becomes a predicate of his property. Marx then argues that, since class is based on property, the disappearance of class differences depends on the disappearance of property as the determinant of status.

It was from Hegel that Marx derived his view that reality is not a mere objective datum, external to Man, but is shaped by human agency. For Hegel this shaping was performed by consciousness. Marx extracted, as he did elsewhere, the activist element of Hegel's doctrine from its metaphysical background and combined it with elements of a materialist epistemology. It thus ceases to be merely a reflective theory but becomes a vehicle for shaping and moulding reality. The activist element is clearly expressed in Marx's philosophical premise that the initial creation of the world is by Man. By acting on the external world and changing it, Man at the same time changes his own nature. Work, then is Man's specific attribute; activity, labour, is Man's process of self-becoming. Man's powers will be fully realized only under communism. A phenomenological-Marxist reading, as outlined above, suggests that the revolution starts in the realm of consciousness which will cause a change in the nature of social relations and social structure. In such a society the State will disappear and private property be abolished. For Marx then, Hegelian logic, inverted, offered the key to changing the world.

Marx's epistemology does not have a mechanistic view of materialism. Much of what is known as Marxist materialism was written not by Marx but by Engels, whose views were often vulgarized versions of Darwinism and biology. Plekhanov, Kautsky and Lenin did believe in such a mechanistic materialism; they held that consciousness is a mere reflection of the objective world, the material environmental condition of Man's existence. Marxism has often been filtered from sources such as these.

Feuerbach, too, held a reflectionist view of consciousness. Though he believed in the necessary progress of human history, he nevertheless also held a passivist view of human existence, i.e., that Man is determined by objective material conditions. Marx believed that the weakness of Feuerbach's philosophy arose from its mechanistic materialist conception and was against such a reflectionist view of consciousness: 'If a man is a product of material conditions he can never emancipate himself from their impact . . . If the world is not of man's own making, how can he change it?' Marx therefore subjected Feuerbach to a critical examination, and wrote the *Theses on Feuerbach*, which contain the essence of his criticism.

Another difference between Marx and Feuerbach was that the latter saw the unity of Man and Nature expressed by Man being a part of Nature, while Marx sees Man as shaping Nature and, in turn, being shaped by it. That is to say, Man does not exist merely within Nature but shapes Nature, and this act shapes Man in a constant interaction between subject and object.[5]

Consciousness is therefore from the very beginning a social product. And human nature itself is the ever-changing product of human activity, of history. The unity of Man and Nature is carried out daily in Man's real economic activity. Man satisfies his needs through his contact with Nature, but also this act creates new needs as well as the possibilities for their satisfaction. It is this never-ending dialectical pursuit of their creation and satisfaction that constitutes historical development.

The Marxian Synthesis: Man and History

Historical development is never reduced, however, by Marx to linear causal terms. Reality is for Marx a human reality not only because it is shaped by Man but also because it reacts on Man himself. This helps us to understand the distinction between what used to be called the 'material base' and the 'superstructure', 'the productive forces' and the 'productive relations', or again, as Engels would have put it, between 'matter' and 'spirit'. The former, productive forces, can now be seen as conscious human *activity* aiming to preserve the conditions of human life. The latter, productive relations, can be understood as human *consciousness* which furnishes reasons, rationalizations, legitimations, justifications for the specific forms that activity take.

This shows, in a way, how Marx's epistemology occupies a middle position between classical materialism and classical idealism. Consider, for example, Marx's view of the 'individual' and 'society': for him they are not two mutually exclusive entities; each concept includes within itself certain moments of the other. The dichotomy between being and consciousness can be bridged by a radical view of the unity of the individual and society. The individual is the *social* being. Thought and being are indeed distinct but they also form a unity. As 'society' does not exist, according to Marx, as an entity distinct from individuals, change in individuals is inevitably change in society, and change in social circumstances is also change in individuals.

It has already been suggested that Marx's great achievement lay in utilizing certain aspects of the politics and philosophy (while rejecting other aspects), largely of Hegel and Feuerbach, and creating a synthesis destined to create a doctrine and a movement. There were two main features of Hegel's system that Marx came gradually to reject: first, Marx rejected Hegel's notion of total comprehension which leads to the reconciliation of mind with the world as it is, instead of turning thought into an instrument for transforming the world. While the Young Hegelians still believed in the efficiency of theoretical criticism, the young Marx was synthesizing Owenite socialism and Ricardian economics, and wielding German philosophy with his knowledge of the French proletariat to form a revolutionary doctrine.

Second, Marx rejected Hegel's justification of the State, and the maintenance of the *status quo*, a situation in which individual men were subordinate to its demands. Marx's views are also directly opposed to that of the positivistic-organicists and functionalists who, beginning with assumptions about society, treat them as if they were objectively valid, and come to reify society. In spite of these rejections, there was a feature of Hegel's philosophy with which Marx was in agreement; they shared a philosophy of history.

Hegel had convinced him that the totality of the world is an ordered whole which the intellect can comprehend and master. Marx obtained from Hegel the notion that there is an objective meaning in history, and that history is the progressive self-creation of Man. It is a process whose driving force is human labour; Man produces both himself and his world and he does so through practical activity which modifies his own nature at the same time that it transforms external nature. History is thus the record of this transformation. Marx emphasized that Man should be viewed historically; what he makes of himself depends on the interaction of his forces with the environment, and the man made institutions of society. The Marxian critique of society is motivated by society's failure to realize Man's potentialities. Freedom, to be genuine, must be universal; hence the individual is free only if all other men are free. These utopian thoughts are derived from Hegel's philosophy of reason and Feuerbach's conception of human nature. Marx uses the Hegelian dialectic of subject-object so as to eliminate the one-sidedness of a mechanical materialism which posits Man as a passive receptacle of an unchanging Nature. But on the other hand he also sees that Man's self-creation involves the real needs of empirical human beings which Hegel had neglected. For Marx, Man is truly himself in so far as he is able to recognize himself in the man-made universe which surrounds him. Alienation is the failure to attain this self-realization. The overcoming of alienation is therefore the ultimate goal of the historical process, the time when all the potentialities of Man's nature are realized. Two contradictory ideas exist side by side: alienation, the notion that Man is impotent to act, and the other side of the coin, the notion that Man's world is nothing but his praxis, his human activity. I shall trace now the evolution and meaning of these terms from their Hegelian background in order to grasp more fully the significance of Marx's social and political thought.

Two Views of Alienation: Hegel and Marx

For Marx, work is the essentially human activity; only men are uniquely capable of deliberate acting upon and changing the world. This was in contrast to Adam Smith, who held that leisure was man's ideal state and that work was a coercive activity. But Marx denies this, and states that work realizes human spontaneity and has the highest potential value. In society as it is, work is coercive not because of its nature, but because of the historical conditions under which it is performed. Under the conditions of capitalist economy, production is conducted in such alienating circumstances that work, man's creative activity, the process we call 'objectification', becomes a process of dehumanization.

Marx argues that it is the nature of Man to produce objects in which he mirrors himself, to surround himself with a man-made universe. But the objects, the products of the worker's creative self-realizing activity, are taken away from him. He is unable to own the product of his work, and becomes estranged from his own creation which confronts him as something hostile and alien. This alienation of Man from his own product also involved his estrangement from other men. The precondition of existence is labour, but under capitalism labour itself has become a commodity.[6]

> The worker is related to the product of his labour as to an alien object. The object he produces does not belong to him, dominates him, and only serves in the long run to increase his poverty. Alienation appears not only in the result, but also in the production and productive activity itself. The worker is not at home in his work which he views only as a means of satisfying other needs. It is an activity directed against himself, that is independent of him and does not belong to him. Thirdly, alienated labour succeeds in alienating man from his species. Species life, productive life, life creating life, turns into a mere means of sustaining the worker's individual existence, and man is alienated from his fellow men. Finally nature itself is alienated from man who thus loses his own inorganic body.

Marx states that Man is alienated from Nature, from himself and from humanity, and that these aspects are interconnected. Work becomes not the satisfaction of a need but only the *means* for satisfying other needs. A worker's life becomes for him only a means to enable him to exist. In other words, the human subject becomes the object of his own products; seen in this light, capital is man's alienated self.

Like many of Marx's ideas, the notion of alienation comes directly from Hegel, but again it is not just a question of derivation but of confrontation with Hegel's ideas. Marx's criticism of Hegel's notion of alienation is a re-statement of his general critique of philosophical idealism. But before we turn our attention to that, let us take a brief look a Hegel's view of alienation.

Hegel's View of Alienation

Hegel believed that there was only one world, the world of spirit or idea, and that therefore the distinction between myself and the outside world was delusory. As long as Man distinguished between himself, subject, and the world, object, alienation was inevitable. The world is mine, but by treating it as a separate object, I conceal this from myself; this is estrangement. But how is it overcome? Hegel suggests more knowledge; knowledge is the re-possession within myself of what has been falsely divided from me.

Marx was particularly drawn to the notion that there is only one world; the notion that Man exists as part of the world and cannot be outside it. There can be no value therefore outside humanity itself. The similarity between Hegel and Marx was that they both insisted that it was wrong to think of Man as separate from the world. When men do think with this separation in mind they are alienated; there are not two worlds but one. The crucial difference between the two writers seems to be this: Hegel stressed possession of the world by knowledge, but Marx rejected the Hegelian view of the primacy of thought or spirit and emphasized concrete reality, the way that men mastered or possessed the world by working upon it. The overcoming of alienation was not a matter of merely knowing or understanding more, not just a matter of consciousness subject to elimination by another state of consciousness. Marx objected to the implications that followed from such a view: Hegel considered all objects as mere projections of consciousness and so reduced Man to his inner self. But such a reduction of Man to his inner self accepts an image of Man as isolated from his fellow-men, and thus denies him self-development and self-creation. Another of Marx's objections was to Hegel's mode of thinking that history ceased to deal with concrete events and was reduced to the act of thinking. In contrast to Hegel's idealist position, Marx maintained that alienation was rooted in the historical situation and its consequences, and that it could be overcome by action that altered the circumstances of one's life.

Marx's View of Alienation

Alienation, in its different forms, remains a central concept in all of Marx's work and shows the continuity of his thought. He discusses many types of alienation: religious alienation, one could say, was when God had usurped Man's position. Philosophical alienation was when philosophy was merely speculative, concerned only with abstractions; pure thought which reduced man and history to a mental process. There was political and economic alienation also. They all contained the common idea that Man had forfeited to someone or something what was essential to his nature. In all these different forms some other entity obtained what was proper to Man – the right to be in control of his own activities. This alienation in real life is reflected also in the form of its ideology. For example, political economy is considered to have objective ontological reality with 'laws' that independently regulate human activity. Once again, the human subject becomes the object of his own products; that is to say, alienation makes Man a predicate of his own products. Objects, commodities, the products of Man become his master, while Man as worker becomes an object-less being.

The necessary consequence of such a system, of the external relation of the worker to Nature, to others, to himself, of alienated labour, is private property. Marx maintained that property was not the realization of personality but its negation. The possession of property entails its non-possession by another. Marx's solution to these problems was the abolition of capital and of all property relations. To abolish alienation, another necessary prerequisite would have to be the abolition of the division of labour. At present, the division of labour reduces Man since it makes a man's occupation into his main characteristic.

Marx stated that in present societies the creation of objects, instead of helping Man to realize himself, causes alienation, but in future societies objectification will lead to the unfolding of all human potentialities. Instead of antagonism there will be mutuality: 'The positive abolition of private property and the appropriation of human life is therefore the positive abolition of all alienation, thus the return of man out of religion, family, state, etc., into his human, i.e. social being.[7]

The society that will abolish alienation will abolish not labour but its alienating conditions.[8] The abolition of the division of labour entails the abolition of the distinctions that prevent Man from being truly human. The coming of communism will mean that men can live in a society where they are no longer estranged from themselves; it will mean the resolution of the conflict between Man and Nature, and the realization by Man of freedom and of his universal humanity.

Marx's View of Praxis

It is a part of my argument that there is continuity in Marx's thought and that the theme of alienation preoccupied him continuously. What was philosophically postulated in his early work was empirically verified in *Capital*, using the tools of classical economics. A necessary prerequisite for the abolition of alienation was to be the abolition of labour and capital. This was to be achieved through revolutionary praxis, the fusion of thought and action, of theory and practice, of philosophy and revolution, for the cause of human liberation. For a fuller understanding of some of the contradictions and problems concerning theory and practice we must look first at Aristotle, Hegel and other philosophers before we see how it was developed by Marx.

Some of the problems concerning theory and practice can be seen in a work as early as Aristotle's *Metaphysics*, where he makes a distinction between theoretical and practical knowledge. *Theoria* aims at a general truth, is comprehensive, and seeks to know the world and understand it with the sole aim of knowledge itself. The more this sort of knowledge is related to principles and general rules the more it is theoretical. *Praxis*, on the other hand, is practical knowledge, it is instrumental. While theoretical knowledge, then, aims at the universal, the permanent and the eternal, practical knowledge is particular, applicable and momentary. Both theoria and praxis are different modes of knowledge. The two concepts are defined as to be mutually exclusive; no kind of knowledge can therefore be simultaneously both particular and universal, both applicable and inapplicable. We now use the term 'praxis' to mean 'the unity of theory and practice', but this, from a strict Aristotelian point of view, would be quite meaningless. How, then, did the meaning of the term change?

Hegel began the shift in the traditional meaning of the terms. He believed that the object of thought, the universal and the eternal, could be consciously created by thought, that the object of theory could be shaped by human consciousness. This is partly expressed in the famous quotation: 'What is rational is actual, and what is actual is rational.' Inevitably those who underlined the notion, 'what is actual is rational', justified existing reality and drew politically conservative conclusions from it. There were others, however, who emphasized that 'what is rational is actual'. This was taken to imply that whatever can be shown to be rationally valid will ultimately be realized. This can be seen as a call to shape the world according to Reason.

Among the thinkers who stressed this view, the linking of Hegelianism with some sort of notion of an historical future, was a Polish writer named Cieszkowski. He is important in that there are many similarities between his thoughts and those of Marx; both believed in praxis, the unity of theory and practice, and that philosophy must be applied in the service of a future society. Moreover they shared the view that the precise form of utopian socialism of the future society could not be predicted. Let us first consider Cieszkowski's contribution to the development of the term 'praxis'.

August V. Cieszkowski was critical of Hegel's denial of the possibility of recognizing the future prior to its becoming the present, or rather the past. In Cieszkowski's view[9] the task of philosophy was to find out the connections between historical actuality and the future. He therefore proceeded to create a synthesis of the future out of the antitheses and contradictions of the historical past, as described by Hegel. In brief, Cieszkowski was pointing out that the Self can become a concrete Self only through action related to external objects. In thought, man's relation to the world remains abstract; he can express his actuality only through an active relation that causes objective results.

Cieszkowski therefore suggested that philosophy must

become *applied* philosophy, that it must have an impact on life, on our social conditions and problems. A philosophy of the future would thus be a transcendence of philosophy beyond itself. On this point, as in many others, he clearly prefigures Marx. Another of his insights, which has a striking resemblance to Marx's own views, concerns those utopian socialists who tried to impose their vision, their prescriptions from the outside, instead of attempting to shape the new reality from within existing conditions. Not only can future society not be discussed without a prior analysis of the present, but it is not possible to predict the details of the future precisely. All that we can have is a general outline of the mainstream of future development.

A criticism that can be made of Cieszkowski's work is that the historical content of the social problem is hardly mentioned. His main weakness was that he, unlike Marx, did not envisage a historical subject, like the proletariat, that could carry out his postulate of radical change. Lacking a motor, he could not develop a theory of social action.

The Young Hegelians like Ruge and Hess further developed the concept of praxis, the new revolutionary relationship between theory and practice. They pointed out that attempts to solve problems such as alienation theoretically inevitably fail because the problem and its solution involve social practice. Thus praxis came to have a new meaning: the revolution cannot be an outcome of mere theoretical criticism, it has to manifest itself in social action. The ultimate end of theoretical emancipation is practical emancipation. Marx was to develop further the theory of praxis by giving it a concrete historical content.

Marx was highly critical of both German idealism and traditional materialism because they both stopped short of changing reality. He thought that philosophy should always be related to historical actuality, but in the way it was often practised the link between reality and reflection was severed. This, according to Marx, might cause the illusion that the object of philosophy is itself. A merely contemplative attitude contains its objects in its contemplation and is thus object-less. In this view, philosophy represents an illusory realm of essences divorced from the world of material existence. Feuerbach, too, was limited in that he held that the task of philosophy was to supply an adequate consciousness about the world. It was Marx's view that praxis, the unity of theory and practice, transferred man from an object-less world into the sphere of objective activity. Philosophy, in ceasing to be contemplative, must become the theory of revolution; its ultimate task was not merely to comprehend reality but to change it. This view is illustrated by the following well-known quotations:[10]

> It is only in a social context that subjectivism and objectivism, spiritualism and materialism, activity and passivity, cease to be antimonies. The resolution of theoretical contradictions is possible only through practical means, only through the practical energy of man. Their resolution is by no means therefore, the task only of the understanding, but is a real task of life, a task which philosophy was unable to accomplish precisely because it saw there a purely theoretical problem.
>
> The question whether human thinking can pretend to objective truth is not a theoretical but a *practical* question. Man must prove the truth, i.e. the reality and power, the 'this-sideness' of his thinking in practice. The dispute over the reality or non-reality of thinking that is isolated from practice is a purely *scholastic* question.

Shlomo Avineri argues that Marx believed strongly in the value of proletarian associations; because for him they united the subjective aspect of consciousness with the objective aspect of social conditions and organizations. Avineri suggests that for Marx they did not have a narrowly political or even a trade unionist significance; they were, potentially, what the future society would be in practice.[11] They are seen as means of creating now the social texture of future human relations. In this reading of Marx, it is held that the political movement would grow out of the economic struggle. Seen in this light, working-class associations are the means for the organization or proletarian self-consciousness. This is the subjective element, but there is also the objective element, the organization of social conditions. It is this dialectical relationship in revolutionary praxis that leads ultimately to human emancipation. The end results of the revolution are thus historically formed and determined during and by its occurrence. In this view the question about the inevitability of the revolution breaking out because of the internal contradictions of the capitalist economy becomes difficult to ask, because such a mechanistic and deterministic view, derived largely from Engels's work, sees in Man and in human will only an object of external circumstances and political manipulation.

It was Marx's view that theory must evolve an adequate interpretation of the world before it will be able to change it. But a change in consciousness is also required; when a worker comprehends that under capitalist production he is degraded to the status of a mere object, he ceases to be an object and becomes a subject. A self-change, then, is needed in the proletariat. This consciousness becomes the motor of revolution, and its dialectical nature transcends questions such as determinism versus voluntarism. According to this view, if the proletariat is still unaware of its own historical position, if it does not possess an adequate world-view, then the objective conditions by themselves will not create the revolution. If, however, the proletariat grasps that by shaping its own view of the world it also changes it, if such a revolutionary consciousness exists, then the revolution is bound to happen. Avineri contends that the activist and practical elements of this consciousness imply that circumstances will change with the self-change of the proletariat. Moreover, under these conditions, it could be said that the revolution is already taking place. It could be argued against Avineri, however, that there is an absence of proletarian class-consciousness and of this he gives no account.

Marx was always concerned with a theory of society and explanations of social change. Why had capitalism come into existence only in Europe? What was the genesis of bourgeois society? Unlike Taine or Tocqueville who merely described historical links connecting successive stages of society, Marx wanted to find some kind of logic in the pattern of events. It is a matter of controversy whether he states that these stages arise as a matter of necessity or not. For reasons which will become evident as we proceed, I take the view that Marx's historical account of the genesis of capitalism should not be seen in a deterministic manner as a universal law of development. Taking a unilinear view of history common in his time, Marx described Asiatic, ancient, feudal and modern

An Introduction to Marxism

modes of production as 'progressive epochs in the economic formation of society'. Slavery, feudalism and capitalism were definite phases in the development of western society. The rise of capitalism involved the creation of the modern proletariat. 'Capital' and 'labour' presuppose each other, indeed the capital–labour relationship is central to the functioning of capitalism. Marx argues that the prior development of capitalism is necessary for the realization of socialism. This does not, however, imply a deterministic concept of necessity. Capitalism is necessary in so far as the next stage dialectically unfolds the principles inherent in capitalism itself. The contradictions inherent in bourgeois society and political liberalism, the polarization of wage-labour and capital, will give rise to socialism. In this process capitalism will be simultaneously realized and abolished. The proletarian State will be the first State in history to use political power for universal, and not partial, ends.

This, then, in brief, is one reading of Marx's theory of social structure and change. The impetus comes from 'the sub-structure', but the emphasis is on Man's understanding of processes and contradictions. The future development towards socialism depends on the prior existence of conditions which make this social change possible. Conditions never give rise to ideas but make their realization possible; they can be understood and guided. It is obvious that the existence of communist ideas precede the conditions necessary for their realization. But what are these conditions? It is difficult to be explicit about this because nowhere does Marx give directives, or provide a list of rules. He even refused to prophesy about the way revolution would occur in any particular country. The transformation of society, for Marx, is always revolutionary, since it implies the transformation of the determined into the determining. Such a transformation suggests a revolution in human consciousness, in human praxis. The exact circumstances in which the revolution will be carried out cannot therefore be pre-determined. Marx has also little to say about the future society. His sketches are few and fragmentary, partly because he was aware that his rivals, the utopian socialists, did construct detailed blueprints for the new communist society. His hostility to them was based on his belief that communist society would be determined by the specific conditions under which it was established, and of course these conditions could not be predicted.[12] Ironically, after Marx's death in 1883, there was a gradual abandonment of these ideas. We must now look for some reasons for this drift towards a deterministic, scientific rendering of Marx's thought.

The Drift Towards Positivist Marxism

After the death of Marx, it was Engels who was chiefly instrumental in giving shape to what became known as 'orthodox Marxism'. For Engels, socialism was above all scientific, and the active agents of progress were disembodied entities, reifications such as technology, science or the industrial revolution. He emphasized that these agents of progress were for the satisfaction of human needs, while in contrast, Marx had underlined the transformation of human and social nature. This was perhaps, in part, due to Engels's inability to see the greatness of Kant, who had pointed to *the creative role of the mind in shaping the world of experience* present to individual consciousness. For Marx, too, as well as for Kant, the world of experience was not simply given but was mediated by the human mind. In the *Theses on Feuerbach* Marx attempted to take account of Kant's critique by synthesizing materialism and idealism: mind was no more a passive receptacle of sense-impressions than Man was simply the product of social circumstances.[13] What Engels did was to replace the constitutive role of conscious activity, Man's ability to rearrange the world of which he formed a part, by a faith in science. In other words, Engels re-formulated the original credo expressed in Marx's early works (1843–8) in such a way as to make it closer to determinism and positivism.

The earlier Marxian version was that the dichotomy between idealism and materialism would be overcome and that the 'realization' of philosophy through action would transform the world. But Engels replaced praxis by the new scientific doctrine which stated that the course of history is governed by inner general laws which we can discover. It is from Engels's philosophical writing, his amalgamation of philosophy and science, rather than from Marx that dialectical materialism is derived. Dialectical materialism was thought of as 'a universal science'; nature and history were subject to immutable laws, the determined goal of this process being socialism.[14] This scheme was basically an amalgam of Hegelian and Darwinian concepts. The basic analogy used was of Darwinian evolution, so that just as Darwin discovered the law of development of organic nature, so Marx discovered the law of development of human history.

There has always been an unceasing tension between the idealist core of the Marxian version and the materialist science surrounding it. The latter view has been expressed in many works and has been so influential that many sociologists have drawn their mental pictures of the world from it. To put it briefly, while Marx thought that Nature and Man are complex realities whose interaction is studied in society, writers such as Engels conceived of Nature as an independent reality external to Man, from whose operation historical laws could be derived. There was now a cast-iron system of laws; history was seen to be subject to immutable laws from which the inevitability of socialism could be deduced. Capitalism had once performed a revolutionary role in doing away with pre-industrial forms of society. Now it was the task of the proletariat to set free the industrial revolution from the control of the institutions of bourgeois society.

This progressive abandonment of the critical theory of Marx's early work led to the transformation of Marxism into a scientific doctrine, 'scientific' socialism. Engels and other interpreters and definers of Marx transformed his vision into a causally determined process. Instead of the original dialectical method, praxis, in which critical thought was validated by revolutionary action, the accepted reading has come to be of the logic of history as a causal process in which there is little room for the notion that history may be created by human action directed towards the attainment of a truly human society. Thus began the drift towards positivism and scientism. It is a crucial part of my argument that this emphasis on the scientific leads to a vulgar deterministic communism which denies the important scope and significance of praxis. But obviously for any praxis (the unity of theory and practice) to be possible, there must be presuppositions about the nature of the world and of Man. It is therefore to Marx's conceptions of reality and human nature to which we now turn. This will form the basis for a discussion on the meaning of alienation, and its manifestations in schools.

Chapter 9

Alienation and Schooling

This chapter deals with one of the major concerns of humanistic Marxism: alienation. I begin by outlining Marx's relational conception of reality and his view of human nature. This forms the foundation for a discussion of the meaning of alienation. After outlining what is called 'the general logic of commodity production', it is argued that the same process takes place in the case of knowledge. Under the conditions of capitalism, education is conducted in such alienating circumstances that it becomes a process of dehumanization. This has been accurately depicted in the writings of the de-schoolers, but Illich's solution, that each individual is responsible for his own demystification, is an idealist one. It is unlikely to be practically realized, because what is necessary to overcome alienation is not only theoretical criticism but social action. Attempts to solve problems such as alienation theoretically, through a phenomenological emphasis on the power of consciousness alone, inevitably fail because the problem and its solution involve social practice. The discussion on the de-schoolers is followed by a Marxist analysis of education. I believe that to fully comprehend the alienation that is prevalent in our society it is necessary to have a Marxist framework, and suggest that Bertell Ollman's work on Man in capitalist society provides possibilities for constructing such a theoretical framework. I begin to do so here by applying some of Ollman's insights to education, particularly to pupils, teachers and knowledge. My argument in this chapter is simple: education is a mode of production involving pupils and teachers, and knowledge is both private property and cultural 'capital'. Schools are factories.

Marx's Relational Conception of Society

In contrast to the positivist version of Marxism mentioned in the concluding sections of the last chapter, this section outlines a Hegelian reading of Marx's conception of reality. The view presented has been called by Bertell Ollman 'the philosophy of internal relations' and includes within it the concept of dialectic. It is argued by Ollman that Marx's words are meant to express a conception of things and their inter-relations.[1] But even these inter-relationships are not fixed but are changing. Marx conceived society relationally. That it to say, capital, labour, value, are all grasped as relations. Relations are internal to each factor, and when a relation alters, the factor itself alters — its appearance and/or function has changed sufficiently for it to require a new concept. Thus Marx often uses the same expression to refer to different things, and he often uses different expressions to refer to the same thing.

Marx is saying that for this factor in this context, this is the influence most worth noting. Each social factor has the potential to take the names of others when it functions as they do. Each social factor is internally related to its own past and future forms, as well as to the past and future forms of surrounding factors. All social change is conceived of as a coming to be of what potentially is. Thus naming attaches to a function, which in turn is conceived of within a relational whole. Marx, then, had a relational conception of reality but Hegel, perhaps, best expresses this conception. For Hegel, truth is a whole and what we say about particular things is partial truth. He suggests that through their inter-relations things are more than they appear. Marx, of course, never criticized the relational scheme itself, only *how* Hegel chose to apply this framework. It has already been emphasized how, even before Marx, the Young Hegelians replaced Hegel's World Spirit as subject with Man. When Man becomes the subject, the individual becomes an actor instead of being just a passive observer. Marx thus took over Hegel's concepts and endowed them with fresh meaning by removing their idealistic content.[2] Subsumed under a philosophy of internal relations is the concept of dialectic, which we will now examine.

In this section I propose to take the dialectic from its

Hegelian background and consider it within Marx's philosophy of internal relations of which it forms a part. As Ollman has noted, the dialectic has several functions: first it is a method of exposition – a way of seeing things as moments in their own development in, with, and through other things. Second, it looks for relationships, not only between different entities, but between the same one in time past, present and future. In a sense this text is an attempt to show how phenomenological Marxism and education can be studied from different angles and approaches, in ways that are interconnected and for ever in flux. Thus in this book each subject is dealt with from many vantage-points and each subject is followed out of, and into, different contexts. Thus what is being continuously stressed is that the basic unit of reality is not a thing but a *relation*.

One of the more important principles of the dialectic is termed 'the mutual penetration of polar opposites'. Consider these examples: identity and difference, cause and effect, necessity and chance, positive and negative, love and hate, good and bad. Now from the point of view of dialectic as outlook, it could be said that these qualities which 'appear' opposite and distinct are in reality joined by internal relations. Thus the truth of any contrasting observation depends on the angle or point of view of the observer. Moreover the dialectic knows no either/or, to it everything is 'both this and that'.

Another principle of dialectical thinking is the 'development through contradiction'. An example often given is that of capital, which includes the proletariat and the capitalist among its components. The resolution of this contradiction is sometimes called the 'negation of the negation', referring to the fact that capital itself emerged out of similar contradictions in the entities that preceded it.

Four points are particularly noteworthy from what has been said so far. Each entity is internally related to numerous others in a setting which is for ever fluctuating. Second, entities experience qualitative changes with an alteration at some point in quantity. Third, each entity appears quite different, even the opposite, of what it does now when looked at from another angle or for another purpose. Fourth, each entity was something which progressed through repeated conflicts between its parts; that is to say, reactions against what went before.

It should not be thought that this mode of theorizing – what Ollman calls the philosophy of internal relations – is without difficulties. It *is* difficult to think relationally. This may be partly because the bivalency of standard logic; true-false, fact-value, may have become deeply embedded in our culture, and meet an apparent need for decisiveness, for determinacy. The extent to which thinking relationally may be difficult because of our upbringing in a capitalist society should also be considered.[3]

Let me summarize the importance of the philosophy of internal relations. Marx suggests, then, that we view reality as a whole, in flux, and composed of internally related parts; that we take change and interaction as necessary rather than contingent. Second, we should treat the relational view as a working hypothesis. It teaches us how we should try and look at everything (rather than describe how we do or ever will). It is because some critics have not understood the relational view that they have misunderstood Marx. If they had utilized this view, many of their 'difficulties' would be resolved. How else – but by such a philosophy of internal relations – could sense be made of statements such as these? 'Theory is material force', or 'Religion, family, state, law, morality science, art, etc., are only particular modes of production'.[4]

Because of the dominance of positivism, this philosophy has been largely ignored until recently. With it one can challenge narrow entrenched, scientistic philosophies. The dialectic, it seems to me, is one of the main features of 'the philosophy of internal relations'. The dialectic is an alternative mode of theorizing to the limitations imposed upon us by conventional logic. The traditional view holds that A = A. A cannot at the same time be not-A. Now, dialectics does not deny this, but goes on to say that nothing is merely self-identical and self-contained. Nothing concrete and real is merely positive. Things which are merely positive, which are merely what they are, are abstract and dead. All real things are part of the world of interaction; everything is in flux. Dialectics, then, regards things in a process of motion and as essentially interrelated. It believes that all concrete things are contradictory. There are contradictions in reality. A contradiction is not mere accidental conflict, but essential conflict; it is opposition within a unity. The outcome of a concrete contradiction, by the process which Hegel called '*aufgeben*', results in a new thing.[5]

Now that an exposition has been given of a way of understanding Marx, we can proceed with one of our main purposes, which is to examine the relationships between a phenomenological Marxism and a view of education from such a perspective. But before we turn our attention to such topics, let us look at some questions concerning nature and society, and in particular, Marx's conception of human nature. Once Marx's view of Man's needs, his powers, the nature of human activity and work, are understood, and a vision of a possible future given, alienation, in its educational context, can be more adequately grasped and challenged.

Marx suggested that we study first human nature in general and then human nature as modified in each historical epoch. He begins with what is common to all men: powers and needs. Every man, because he is a man, possesses certain powers and needs. Power suggests potential, the possibility of becoming more of whatever already is; need refers to the desire one feels for something, usually something not immediately available. A power is whatever is used that 'fulfils' a need. To know any power is therefore to know its corresponding need, and vice versa.

Marx also makes a distinction between natural and species powers and needs. Natural powers and needs are those Man shares with every living entity. Labour, eating and sex, for example, are the powers associated with natural man. The easiest way to grasp Marx's notion of Man as a natural being is to view him as not yet a man but still an animal. Man has impulses and abilities which enable him to realize his goals. But what sets Man apart from the rest of the animal world are species powers and needs – those that Man alone possesses. Species man is a being for 'himself', with self-consciousness – an individual active in pursuing his own ends. Man's species powers of seeing, thinking, feeling, loving, are possible only because of his natural powers. For Marx, the individual appropriates nature, and makes it in some way a part of himself. At the same time Man, in every sphere of his life, is involved in objectification. That man is inescapably social is continuously stressed by Marx. Work, creativity, must be done with and for others, and consequently, he is a social being. People are invariably in a close relationship with one another because their needs, and the manner of satisfying them, create between them reciprocal links such as sexual relations, exchange, division of labour. An individual cannot escape his dependence on society even when he acts on his own: the materials; skills; language itself, with which he operates; are social products.[6]

According to Marx, Man's activity is planned, purposive, flexible, conscious and willed. He develops his capacities and transforms his nature. He makes an important distinction between labour and work; labour is thought of quantitatively, it is an alienated form, but *work is conceived of qualitatively, as potential*. Marx talks of work as a life-activity, need; it expresses Man's powers. Man is forever remoulding Nature, by thus acting on the external world and changing it, he at the same time changes his own nature. There is no clear distinction in Marx's writings between creativity, activity and work. Obviously creativity focuses on the uniqueness of the product and its source in Man; activity involves purposeful endeavour, and work points to material production as the prime area of activity. But as Ollman has justly remarked, not all activity is work, nor is all work creative. A given case of activity and work is also one of creativity when it involves human powers to develop positively. But not all work is creative – work in a capitalist society does not aid Man's powers to mature but is felt as alienation. As we have seen, Marx believes in a unity between man and nature, and anything which diminishes the individual's role as initiator is seen as rending them apart.

Alienation and the De-schoolers

It has been stressed that, for Marx, work has the highest potential value and that it is coercive in society as it is, not because of the nature of work itself, but because of the historical conditions under which it is performed. The worker's alienation in the means of production finds expression in all areas of his life. The same misconceptions of the place of Man's creations can be seen in all spheres of activity: class, state, religion, family, ethics, art, science, literature, education. In this section I will begin with an outline of the meaning of alienation, particularly the separation of Man from activity. Marx's analysis is then applied to some aspects of education, and the notion of dehumanization is exemplified by a discussion of the work of the de-schoolers. There are then sections of 'the school as a factory' in which pupils and teachers are conceived as workers, and the notion of knowledge as private property.[7]

Alienation can occur when Man is separated from his activity, his own products, from his fellow-men and his species. To be concise, whereas Man makes himself through labour, under capitalist conditions of production, he destroys himself in the process. The object is taken away from him and to the extent that the object embodies his subjectivity, capitalism deprives the subject of his subjectivity and humanity.[8] Parts of his being are split off and undergo their own transformation. They attain an independent life, take on needs which the individual is then forced to satisfy. The subject is reduced to the level of object, *which however must remain minimally a subject so that he can continue producing.* Simultaneously, his product becomes first a commodity (in fact, this process is sometimes called 'the general logic of commodity production') on the capitalist market, and subsequently capital. Thus alienation results. The original producing subject is reduced to the level of an object to be bought and sold in the labour market just like any other commodity. The object that he originally produced, in becoming capital, becomes the abstract subject. Capital thus functions as if it were a subject, alienating worker and capitalist.

Instead of developing the potential inherent in Man's powers, capitalist labour consumes these powers without replenishing them. In so many aspects of education the potential inherent in individuals is neglected and the person thought of as a commodity on the market. That is to say, 'potential' is regarded only in terms of usefulness to 'social needs'; instead of being developed, it is exploited.

Marx did not directly write about education; he elected to analyse political economy. If we wish to understand what is going on in our classrooms by using a Marxist analysis, we are

135

faced with the problem of using what we take to be his method, his conceptual scheme, or of attempting to formulate new concepts to study this field. Having decided on the former course, our discussion of schooling and alienation can be no more than a 'translation'. In using the short chapter entitled 'Estranged labour' in the *Economic and Philosophic Manuscripts of 1844* on the basic relations of alienation, and trying to apply these to education, we are perhaps making no more than an analogue. This section on schooling and alienation is largely based on the acceptance of two propositions: first, Marx's view of the relation between Man and Nature. In the previous section we referred to one of the basic ideas of dialectical materialism, the view that Man has possibilities which can be realized only through his work. Moreover, he possesses consciousness, and is conscious of himself as a member of a species. Second, the following account also assumes that a philosophy of internal relations is a useful mode of thinking. Such a philosophy suggests that we take as a basic unit of reality not a thing but a Relation. This means, as Ollman makes clear, that when we speak of Relations we seek relational, not causal, explanations; we don't go back in history to posit first causes and sequential chains but view historical developments as temporal relations having dialectical ties. It will be remembered that Marx viewed 'religion, family, state, morality, science, art, etc.' as particular modes of production. A mode of production, according to Marx, 'must not be considered simply as being the reproduction of the physical existence of the individuals. Rather it is a definite form of activity of these individuals, a definite form of expressing their life, a definite mode of life on their part.'[9] For Marx this means an expression of the alienation of social relationships within and through capitalism. It will be argued that, as an expression of alienated production, education is treated as a thing. It has become fetishized and is attributed with powers usually given to man. Education thus comes to be reified, that is to say, it comes to be seen as a power over and above man, and therefore beyond change.

This same alienating process takes place in all areas of knowledge and life. We can take as an example science and science-teaching. Scientists produce commodities through their specialized labour. But instead of developing science to attain humanist goals, science and its products are today separated from the subject, the scientist who produces it. It can be said that science has lost its purpose, and instead of remaining a means has become its own criterion. Having lost sight of its subject, science has become bourgeois science.[10]

Not only scientists, but all men, inevitably objectify themselves through labour, but what is so destructive in the process of alienation is that workers have no control over what becomes of their products. The products of capitalism begin to control their producers. Individual subjects are reduced to the level of passive objects. This passivity is related to another important element in alienation, the feeling that Man has forfeited to someone or something what was essential to his nature; the feeling that some other entity had obtained the right that he should have to be in control of his own activities. Man is dehumanized.

I wish to suggest that under the conditions of capitalist economy education is conducted under such alienating circumstances that it becomes a process of dehumanization. One of the most accurate depictions of the dehumanization involved in prevailing conceptions of education is to be found in the work of the de-schoolers, Illich, Reimer, Postman and others.[11] While disagreeing with much of their analysis and many of their remedies, their descriptions of schooling nevertheless seem mordantly correct.

Illich's argument, briefly, is that this dehumanization is partly a consequence of the institutions that we created, which have now grown so powerful that they shape not only our preferences, but actually our sense of possibilities. The more we become trained in the consumption of packaged goods and services the less effective we become in shaping our environment. We live in a society where demand is engineered through publicity to stimulate the production of more commodities. But how are schools involved in this process of dehumanization?

Schools actually operate in such a way that schooling has become anti-educational, anti-social. They have the effect of tempering the subversive potential of education in an alienated society. Several methods are used: for example it is generally accepted that only those who have been schooled into compliance on a lower grade are admitted to the higher reaches. Despite the claim that teaching is non-political, schools indoctrinate the child into the acceptance of the political system. Schooling is a form of indoctrination to fit children passively into the acceptance of an ideology that keeps them 'democratically in place'. For all children that come to accept this view, or at least do not struggle against it, there is ritual certification. In *Deschooling Society* Illich argues that the notions that are being indoctrinated by the schools include the following: first, they naturalize the divine origin of social stratification with much more vigour than the churches have ever done. Second, children are schooled into disciplined consumption, the myth of unending consumption. Third, schools initiate young people into a world where everything is measured. It seems that once people have the idea schooled into them that values can be produced and measured, they tend to accept all kinds of rankings. This is, in my view, a manifestation of the culture of positivism.

It is not my purpose here to present a critique of Illich; but because he is so readily set up as an educational guru, it should be mentioned that he too can be charged with holding philosophically idealist views which have little chance of being realized *in practice*. Illich believes that fundamental social change must begin with a change of consciousness in ourselves. In other words, he suggests that these problems must be attacked on an individual rather than a political level; he says nothing about power. Since the institutionalization of values occurs not through external coercion but through psychic manipulation, so its rejection is a psychological act of individual will: each individual is responsible for his own demystification. I have argued consistently that such a stance, the stress on mental de-reification, though vital, by itself changes nothing. (A clue, perhaps, for his popularity among some educationists?) It is, in a sense, a rejection of political action. What is the point of merely ending manipulation while maintaining the basic economic institutions of capitalism?[12] This is what Illich seems to want, but in such a society education and equality are consistently sacrificed for the sake of the accumulation of capital. Un-alienated education can perhaps be a result only of the revolutionary transformations of the basic institutions *and* consciousness. Nevertheless in spite of these criticisms, Illich is still saying something important. He reminds us that everything must be doubted. He points to the fact, but without using a Marxist vocabulary, that pupils have become estranged from knowledge and that it confronts them as something hostile and alien. He makes us raise questions such as: Should education be compulsory? What then should we do about the curriculum? How often do we examine and criticize our institutionalized practices? We keep returning to the same question: What forms of social action can we undertake so that alienation can be overcome?

Pupils, Teachers and Knowledge

There has been much discussion on the meaning of alienation and estrangement. Some writers have held that they have different emphases. Alienation lays stress on what it is that Man has given up and its subsequent relations to the donor. Estrangement tends to stress what is left — the state of the individual upon, and after, giving. According to Marx, alienation arises out of the division of labour. The further division of labour develops the smaller is the task assigned to each individual. (This is one way in which the increasing pressure towards subject specialization by the teacher and pupil can be understood.) The division of labour arises in society as part of a complex which includes class divisions, exchange and private property. Alienation appears wherever the division of labour is the operative principle of economic organization. If we accept this supposition and view education as a mode of production, questions that emerge are: Can we usefully think of school as a factory, and if so, what are the products that are being made? Obviously the three related entities that we should consider are pupils, teachers and knowledge.

Let us consider pupils first: pupils can be seen both as workers and as commodities that are produced. Within the school the pupil has labour potential. He exchanges the product of his labour for objects; house points, grades or examination certificates are metaphors for wages.[13] On leaving school the pupil exchanges these products for different occupations that have already been graded, there being, generally speaking, a relationship between qualifications, status and salary. Pupils' activity in school, then, is a relation and expression of activity in society. Like other workers, pupils have needs for objects to fulfil their powers but they are not given the opportunity to acquire these objects. Cannot the claims for relevance in the curriculum, and student consultation in the content of their courses, be seen in this light? In this process pupils are transformed into products, commodities to be sold on the market. Pupils are categorized only in terms of certain characteristics that ideal pupils should possess: interest, discipline, ability, intelligence. In this process, what is the role of a teacher?

The teacher too is a worker whose products are, in a sense, his pupils, but in the situation in which he works what he does merely affirms their character as capitalist products. The teacher then is a producer, and everything outlined above about the pupil, and what follows shortly about knowledge, also applies to the teacher as worker. The social relations of pupil and teacher are thus internally related. There may be an inherent contradiction here, because a teacher is not only a producer but is also an employee of those who wish to *reproduce* society as it is. Some teachers of course see themselves as members of the bourgeoisie, but even teachers who see themselves as proletarian may become involved in actions which are against their long-term interests. It is perhaps because of these sorts of contradictions that the classroom situation is so often experienced as one of conflict.

It has already been noted that teachers and pupils are seen in terms of what they can produce, and so the productions that are valued are those that can be easily assessed. Many students become constrained by marks, grades, examinations, qualifications. The processes involved in grading and assessing influences teachers as well, affecting their relationships, how they teach, and, as we shall see, the curriculum itself.[14] Marx, commenting on such alienated labour, had expressed the view that Man was social, endowed with a capacity for seeing his life activity as an object of his will and consciousness, but that his life had become a 'means to life' and not life itself. It is possible that from the work of pupils and teachers schools gain status, for example O- and A-level passes add to a school's prestige and its ability to attract certain types of staff and students. Status, then, can be seen as a form of profit.

In alienated labour, Man's product 'exists outside him, independently as something alien to him and that it becomes a power on its own confronting him'. If we think of the product as 'knowledge', one can see the force of Maxine Greene's argument that the prevailing tradition of the 'liberal philosophers' presents forms of knowledge as 'objectively existent, external to the knower — there to be discovered, mastered, learnt'. The worker's product — in this case knowledge — is often alien to students in that they cannot use it; it is often too narrow, specialized, unrelated, abstract. The student has no control over what he makes, or what becomes of it. 'Knowledge' gains in power the more the pupil or student spends his own, and even acquires qualities, suitably altered, that the student loses. Students then lose confidence and look upon themselves as mere 'appendages' of their products; thus gradually 'knowledge' begins to control the producers.

Private property is the material expression of alienated labour. In short, from the point of view of a philosophy of internal relations, private property means what capitalism does. It has been suggested by Basil Bernstein that in the educational context 'capital' can be thought of as cultural capital, and that the prevailing view of knowledge in our society is as if it was 'private property'. He writes: 'Children and pupils are early socialized into this concept of knowledge as *private* property. They are encouraged to work as isolated individuals with their arms round their work.'[15]

Marx makes a distinction between 'exchange value' and 'use-value' which I later wish to use to speculate on aspects of knowledge. He regarded exchange value as the ratio at which a product exchanges for others; that is to say, its trading power or ability to relate to other products on the basis of embodied labour-time. Exchange value corresponds to the *quantitative* aspect of labour. In contrast, use-value is not simply that for which an article is used but is a specific relation between the worker and his activity, between the product and other men. A commodity is a use value because it has the power to satisfy some human need. Use values, then, corresponds to the *qualitative* aspect of labour. Now, just as in a capitalist society, articles such as guns or objects of little durability will be produced, objects typical of an alienated society – I wondered if I could make here an analogy with 'knowledge'. Could the alienated character of capitalism be read from the characteristics of the sort of knowledge produced? An interesting speculation would be: How and, in what ways, does the use value of knowledge express production relations?

If knowledge can be seen as the pupils' product, as has been suggested above, that knowledge is, in a sense, both the result and the cause of alienated labour. In many of our schools it is the product, knowledge, that determines what the pupil-worker does. The power of any of the worker's products over the worker, Marx wrote, always reflects the power of the people who dominate it and use it as an instrument. In this process knowledge is categorized into hierarchies and invidious distinctions such as between theoretical and practical work are made. In our positivist culture there is an emphasis on abstract objective knowledge but such a view emphasizes knowledge at the expense of man. Knowledge is so often lying outside, above, beyond both teacher and pupil. The more teachers and pupils 'spend' themselves working on knowledge (usually discrete subject areas separated from the real world), the more powerful and coercive this reified knowledge seems to become. The pupils knowledge is taken away from him, or to be more precise, he dissociates the knowledge from himself, because the pupils needs or individuality is not considered. This is not difficult to understand because the knowledge did not belong to him in the first place but was set up *for him by others*.

It is possible, therefore, for pupils and teachers to see each other as *opposed* to one another, of being in competition – teacher against pupil, teacher against teacher, pupil against pupil. This split is analogously a manifestation of class, which is an expression of *reified social relations*. The development of IQ and attainment tests (and other techniques to stratify pupils and create hierarchies) is an expression of the alienated social relationships, of class, exerting their influence.[16] Class, labour and value are expressions of Man's alienation in capitalism, and are interdependent as people, activity and products. Ollman suggests that the Relation, class, is also a component of the Relations labour and value, and they of it. Any account of schooling and alienation therefore that was to be more than a general description would have to analyse not only class, but labour and value, to an extent that is not possible here. Work, education, knowledge – everything is metamorphosed into money, the substance in which the relative worth of things is reckoned. Over a period of time money replaces all other commodities as the object of practical effort. In a society dominated by private property and money, all organizations and institutions become class organizations. Neutrality and communality in our schools and colleges can therefore be ruled out. The power of money to buy is a function of people's necessity to sell what they have. Consider for a moment the power of money of those that provide and sustain hierarchical forms of education; of those that define valid knowledge in the form of 'reports', textbooks, research, and how wealth and power influences schooling not only here but in the less developed countries of the Third World.

This point can be summed up quite simply: those who control what is needed have interests other than, and hostile to, the interests of the persons in need.

There are in education, for example, theories about ability, interest, motivation, intelligence and deprivation. Most of these theories do not demonstrate how they arise from the 'facts' that they are supposed to explain, but take for granted what they are supposed to explain. How do educational theories (and theories about education) that are in opposition to the interests of teachers and pupils become institutionalized? How do theories become converted into abstractions that are taken as natural and immutable laws? These are some of the questions to which, as yet, we do not know the answers. Theoretical work on problems such as how do ideologies work? have hardly begun. What is it (if anything) that institutionalized educational theories have in common? It has already been noted that out of many contending theories *some* become institutionalized; the theories, for example, of Hirst, Piaget and Bernstein. These theories stress that the forms of knowledge have a necessarily *logical* existence. The growth of logical reasoning is said to have a *genetic* basis. Restricted and elaborated speech codes are located within the individual *family*. An interesting project for research would be to draw out from these theories the implicit assumptions that theorists have about, say, science or rationality. The above theories, because they point to certain structural features that are difficult to locate and therefore remedy, may have conservative implications. Is it a coincidence that the theories and practices that are *aided* in this process of becoming institutionalized all seem to share certain features? There is also the question of how theories are used or distorted in the process of popularization. This has happened to Bernstein's theories, and he has written of how his work has been used in this way, and how the emphasis on the individual family has prevented the issue from being seen in a wider class, political, context. These theories conform in their characteristics to ideologies, and what is really important is that they are used to legitimate classroom practices and become the criteria for evaluation. Indeed we now have a rapidly increasing number of 'evaluation' experts rapidly creating 'a discipline', and becoming so influential that they 'assess' all curricular research and innovatory programmes.

In our society, it has been argued, knowledge is thought of as property; it is capital. But the possession of knowledge as property is not the realization of personality but its negation. The knowledge that is connected with economic rewards, high-status knowledge, is kept in such a way that it entails non-possession by others. At our desks we work privately, putting our arms round our work to hide what we read and write. Access to many subject areas is limited to a selected few; moreover, the dominant conception of knowledge inverts the relations between the human subject and the world of object, and is thus transformed from an object of the will into a master. To say this is to say that men have become a *predicate* of knowledge. The lives of many wo/men have been greatly influenced by the 'value' that is placed on the knowledge they possess – what could be called their 'knowledge position'. Since 'class' in our time is largely based on knowledge, the disappearance of class differences would depend partly upon the abolition of the distinctions between high- and low-status knowledge as one of the main determinants of 'success' in our society. High-status knowledge, you may recall, could be characterized as abstract, unrelated, written and conceived in terms of the individual; 'low-status' knowledge is usually that which is practical and oral. These distinctions and the notion of knowledge itself as property, capital, is one that we have consistently opposed. This view which sees knowledge as of a factual, real, external and independent character is often based on epistemology that sees certain forms of knowledge as having a necessary logical existence. Truly this is knowledge serving the needs of a system; detached from the knower, and therefore 'neutral' – which is one of the features of positivism. This prevailing conception of the 'liberal philosophers' of knowledge detached from the knower may be a case in point of the separation, the lack of relation between subject and object. The disenchantment that some students feel for the concept of 'education as initiation' into worth-while activities, widely interpreted as having elitist implications, may stem from the recognition that this particular philosophy is not related to historical actuality. I suggest that in the way the subject has been defined the link between reflection and reality has been severed – and so it always stops short of changing reality. It was Marx's view that the ultimate task was not merely to comprehend reality but to change it. This is the project on which the 'new' sociology of education is engaged: it has drawn attention to the ways knowledge is used to create and sustain hierarchies. The implications of what we are saying are that we should be working towards the abolition of capital and of all property relations. This would mean that knowledge as property too would be overcome and transformed.

I want to turn now to some objections that could be made to the above account of alienation and education. First, it could be argued that the connection I have made between commodity production and education is based on an argument by analogy, and that this is an inadequate form of analysis. Second, it could be said that I have given the impression that the education system produces pupils as 'units to be slotted in', and that such a view oversimplifies the education process. To get at the specificity of the factor of education under capitalism, we should look at the ways in

which production in the school is *not* identical to the forms
of commodity production and cannot be conflated with it. I
concede that the contents of this chapter, a form of humanistic
Marxism applied to what happens in the schools, is very
general. Nevertheless, I hope that what I have described
makes some of the contradictions apparent, and that these
may point to action. It could be said that a discussion of
schooling and alienation doesn't have the centrality, the
force or the relevance that Marx's discussion of private
property has, but I have attempted to argue that the relation
of teachers-knowledge-pupils — is an important one. According to Ollman, the family, ethics, art or literature could have
served just as well to tell the same story.

But I think a more important criticism is that many of
the weaknesses in my account of alienation and education
arise from the framework used; that is to say, from Ollman's
rendering of Marx. I will now make some critical comments
on Ollman's position.

Ollman's book is the work of a philosopher, and it reflects
its author's concern for *language*. Many Marxists do not
accept Marx's account of Man's relationship with Nature as
depicted in the *1844 Manuscripts*. Nor do they find the
concept of alienation useful. They would argue that both
conceptions derive from his early Hegelian period, when he
was very much concerned with individual consciousness and
creativity and had not realized the primacy of the mode of
production, the importance of economic categories.

It could be objected that because of these idealist tendencies,
Ollman's account brackets out notions of revolutionary
change. There is no 'motor', as the proletariat is missing.
From within Ollman's view of Marxism, it is difficult to
formulate questions concerning the proletariat. Are teachers,
for example, members of the petty bourgeoisie or are they
segments of the proletariat, the agent of change? Should the
struggle within schools, for example, be seen in the context
of the struggle outside, the oppressed inside joining the
oppressed outside? Views on such matters are closely related
to the version of Marxism that one holds.

In Ollman's work, then, there is an absence of any conception of history and the proletariat. As in other idealist
versions of Marxism, the importance of the materialist

conception of history, and of economic factors and categories, is insufficiently realized. What are Ollman's own views about this?

Ollman admits that working with internal relations (the organizing principle of Marx's epistemology) leads to some distortion, but he argues that this is inevitable as it depends upon what one begins with and focuses upon. His main self-criticism is this:[17]

> Alienation treats labour, value, capital, class, state, etc., as forms of each other and as expressions of a common totality with the main negative result that social transformation (the core subject of Marxist history) is seriously underdeveloped. The primacy of the mode of production and the objective facet of social and economic contradictions in particular suffer from this focus on alienation — that is the materialist conception of history.

It is because of this damaging admission that I will examine in the following chapters some current developments, forms of materialist Marxism, that stress the importance of historical and economic factors. Let us turn now to a consideration of the work of some American theorists who, in reinterpreting the history and political economy of education and relating it to the development of capitalism, are having a considerable impact on the sociology of education.

Chapter 10

Current Developments:
The Primacy of the Mode of Production

There are several significant new developments that are influencing current conceptions of the nature and role of the sociology of education which should be considered. At the end of the last chapter I mentioned some of the limitations of idealist (or Hegelian) Marxism. I now, therefore, move on to a discussion of factors, underdeveloped by Ollman, such as ideology, history and political economy. These are the concepts in terms of which problems are now being increasingly posed. Questions such as: What is the relationship between education and ideology? How does the capitalist system use education to reproduce itself? In what ways does the State intervene in the educational process? How is the power of the State used to foster the development of capitalism and be its guarantor?

In order to outline some of these current developments I have divided this chapter into three distinct sections. I propose in the first to offer a contrast to the 'humanistic' Marxism discussed so far. To do this I give a brief introduction to the French theorist Louis Althusser, and focus on his contribution to our understanding of education and ideology.

In the second section I consider the importance of some selected American historians and political economists of education. The theme of the first section – that the assumptions of the educational system are ideological – is continued, but in a more concrete form. Althusser and the American theorists have this in common: they believe that the economy is determinant, and are concerned with the mechanisms by which society reproduces itself. They believe that, in order to exist, every social formation must reproduce the productive forces and the existing relations of production. I introduce the reproduction theses of Samuel Bowles and Herbert Gintis only briefly in the second section, as I provide an extended discussion of their views in chapter 11. My argument in this chapter is simple: to understand fully educational issues one must first know the forms in which they relate to *the mode of production*. The third section, therefore, is a discussion of contemporary monopoly capitalism. This provides a materialist base for a subsequent critical analysis of education and political economy, of schooling in capitalist society.

The Contribution of Louis Althusser: Education and Ideology

Education is involved in ideological work. By this, I am not saying that education is controlled by members of a ruling class, or that it merely represents 'the ruling ideas of the ruling class'. Of course the view that education is controlled by a single conspiratorial group is too simple and reductionist. In ways that are as yet unclear, mass schooling does manage to form a consensus. Consider how in the schools the curriculum, indeed 'school life', is treated so as to present 'both sides'. All ethical and political matters are presented as if to give 'a balanced picture', the liberal view. As other premises are not accepted, it is difficult to change the 'givens'. That is to say, the terms of the debate are limited — by the limiting structures themselves. We know that advanced industrial societies are very dependent on ideology, as it is partly through ideology that society *reproduces* itself. But can we develop a theory which enables us to understand education within an overall view of capitalism, as a historical phenomenon, both as a mode of production and as a system of social relations? A theorist who has made a preliminary attempt to outline a method to do this, to link education with politics and the state, is Louis Althusser.

Althusser rejects the humanist interpretation of Marx. He sees the early works of Marx, which emphasize alienation and the 'human essence', as being ideological and unscientific.[1] These works are expressions of Hegelian idealism, and idealism is often the basis of a form of humanism, a bourgeois ideology.

In Althusser's view, Marx himself rejected the 'anthropological problematic' of his early work and went on to construct new scientific concepts such as the forces and relations of production. He draws therefore on Marx's later, post-1848, work where his unit of analysis is not the individual but the social formation. It is argued that in any social totality there are four distinct levels, or, to use Althusser's term, practices: the economic, the political, the ideological and the theoretical. Although the economy is determinant *in the last instance*, the dominant role may be taken by the others at different times. There is therefore not a simple dialectic of economic base and superstructure, but a complex unity of separate and specific levels of practice which may be relatively autonomous. There is a necessary unity between all the contradictory levels composing the social totality, and yet each level possesses relative autonomy. This means that the unity of the totality is a unity of complex of 'instances' at uneven stages of development relative to each other. Therefore there is not just one contradiction, between capital and labour; in the structural totality there is the possibility of a multiplicity of contradictions which may be related to each other in complex ways. An advantage of this conception of the whole, as a complex unity necessarily related by relatively autonomous instances, is that it rules out any form of reductionism.

Althusser writes of his views on the relationship between the social totality and education in his essay 'Ideology and Ideological State Apparatus'.[2] He conceives of the social whole as consisting of base and superstructure. The economic base is a unity of the *forces* of production and the *relations* of production. The superstructure has two levels or 'instances', the law and the State. The repressive apparatus of the State includes, for example, the police, courts, prisons, the Head of State, the government and administration. There is a distinction between State power and State apparatus; the objective of the class struggle, of the proletariat, is to seize State power and replace it with a proletarian apparatus. Ultimately its aim is to *destroy* State power and every apparatus.

However, there is a second level or instance of the superstructure where there are many ideological State apparatuses, the religious, legal, ethical, political — and the educational.

The relationship between the superstructure and the base is of reciprocal action, the superstructure having relative autonomy from the base. This type of conceptualization enables many subtle combinations to be woven from the interplay of the above. Moreover one implication of this is that we have to shift from our conventional way of thinking of a cause as a thing, a distinct identifiable entity to treating it as *a relation*.

Following Gramsci, Althusser says that no class can hold State power without exercising hegemony over and in the ideological state apparatuses (ISA). There are, then, structures whose specific role is to mystify the workings of social formations through ideologies (an ideology being an imaginary representation of reality, the mystified form in which men experience the relation to the world). The existence of ideologies, however, is material; they always express class positions. This is because an ideology always exists in an apparatus and its practices. Education is one such apparatus. He suggests that, in order to exist, every social formation must reproduce the productive forces and the existing relations of production. And so ideologies are used – all of them contributing to the same result: *the reproduction of the relations of production.* He contends that education reproduces capitalist relations of exploitation. In medieval times the dominant ISA was the Church, but now the Church has been replaced by the school. The school is the institution where children are provided with the ideology which suits the role they have to fulfil in class society. In other words, individuals are moulded into subjects that fit the needs of capitalism. Second, in the school, children are taught 'know-how', but in forms which ensure subjection to the ruling ideology.

It can be said in criticism of Althusser that his system implies a very passive, deterministic, view of man. In his view, history moulds individuals.[3] The message of his Marxism is: theorize. Now, I believe that theory, ideas are important. They are important because they can be translated into collective social and political forces. But the dilemma is that though theoretical work needs to be done – urgently, the theoretical enterprise too often becomes a detached form of activity. This could be said of Althusser's philosophical, theoretical, practice; at times it seems to bear little relation

151

to the class struggle. In short, his version of Marxism neglects the problem of the unity of theory and practice. But, in spite of these criticisms, Althusser is an important and influential theorist. For us he has reformulated the problem that must be solved: precisely, how does the structure of the whole operate upon the parts? This is the urgent task *we* must complete.

The Contribution of American Historians and Political Economists of Education

I believe that it is also important that we consider the work of certain American historians of education. Why? They are important because they are researching the origins of American education and showing that its assumptions are ideological and rooted in class-interest. Writers such as Clarence Karier, Paul Violas and Joel Spring are interested in the role that the 'liberal' has played in the development and maintenance of the corporate state. Karier, the historian on which I shall focus my remarks, throws valuable insights on the ideologists that have dominated American intellectual life for half a century — liberals such as Jane Adams, Charles Cooley, James Conant and John Dewey. He asks: What were the assumptions that guided their perceptions? These, after all, helped to bring about the reality they created. Some of the main assumptions of the above liberals included the belief that progress was possible through social melioration, and that institutions might be *adjusted* as to usher in the American Dream.

Second, they saw the solution to the problem of the poor, the black, the disinherited, not in questioning the system but rather in allowing more of the disinherited to enter the growing middle class.

Third, they believed in a meritocracy in which the professional expert would play in increasing role.

And fourth, with respect of education, the liberal supported the creation of a mass system of schooling dedicated to filling society's need for citizens capable of adjusting to an industrial system. Of course, these assumptions overlap. In Karier's work the central concern seems to me to be to reveal the conservative implications of liberalism (such as that of John

Dewey), the *functions* of mass schooling and its connections with the corporate liberal state. These are the topics of the section that follows.

Karier has taken, as a case study of liberal ideology, the life and work of John Dewey. Philosphically Dewey believed in pragmatism; a philosophy, Karier writes, for those inclined to calculate consequences so as to survive. In ethics, this view emphasized efficiency as a principle. (The basis of Dewey's criticism of the old psychology was that it was inefficient.) This stress on efficiency led to a form of expediency which can only be described as moral dexterity. C. Wright Mills characterized this type of pragmatism as technologism, and indeed many students trained in this way of thinking fitted easily into a form of instrumentalism, a world in which values become ends, and ends become subordinated to means. American pragmatic philosophy was functionally useful in developing a capitalist system, but it failed to deal with the moral issues of the day, issues of the struggles of men in history.[4]

Dewey's view of history was that it was the struggle with Nature, not of men against men, classes against classes. The violent history of the Indians, the blacks, the immigrants and of the labour movement, was missing. There was no conflict, no violence; a classless history. What Dewey generated in his school at Chicago was a middle-class history that eschewed conflict and violence and supported the organizational thinking of the new middle class. When, however, Dewey did recognize the existence of social conflict, his solutions were the intelligent use of education for social control and the employment of experts.

In accordance with the new liberal ideology that he helped to construct, Dewey turned not to the masses for social guidance, but to the expert. Karier writes that 'this ultimately led to the rise of bureaucratic meritocracy, whose members talked about democracy and education without seriously threatening the power elite that controlled the system.'[5] Believing in the scientific method, in objectivity, he stressed the importance of the new professional expert whose function was to inform the lower classes. Through extensive research Karier convincingly shows that Dewey was the philosopher, the ideological spokesman of the middle class, and that a

153

liberal educational reformer, like the liberal political reformer, is, in effect, a conservative. He was also a good pragmatist, and, like other liberals, was committed to flexible, experimentally managed, orderly social change that included a high degree of manipulation and expediency. He thus never seriously challenged the power sources within society. Indeed, his belief in pragmatism, the new professional expert, American nationalism, combined into a vision of industrial society that was fundamentally inegalitarian.

Let us move on now to another area with which the American historians of education are greatly concerned: the provision of mass schooling. Karier contends that throughout the history of American education, schools have been used as instruments to teach the norms necessary to adjust to the changing patterns of the economic system. Primarily, schools transmit the values necessary for the maintenance of a business ethic. In his view, mass education functioned along three distinct but overlapping lines: One, the training function, which in co-operation with business and industry assisted youth to fulfil occupational requirements in an increasingly complex system. Two, the holding function; the school not only kept children off the labour market, but it also maintained a viable manpower pool for capital. Three, the testing and sorting function.

The school as an instrument of social control can be clearly seen in the way it differentiates pupils so that their training prepares them for a particular social slot. Among the means used are the differentiated curriculum, and testing. Karier writes[6] that

> it was men like Thorndike, Terman and Goddard, supported by corporate wealth, who successfully persuaded teachers, administrators and lay school boards to classify and standardize the school's curriculum with a differentiated track system based on ability and values of the corporate liberal society. The structure of that society was based, then, on the assumed meritocracy, a meritocracy of White middle-class management-oriented professionals.

The tests that L.B. Terman devised were based on an occupational hierarchy that was, in fact, the social class system of the corporate liberal state then emerging. It is no different today; selective differentiation in the school is to prepare pupils for selected social roles in society. Intelligence and achievement tests used throughout American society are a vital part of the infrastructure that serves to stabilize and order the values of the corporate liberal society. Repeatedly, psychologists and others have attempted to link ability to the meritocracy but have not questioned the values inherent in the meritocratic principle itself. Few are willing critically to doubt the validity of the system. Corporations have played a major role in maintaining this system, and they have also shaped educational policy. Foundations such as Carnegie, Ford and Rockefeller have defended their vested interests by influencing educational debates at critical points when the system has been in acute danger. Karier argues that there was an alliance between government and corporate wealth, and that it became welded together, after the Second World War, in the form of the military industrial state: 'This was a world of burgeoning Government bureaucracies effectively allied with corporate wealth which fashioned a mass system of schooling to maintain corporate security at home and abroad.'[7]

Liberals have been deeply involved in this process of the school becoming a custodial institution designed to maintain social order. Karier writes: 'They could not escape the fact that many of their own personal values were embedded in that corporate liberal state that they helped make intelligible if not justifiable'.

It is sad, but perhaps typical, that no such school of historians of education is doing similar work in Britain at the present time, because in numerous ways we have much to learn from these researchers' critiques of dominant capitalist ideologies. As Karier has pointed out: 'Liberal history does not connect with and add meaning to our present world. If one starts with the assumption that this society is in fact racist, fundamentally materialistic, and institutionally structured to protect vested interests, the past takes on vastly different meanings.'[8]

The Adaptation of Education to the Needs of Work

Besides the American historians of education, another major

influence on contemporary sociology of education is that of 'political economy'. A work which exemplifies this trend is Bowles and Gintis's *Schooling in Capitalist America*.[9] Gintis has suggested that though C. Wright Mills, Sweezy and others were writing on this and similar topics in the 1930s, a political economy of education has been slow to emerge. Since that time Marxism has developed, broadly, in two forms:

1   Humanistic Marxism, as developed by Lukács, Gramsci and Karl Korsch, which largely focuses on the super structure. This version of Marxism, drawing on the earlier Hegelian works of Marx, stresses the freeing of individuals, and the abolition of need, but it has the weakness that it is philosophically idealist, and neglects economic factors.

2   'Structural' Marxism, as expressed in the work of Althusser and Nicos Poulantzas, rejects the above 'humanist' view as ideological and stresses the 'scientific' character of Marxism.

In Gintis's view both versions are misdirections; socialism has to be defined materially. Historically, under feudalism, there was both material and personal dependence. With the bourgeois revolution against the aristocracy personal independence (of a nominal sort) came about, but material dependence continued. As Marx noted, there cannot be change in distribution without change in the mode of production, and as exploitation occurs at the point of production, what is of crucial importance is control of work relations. It is under socialism that we will reach the final state of personal *and* material independence, when there will be a true democracy in which workers control the entire work process.

Political economy is seen as an alternative general Marxist theory which avoids the weaknesses of the prevailing versions mentioned above and can form a base on which a Marxist sociology of education can be built. In Gintis's view, the State functions not by ideological forces, as these are insufficient, but by *reproduction*. Education produces the labour force; it produces workers for capitalism. He argues that it is neither force, nor ideology, but a third element that is of crucial importance – *the production process*. The production process not only produces but reproduces the whole set of social constellations. The education system, then, *is part of the State*. But there are problems here about adequately conceptualizing the nature and the mechanisms of the State. The 'base' and 'superstructure' distinction is obviously too simplistic, but so also is the view that the State is merely 'the executive instrument of the ruling class'. There is also the view of the State as a structural entity having a dynamic of its own. Now this theory, Gintis argues, is historically false because it denies human praxis. There is no recognition that there is an uneven class struggle in which workers do have *some* influence. We are, then, in a situation where some serious research needs to be done into problems such as these:

To what extent is education not a service for people, but a tool for the State machine?

Is the State machine a reification, or is it an apparatus of certain people?

And is the State monolithic, or contradictory in the sense that it contains progressive elements within it?

In most States, education has moved from the private to the public sector, from the family to State schooling, but as to questions such as why and how does the State intervene we know little. Adequate theories of the State do not as yet exist.

I suggest that to begin to comprehend the issues involved in the political economy of education, it is important first to know the forms in which contemporary monopoly capitalism has developed.

On the one hand we are told that because of science and technology more education and skill are required, and yet, on the other, more bureaucratization and alienation appear. Why is this? After all, the main discontents under capitalism are centred not on its inability to provide work, but on the nature of the work it does provide, on the appalling effects of the processes involved. Even prosperity and unemployment cannot remove these discontents because it is *capitalist social relations* that produce the manner in which labour processes are organized. It is important to study these processes, to enquire: How has the nature of work been transformed in the twentieth century? What are the roles of scientific management and technology? We know, for example, that a change in social forms as in the Soviet Union does not necessarily lead to an automatic transformation of the mode of production. In the section that follows I will give a rendering of Harry Braverman's *Labour and Monopoly Capitalism.*[10] My exposition of this work is intended to provide the context so necessary for any discussion of education and political economy, of schooling in capitalism. He begins his analysis of 'the capitalist mode of production' by a consideration of 'labour'.

The Capitalist Mode of Production

Human beings act upon Nature and change its forms to suit their needs. But while the work of other animals is instinctual, human work is conscious, purposeful; it involves conceptualization, and we have symbols, language, to do this. By acting on Nature, then, we change our own nature. This human capacity to perform work is 'labour power'. Under capitalism, workers are separated from the means of production and therefore must sell their labour power, for a period of time, to others. They have no other way of gaining a livelihood. On the other hand, the capitalist wishes only to enlarge a 'unit of capital'. The labour process is thus shaped by the accumulation of capital. As human labour is infinitely malleable, and vastly productive, 'the surplus product' is continuously enlarged. The capitalist increasingly comes to dominate the labour process, and takes up every means of increasing the output of the labour power he has purchased. It becomes essential for the capitalist to take control over the labour process, to remove it from the hands of the worker into his own.

A feature of the new social relations developed by capitalism was the division of labour. All known societies have divided their work, but capitalism developed a new form: it systematically sub-divided the work of each productive speciality into limited operations. What is new is the sub-division of labour *within* an occupation. What happens is this: first, each part of the work process is analysed into its constituent elements. But not only are the operations separated from each other, they are assigned to different detail-workers who are unable to carry through any complete production process. Labour power is cheapened by breaking it up into its simplest elements; crafts are divided into individual parts, occupations destroyed. Labour power becomes a commodity organized according to the needs of employers who are seeking only to expand the value of their capital.

One of the ways capitalists attempt to increase the unit of capital is by developing management methods, 'Taylorism'. This method of work study analyses it on behalf of those who manage it, rather than those who perform it. Management has no other purpose that to extract from labour power the maximum advantage for the capitalist. Scientific management prescribes the actual mode of performance of every activity, the control and dictation of each step of the process. As an example, Braverman relates (from F.W. Taylor's Principles of Scientific Management[11]) the methods by which the originator of time and motion study persuaded a Dutchman named Schmidt to increase the loading of pig iron from $12\frac{1}{2}$ to 47 tons a day.

All the decisions that are made in the course of work are made by management, their purpose being the control of labour. But how is this done? First, the labour process is dissociated from the skill and knowledge of the worker, from his craft and tradition. Second, there is separation of conception from execution. Mental labour is separated from manual labour, but mental labour itself is then further subdivided into those who conceptualize, plan for others, and those who execute the work. In this process, workers lose control over not only their instruments of production but also their labour, and the way it should be performed. Though the worker's output enlarges, the worker himself is cheapened as the training required decreases. Workers perform the simplified job-tasks but without comprehension of the underlying reasoning. The monopoly of knowledge by management is used to control the steps of the labour process and its mode of execution; conceptualization is separated from execution.

Because of this separation, the labour process is now divided between separate sites and bodies of workers. The production units operate like a hand, watched, corrected and controlled by a distant brain. But hand and brain have not just become separated – they are hostile towards each other as conception becomes even more limited to a few. New workers are being continuously brought into a process unknown to them, and they take the organization of work, and the low-skill requirement, as given.

The capitalist mode of production is continually extending, and in each generation workers are continually being habituated. There is a necessity for adjusting workers into work in its capitalist form. An industrial psychology which addresses itself to problems of management (but sees itself as value free – and neutral) has therefore developed and focuses largely on the selection and performance of workers. With the advent of the assembly-line, mangement greatly increased control because it could control the pace of labour. And increasing mechanization leads to unemployed workers going to new industries at lower rates of pay. Other forms of work disappear. Just as the Ford assembly-line system was adopted by other car firms in the industry, similarly the capitalist mode of production destroys all other forms of organization of labour. Other modes of living become impossible.

The incorporation of science, how science became capitalist property, should also be considered. The origins of science are in craft technique; that is to say, science depended on the growth of technology. Stephenson, Watt and Crompton were craftsmen; the steam engine, for example, was perfected by 'working-mechanics'. Gradually the incorporation of science into the capitalist firm began; it became an adjunct of capital, a commodity to be bought and sold. Science itself has become transformed into capital; but how has this occurred? It has already been mentioned that in the first stage of capitalism there is a division of labour where the constituent tasks are performed in series by a chain of detail-workers. Then new methods and new machinery are incorporated, so that the labour process of the worker is reconstituted as a process organized by the management. The 'success' of time and motion study leads to a displacement of labour to other industries. The animating principle of all such work is, of course, the view of human beings in machine terms. But what precisely is the effect of the machine on the labour process?

At first the guidance of tools was always in the hands of the worker. The next step was the removal of the tool from the hands of the worker and fitting it into a mechanism, a machine with a fixed-motion path. Then machines were developed that had a pre-set pattern, a sequence of move-ments that are predetermined. Machines that regulated themselves and made continual adjustments followed. In the next stage, machines with a general purpose are replaced by machines for a particular product, or operation. Now machines can be controlled by tape, and a system of interlocked machines, or a single machine, can embrace an entire pro-duction process. Machines represent technical possibilities but at present serve only the needs of those who own them. They are used as an instrument of control over the labour process. This is because machines can be paced and con-trolled according to decisions made by management. Pro-duction is thus controlled not by the producers but by the owners and representatives of capital. As machines can now be numerically controlled, a worker is relieved of all decisions and judgments; he needs to know less. Automation has hastened this process, which means that (for most people) there is no need for knowledge or training. One consequence of this is that workers are now far less capable of operating their own industries than they used to be. They have lost control of their own labour. Control lies not with the worker, but with the machine that is controlled by the management. As the aim of every firm is the expansion of capital, there is an urge for more productivity, but each advance diminishes the number of truly productive workers. It is a mistake, however, to reify or fetishize the machine; it is a matter of social relations. It is capital that utilizes machinery to separate control from execution.

Let me summarize the main points that have been made so far:

1   There is a separation of conceptualization from and an increasing division of labour within management itself.

2   The application of modern methods of management and machine technology have increased the productivity of labour, but this has also led to a reduction in the demand for labour.

3   The prime aspects of monopoly-capitalism are the growth of scientific management and the systematic use of science. The rapid accumulation of capital has led to an important shift: a small proportion of technical jobs, closely

linked to management, and a larger proportion of lower-grade routinized technical, or unskilled, clerical jobs. What are the social forces at work? First, as the 'firm' is a limiting personal form, the individual owner gives way to the corporation. There is a concentration and centralization of capital, and the functions of management increase rapidly, as do marketing and sales divisions. The corporations induce demand for their products by fabricating customers, whose 'needs' are geared to production. Products themselves are planned to be obsolete so that they have to be replaced. It could be said that corporations are now so huge that their 'internal' planning is in reality social planning; they make the prime decisions, governments merely filling in the interstices.

The centre of social life, of production and consumption, was once the family, but in the last hundred years capital has inserted itself between farm and household. Now everything has become processed and there is a drive for new services and commodities. In this process human relations are replaced by market relations. Capitalism transforms all of society into a gigantic market. Everything must be bought – but only in the market. Gradually, as alternatives are destroyed, we become trapped by a web of commodities. Institutionalization increases, as does 'service' employment; prisons, schools, hospitals, asylums, 'social work' expand. Even innovations become incorporated. There is an atrophy of competence, and labour is alienated.

The role of the State in these processes is an important one, as its power has been used to foster the development of capitalism and be its guarantor. Governments intervene when poverty and insecurity become permanent features, but the discussion becomes limited to disagreements about the scale and scope of welfare. These disputes about reform then become a substitute for revolutionary action.

In the attempt to enlarge capital, management functions of control and appropriation of surplus value have in themselves become labour processes. For example, office work, a labour process in its own right, has become systematized because scientific management methods are now applied. The same principles as those applied to the factory now control the labour process in the office. There is a similar emphasis on standardization and higher production. There is also the division of labour and mechanization, which leads to detail-work. The only difference is that clerical work is *less* well paid that 'blue'-collar work. In the office, management has a monopoly over planning and conceptualization, but mental labour involves manual operations such as writing. It is therefore possible to separate the functions of conceptions and execution, the latter taking place elsewhere – by others. By the use of computers knowledge can be controlled by a few experts. And so, for the office worker, thought is eliminated and work reduced to abstract labour. The application of scientific management and technology has meant that office work has become machine based, routinized, speeded up. The characteristics of clerical and production labour are merging; this is 'the proletarianization of the white-collar worker'. With the decline in the number of male clerical workers and the increase of women workers at lower wage-rates, clerical labour, a product of monopoly capitalism, now represents a large proletariat *in a new form.*

But these different forms of labour are not now important for the capitalist; what counts for him is not the production of goods and services but labour, which produces a profit for capital. Labour and capital are opposite poles of capitalist society. Capital is labour, and yet, at the same time, labour is capital. What has been happening, briefly, is this: the working class has only its labour to sell in return for its subsistence. The mechanization of industry produces a relative surplus of population. Capital moves into new fields; labour then follows into these less mechanized areas of capital accumulation. Because of the 'relative surplus population', wage-rates are low. Machinery is introduced in order to decrease the number of workers in that industry; in the process, skills are simplified and then destroyed, and the 'labour reservoir' then again increases. The resultant shortage of skilled labour in turn makes new processes inevitable. Capital produces this reserve army of labour because unemployment is a necessary part of it. Though sometimes doubted, Marx's law, the absolute general law of capitalist accumulation, is correct: there *is* an increase in the accumulation of capital *and* misery.

In other words, a polarization of income among job-holders has occurred. At one end of the pole there is accumulation of wealth; at the other there is an increase in the mass of lower-paid occupations, many jobs paying less than a living wage; there is unemployment, misery.

Almost all the population are now employees of capital. Management staff who have authority and technical expertise are chosen by capital, the managers sharing in the surplus produced by the corporation. Recently it has been observed that 'the professions' also have tended to become part of the reserve army of the unemployed. Skill, too, has become polarized; a few have scientific knowledge, but for the many there is a fall in skill. Indeed, many specialized technical occupations dispossess workers from scientific knowledge and skill. In short, 'adaptability' has become a synonym for unskilled labour. It should be noted that, similarly, in education, the content has deteriorated for many children (while the time spent in schools by pupils has increased).[12] The problem is that though there can be mastery over labour processes through scientific, technical, and engineering knowledge, this knowledge is largely in the hands of management. It is suggested that a solution to these problems may lie in a truly collective mode of production, where workers are not dependent on experts; where the process of production is controlled by the workers in the fullest and most direct way.

Chapter 11

The Political Economy of Education:
Schooling in Capitalist Society

The last chapter concluded with my attempt to isolate some of the outstanding features of Braverman's views which are most relevant for my present purpose – the understanding of the relationship between education, economics and politics. It is appropriate to have considered Braverman's brilliant analysis of capitalist social relations before turning our attention to the political economy of education, because the latter work, in many respects, *presupposes* a knowledge of his main themes: the forms in which contemporary capitalism has developed; the important historical tendencies such as the expansion of capital, and changes in the division of labour. Let us now see how these changes are related to the educational system, and analyse the ways in which these forces, external to the school system, have impinged upon its operations.

It has been argued by some political economists, such as Samuel Bowles and Herbert Gintis, that schooling was once thought to have an enlightening and equalizing mission, but it is now increasingly seen to have inegalitarian and repressive features. There is a growing awareness among radicals that the educational system mirrors the growing contradictions of our society. All attempts at reform have failed. As for the schools, their role is now seen to be that of reproducing the class system and extending the capitalist mode of production. This view finds its clearest and most consistent expression in Bowles and Gintis's *Schooling in Capitalist America.* It is, in many ways, a bold and courageous book. Rather than attempt a broad analysis of education, economy and politics, I will limit discussion to issues directly

165

raised by their polemical work, which has made a considerable impact on the sociology of education in Britain.[1] I turn now to a detailed consideration of their argument.

The Political Economy of Bowles and Gintis

Bowles and Gintis state that according to liberal reformers such as John Dewey and the 'democratic school' view, the educational system must fulfil at least the following functions: schools must help to integrate youth into the various occupational, political and other adult roles. Second, they should help to promote social equality by equalizing economic extremes. And, third, schools should be concerned with the full development of the moral, cognitive and the aesthetic, for the fulfilment of the individual. These can be called the integrative, the egalitarian and the developmental functions of education. But the main problem is this: In the reality of our society, can the schools really promote either human development or social equality?

It is suggested by Bowles and Gintis that the politics of education is best understood in terms of the need for social control in an unequal and rapidly changing economic order: 'schooling has been at once something done for the poor and to the poor'. The educational system basically is a method of disciplining children in the interest of producing a sub-ordinate adult population. Of course the *forms* of school discipline, the position of the teacher and conceptions of childhood have all changed, but the above objective has remained. In the past there was a stress on obedience to external authority and material sanctions, but this has now been replaced by the internalization of behavioural norms which act as a built-in supervisor. The key term is 'behaviour modification'. The traits and attitudes that the schools reward are docility, passivity and obedience. But is not only the student that has become a mere 'object'; the teacher, too, has been reduced to the status of the simple worker with little control over the curriculum and his activities. In their view, progressive education has never been given a chance to be practised. But why have educational reforms failed?

The failure stems from the contradictory nature of the integrative, egalitarian and the developmental functions in a society governed by the institutions of corporate capitalism. Dewey had believed that these functions were compatible and mutually supportive, but such was his belief in American 'democracy' that he did not fully realize that the hierarchical division of labour in the capitalist enterprise is politically *autocratic*. He had also believed that work could be a natural extension of intrinsically motivated activity, but this is hardly possible in a society where there is a rigid pattern of dominance and subordinancy, and alienated work is the rule. Bowles and Gintis believe that there is a correspondence between the social relations of *production* and the social relations of *education*. Schooling is the essential mechanism of the *integrative* function which allocates individuals to economic positions. It produces a stratified labour force for the capitalist enterprise. The main role of education is the production of an adequate labour force in a hierarchically-controlled and class-stratified production system. Schools, therefore, remain hostile to the individual need for personal development, neither are they vehicles for the equalization of economic status or opportunity. Indeed it is through this correspondence that the educational system *reproduces* economic inequality, and distorts personal development. Education, then, is *an aspect of the reproduction of the capitalist division of labour*. But it should be remembered that the roots of repression and inequality lie not in the educational system – but in the structure and functioning of the capitalist economy.

Capitalist society is determined by the imperatives of profit and domination, but this formally *totalitarian economic* system is in contrast to the formally *democratic political* system. As most workers do not own the means of production, they have to sell their labour power. In the process of production, the worker produces not only material products but himself as well. The economy produces people as well as commodities. One of several institutions which serve to perpetuate the structure of privilege is the family. Like the educational system, the family plays a major part in preparing the young for economic and social roles. Families reproduce the forms of consciousness required for the integration of a new generation into the economic system. Similarly, the educational system plays a central role in preparing individuals for the world of alienated and stratified work relationships. The reproduction of the social relations of production depends on the reproduction of consciousness. How does schooling do this?

First, it produces many of the technical and cognitive skills for adequate job performance. The school produces and labels personal characteristics relevant to the staffing of positions in the hierarchy. It rewards certain capacities, while penalizing others. Schools produce personality traits and forms of consciousness which facilitate trouble-free integration into the existing hierarchic forms. Above all, workers must be dependable and diligent. There are also modes of self-presentation, such as manner of speech and dress, which take on a social-class character. The educational system, through the pattern of status distinctions it fosters, reinforces the stratified consciousness on which the fragmentation of subordinate classes is based. Schools at once supply labour to the dominant enterprises, and reinforce the racial, ethnic, sexual and class segmentation of the labour force. It is argued that major aspects of educational organization *replicate* the relationships of dominance, and subordinancy in the economic sphere. There is a correspondence between the social relations of schooling and of work. This accounts for the ability of the educational system to produce an amenable and fragmented labour force. It is argued that employers have sought to use the schools for the reproduction of profitable types of worker consciousness, through a correspondence between the social relationships of education and those of economic life. But in what ways does the educational system reproduce and legitimate a pre-existing pattern in the process of training and stratifying the work force?

Some streams (or tracks) emphasize rule-following and close supervision. In this way the structure of social relations in education familiarizes the child with the discipline of the workplace, while developing certain modes of self-presentation. Working-class parents often seem to favour the stricter educational methods which reflect their own work experiences, their submission to authority. Working-class schools thus often have a type of social relationship that fairly closely mirrors that of the factory. There is this parallel with industry: successful job performance at low hierarchical levels requires the worker's orientation towards rule-following and conformity to external authority. Successful performance at higher levels requires behaviour according to internalized norms. In brief, some schools seem to stress the future subordinate positions of their pupils and teach docility, while elite colleges, for example, stress the need for self-direction through the internalization of norms, and develop 'leadership'. This differential socialization patterns in schools and within schools attended by pupils of different social classes do not arise by accident. Personality traits conducive to performance at different hierarchical levels are fostered and rewarded by the school system. That is to say, different levels of education feed workers into different levels within the occupational structure; in this way the social relations of education replicate the hierarchical division of labour. As Bowles and Gintis remark: 'The educational system works to justify economic inequality and to produce a labor force whose capacities, credentials, and consciousness are dictated in substantial measure by the requirements of profitable employment in the capitalist economy.'[2]

Alienation and inequality have their roots not in human nature, not in technology, not in the educational system itself, but in the structure of the capitalist economy. Indeed by integrating new generations into the social order, the schools are constrained to justify and reproduce inequality rather than correct it. The primary economic function of schooling is to facilitate the stratification of the labour force. The educational system fosters and legitimates economic inequality by providing an open and ostensibly meritocratic mechanism for assigning individuals to unequal economic positions. It is not geared for an egalitarian but an integrative function – towards the reproduction of economic relations. Education reproduces inequality by justifying privilege and attributing poverty to personal failure. But education, we are continually reminded, is not the source of the problem: 'The corporate capitalist economy – with its bias towards hierarchy, waste and alienation in production, and its mandate for a school system attuned to the reproduction and legitimation of the associated division of labor – may then be seen as a

169

source of the problem.'[3]

The authors, throughout their work, stress the role of education in legitimizing the class structure, and in fostering forms of consciousness consistent with its reproduction. But they argue that they are able to show more than a correspondence between the social relations of production and the social relations of education. They assert:[4]

> We have shown that changes in the structure of education are associated historically with changes in the social organization of production. The fact that changes in the structure of production have preceded parallel changes in schooling establishes a strong prima facie case for the causal importance of economic structure as a major determinant of educational structure.

In their view, the basic underlying contradiction of the capitalist economy is that the accumulation of capital and the widening of capitalist control over production actually undermine the reproduction of the capitalist order. It inevitably creates a growing proletariat and also proletarianization, which, in a sense, increases the potential for working-class action. There is then a tension between growth and stability, a contradiction between the accumulation of capital and the reproduction of the capitalist relations of production. They argue that this is the force behind educational change: the contradictory nature of capitalist accumulation and the reproduction of the capitalist order. Most educational problems do not have roots in the school system but result from the workings of the capitalist economy, the contradictions of capitalism frequently surfacing as contradictions within the educational system. But liberal reformers have not understood this, and believe that social problems can be alleviated through the benign offices of the State. Educational reform movements have faltered because they have not called into question the basic structure of property and power in economic life. Indeed, many reforms have served to deflect discontent and depoliticize social distress, and have actually helped to stabilize the prevailing structures of privilege. There is always the danger of reformers being 'bought over', of co-optation. Ultimately the character of reform depends not only on the *content* of the reform itself, but on the

170

programmatic *context* in which the reform is advocated – and the process of which it is won, as well. What do Bowles and Gintis make of the various educational reforms that are being advocated, the 'alternatives' that we are being currently offered?

In their critiques of the free-schoolers and the de-schoolers, they stress that unequal schooling perpetuates a structure of economic inequality which originates, outside the school system, in the social relationships of the capitalist economy. Education is very much a part of the production and re-production of the class structure. That is to say, a more equal school system will not create a more equal society. What many reformers, such as the free-schoolers, do not do is to place schools in their social and economic context. They do not realize the class basis of educational repression, and do not have a viable strategy to combat it. Bowles and Gintis argue that egalitarian school reform must be explicitly political; that only 'an explicit politicization of the free-school movement, an espousal of a participatory and egalitarian workers' democracy, and a strategy for alliance with all oppressed groups may indeed provide a dynamic basis for the liberation of the schools.'[5]

Bowles and Gintis make a trenchant critique of Illich's ideas on de-schooling.[6] Their main point is that Illich's programme is seen as a 'diversion' from the complex political demands of revolutionary reconstruction. Schools are so important to the reproduction of capitalist society that they are unlikely to crumble under any but the most massive political onslaughts. In the view of Bowles and Gintis, schools neither can nor should be eliminated. It is the social relationships of education that should be altered, so that instead of perpetuating the capitalist system, schools are dedicated to promoting personal development and social equality. Under the present economic system schools have to reproduce the labour force and legitimate inequality, and therefore cannot uphold these other functions. In their words: 'Capitalism is an irrational system, standing in the way of further social progress. It must be replaced.'[7]

Some Criticisms of 'Schooling in Capitalist America'

When one comes to consider Bowles and Gintis's argument, presented in broad outline above, it is noticeable that, apart from the obvious quotations from Marx, there is little reference to Marxist theory. There is no awareness of the vital contributions to Marxist thought by theorists such as Luxemburg, Lukács, Marcuse and Althusser. That this is a paucity, and that it matters, can be illustrated in this way: Bowles and Gintis write.[8]

> The direct application of force by no means insures the maintenance of capitalist power relations, however, in part because its unlimited and undisguised use may be counter-productive . . . The long run success of any totalitarian system requires a widely accepted ideology justifying the social order and a structure of social relationships which both validates this ideology through everyday experience, and fragments the ruled into mutually indifferent or antagonistic subgroups.

Later, when expressing the idea that violence alone is not a stable basis for the exercise of power, they quote Rousseau: 'The strongest man is never strong enough to be always master, unless he transforms his power into right and obedience into duty.' It was Antonio Gramsci who stressed this idea, the notion that class domination is exercised as much as through popular 'consensus' in civil society as through physical coercion by the State apparatus, especially in advanced capitalist countries where education, the media, the law and mass culture take on new roles. Beliefs, values, cultural traditions function on a mass level to perpetuate the existing order – this is the meaning of 'ideological hegemony' – and it entails the task for socialists of creating a 'counter-hegemonic world-view'. In Bowles and Gintis there is no reference to Gramsci's most original concept.[9] But this is not an isolated case; throughout their work they touch upon ideas which could have been deepened and enriched by the use of twentieth-century European Marxist thought. But why is there this limitation? I will argue that it is because of a certain dislocation in their work which arises from the fact that though they have a Marxist commitment, they have a *structural-functionalist* view of society derived from Durkheim and Parsons. Several consequences flow from this. I will suggest that this is the rationale for their epistemology which is positivism, their methodology which is empiricism, and their ontology which is determinism. These characteristics dominate their work. This view also makes sense of their dominant themes: the correspondence between the social relations of school and the social relations of work, and the reproduction thesis, as these too follow from the dislocation in their work.

The positivism of their approach can be seen in their empirical methods; they use a barrage of studies to make their demonstrations statistically. But the method itself is accepted unproblematically. The statistical method is treated as a set of value-free, neutral procedures which they can use as a tool. They do not consider that statistics, like any other theory, contain implicit ordering principles. Theoretical judgments and interpretations are required for making sense of data. And it is not adequately realized that interpretations are made mainly by a reliance on 'common sense' and implicit values. Bowles and Gintis never question their statistical methodology. But I would want to argue that mathematics may be inappropriate for understanding the main characteristic of the social world-meaning. Of course, Bowles and Gintis deal with some serious issues, such as the following. 1. They take us though 'massive statistical data' to show us that 'U.S. education is highly unequal, the chances of attaining much or little schooling being substantially dependent on one's race and parents' economic level.'[10] 2. They have extensively analysed a massive body of data and found that pupils are rewarded for their conformity to the social order of the school, and that traits of creative and mental flexibility are directly penalized in terms of school grades. 3. They argue, for instance, that the widespread assumption among all parties to the debate that IQ is an important determinant of economic success does not rest on compelling empirical evidence. Quite the contrary, IQ is not an important criterion for economic success.[11]

In all this work the value of statistics is taken for granted; statistical evidence indicates that 'this is so'; these data support 'these conclusions'. The findings always seem clear, unequivocal, unproblematic, scientific.

That the statistical method can become reductionist is not recognized by the authors. Consider the following examples: 'Arthur Kornhauser, in his study of blue-collar workers, found that 40 percent of his sample of 407 auto workers had symptoms of mental instability.'[12] And, on the following page, 'only 43 percent of white-collar and 24 percent of blue-collar workers in a large representative sample say they are satisfied with their jobs.' They also utilise work which attempts to quantify aspects of personality and motiviation.[13] Here is an example with a direct relationship with their argument: Bowles and Gintis remark how dozens of radical professional organisations have sprung up across the disciplines. 'These groups give tangible political expression to a growing commitment among students, young teachers, and other professionals that their function is not to administer society, but to change it drastically.' Their method entails the giving of statistical evidence, and it is forthcoming: 'During the late 1960s, radical sentiment among students grew rapidly. In 1968, an opinion poll reported that 4 percent of U.S. students identified themselves as "radical or far left." Two years later, the same poll reported 11 percent as radical.[14] A note informs us that it is from the President's Commission on Campus Unrest, *Report* (Washington, 1970).

The above examples raise many problems concerning the use of statistical methodology. Do we really know what 'mental instability' is, and what its symptoms are? What is the meaning of 'radical or far left'? Surely employers and employees do not agree on what 'job satisfaction' is? There is a disagreement even on terms such as 'blue collar' and 'white collar'. And what is a 'representative sample'? What the sample understood as the meaning of the question; the relationship between what they *thought* and what they said; and between what they said and how they might *act* in a particular political context, are important questions. The work of Cicourel and others who have written critiques of statistical methodology is highly relevant here.[15] Bowles and Gintis even quantify personality traits associated with school and work success. The categories that are used can be seen in Appendix B of their book, where there is a partial correlation of the sixteen personality variables.[16] I do not doubt their thesis that 'the reward system of the school inhibits those manifestations of personal capacity which threaten hierarchical authority,'[17] but to demonstrate it by an analysis of personality characteristics such as 'tactful', 'loner', 'creative', 'frank', 'defers gratification', etc. in this way is highly problematic – an example of the sort of social behaviourism in which the prevailing definitions of the society are accepted.

For me, this raises the question of the attitude of the authors towards statistical work, similar to their own, but whose findings, one assumes, they are opposed to. Let me illustrate. Writing of the early twentieth century, they state that students were channelled into curriculum tracks on the basis of their ethnic, racial, and economic background. This process was soon disguised by another reform, 'objective' educational testing: 'In Albany, New York, it was reported that 85 percent of the city's prostitutes were feeble-minded; 69 percent of the white inmates and 90 percent of the black inmates in a Kansas prison were found to be morons; a study revealed that 98 percent of unmarried mothers were feeble-minded.' It was 'found that 83 percent of Jews, 80 percent of Hungarians, 79 percent of Italians, and 87 percent of Russians were feeble-minded, based on "culture-free" tests.'[18] We smile. It is noted that 'the sophisticated statistical methodologies of Pearson, Terman, and Thorndike lent it the air of exacting rigor previously accorded only to the Newtonian sciences.' (They are aware, too, of the importance of assumptions built into tests such as those of Binet.) But when Bowles and Gintis quote the above, an irony becomes apparent to us: the form in which this data is presented is no different from that which they themselves use throughout their own work. Issues about assumptions, meaning, adequacy, reflexivity are never discussed.

One of the tensions in the work of Bowles and Gintis is their use of different conceptual frameworks. If we accept the notion that concepts cannot be considered in isolation and exist only within a theoretical framework, its problematic, then it can be said that their work is eclectic. This tension arises because though they have a Marxist vision of society, the basic sociological perspective they use is that of structural-functionalism. According to such a view, institutions have specific functions. Bowles and Gintis refer to the integrative, the egalitarian and the developmental functions of education.[19] And, like the school, the family is involved in reproduction: 'This reproduction of consciousness is facilitated by a rough correspondence between the social relations of production and the social relations of family life'.[20] 'The nature of work provides a pattern of prerequisites which affect the nature of personal development in families and schools.'[21] They stress that the work process produces people as well as commodities. But the notion that people can never be produced exactly to capitalist specifications is rarely mentioned: 'The product – including the experienced needs of people – depends both upon the raw material with which the production process begins, and the "treatment" it receives. Neither is by any means under the full control of the capitalist class.'[22] In terms of people, the reason given, 'the raw material with which the production process begins and the treatment it receives', implies some notion of a genetic 'given' and external stimuli. What is typically ignored are the possibilities of meaning construction by actors, their definitions of the situation. That human beings are active agents is only occasionally admitted by Bowles and Gintis; it is under-emphasized because it would run counter to their ontological stance, their *deterministic, passive model of Man*. In other words, they have what Dennis Wrong once described as an 'oversocialized' model of Man. In this model, 'Society' makes people what they are, as they have no free will of their own. They are impelled by the ideas they have absorbed from their social environment the family, the school, the factory. Bowles and Gintis write that, 'just as individuals must come to accept the overall social relations of production, so workers must respect the authority and competence of their own "supervisors" to direct their activities.'[23] Actor-members are always regarded as passive; youth is *accustomed* to the social relationships of dominance and subordinancy in the economic system. This over-symmetrical view does not sufficiently recognize that people have perceptions of stratification and status groups, that these perceptions vary and do not always conform to the model of the 'scientific' observer.

If one accepts such an over-deterministic picture, as Bowles and Gintis do, then there is a problem when one has to explain how radical transformation of society is going to come about. If people are determined to this extent, how can they be creative transforming agents? It is because of this problem that the authors have to draw upon the concept of contradiction. The message of the body of the text is that the working class is made passive. Only in the concluding section is the active, conscious participation and role of the working class mentioned. By the concept of contradiction a revolutionary movement is allowed for. In other words, this concept allows Bowles and Gintis to emphasize docility, the passive, determined reproduction of consciousness, and yet at the same time, in the polar movement of the contradiction, allow a potential for revolutionary movement. What is consistently neglected in their work (apart from the concluding section) is this process in which the working class, through its struggles, *makes itself*. The struggle of the working class against capital is not a theme of this scenario. This is one of the legacies of their structural functionalism. In what ways, then, are they indebted to the Durkheimian – Parsonian tradition?

As their purpose is to show how schools reproduce social relations, they emphasize a form of determinism in which society dominates the individual. Their view is Durkheimian in that this 'society' is exterior, superior, and dominates us infinitely. In Parsons's work, as in Durkheim's, there are binding normative patterns which compel human behaviour. There is conformity to conventions and roles; meaning are fixed and not negotiated. In such a society physical force is not required, social conformity acting as a form of soft coercion. From the Marxist viewpoint of Bowles and Gintis, the crucial difference with this 'order' tradition is that in this (capitalist) society education cannot be truly concerned with its developmental function, the full realization of the individual.

This Marxist commitment, however, is combined with their basic sociological perspective, structural-functionalism. This has important consequences in their treatment of certain aspects in the sociology of education. Their work replicates many features of traditional functionalist texts in the subject.

1   There is an emphasis on form and neglect of content

(the curriculum).

2   There is a stress on the macro-levels of society at the expense of other levels. For example, there is a neglect of classroom contexts and the interaction of teachers and pupils.

3   As we have seen, the pervasiveness of their deterministic ontology is also a characteristic feature. Bowles and Gintis say:[24]

> The educational system. . .neither adds to nor subtracts from the degree of inequality and repression originating in the economic sphere. Rather, it reproduces and legitimates a pre-existing pattern in the process of training and stratifying the work force. How does this occur? The heart of the process is to be found not in the heart of the educational encounter . . . but in the form . . . [This corresponds] closely to the social relations of dominance, subordination, and motivation in the economic sphere. Through the educational encounter, individuals are induced to accept the degree of powerlessness with which they will be faced as mature workers.

My first objection, then, is that they do not consider at all *what* is taught, the curriculum. Questions about knowledge are completely ignored. As the emphasis is always on the *form* of the social relation, there is no recognition by them of the importance of the content of education. It follows that if the curriculum is not considered important, then neither will be the context in which the transmission of the content takes place – the classroom. But one would have thought that, after all, this, the actual teaching of curriculum content, is the everyday reality of most teachers and pupils – not some reified notion of 'the educational system'. Moreover, Bowles and Gintis forget that people do not interpret in a uniform way. Certainly, many pupils and students actively interpret their life-world in ways different from that of the school. The question of subjective meanings is given no place in Bowles and Gintis's work. Indeed, such a recognition would weaken their reproduction thesis, which ultimately derives from a Durkheimian–Parsonian ontology. Agreement with their thesis, therefore, depends partly on whether one accepts their model of Man. Underlying the reproduction process there is an assumption of Man's passivity: 'To reproduce the labor force, the schools are destined to legitimate inequality, limit personal development to forms compatible with submission to arbitrary authority, and aid in the process whereby youth are resigned to their fate.'[25]

One of the consequences of their approach, the total absorption in the macro-level, is that many teachers find it difficult to locate themselves in it. They do not know how to relate *their work* in the classroom to the functions, Bowles and Gintis say, that the educational system is performing. And many of these teachers are actually involved in the construction of curricula in order to *challenge* cognitive domination. Similarly many readers, confronted with Bowles and Gintis's 'Durksonian' determinism, find it difficult to relate it to their own persistent experience of the *possibilities* of human freedom.[26] Just as, on one dimension, a sense of the dialectical inter-relationship between classrooms and the education system is missing, so, also, on another, is the constant existential experience of the dialectic between determinism and voluntarism, coercion *and* freedom.

Bowles and Gintis constantly reiterate their main theme, 'the correspondence between the social relations of production and the social relations of education'.[27] They stress, in many different ways, that 'the educational system's ability to reproduce the consciousness of workers lies in a straight-forward correspondence principle.'[28] I have already suggested that their deterministic, passive model of man is ontologically necessary for them to develop their 'Durksonian' thesis, the integration of new generations into the social order. The link between determinism, reproduction of social relations, and the purpose of schooling, can be illustrated by the following quotations:

> Thus it is clear that the consciousness of workers — beliefs, values, self-concepts, types of solidarity and fragmentation, as well as modes of personal behavior and development — are integral to the perpetuation, validation, and smooth operation of economic institutions. *The reproduction of the social relations of production depends on the reproduction of consciousness.*[29]

> . . . the splintered consciousness of a subordinate class is not the product of cultural phenomena alone, but must be

reproduced through the experience of daily life.[30]

To reproduce the social relations of production, the educational system must try to teach people to be properly subordinate and render them sufficiently fragmented in consciousness to preclude their getting together to shape their own material existence.[31]

Bowles and Gintis stress that schooling produces an amenable and fragmented labour force. It is usually fragmented but, as many teachers in inner city schools argue, it is not entirely amenable. And the same is true of the many struggles of the working class. But as they themselves state at one point; 'The fit between schooling and work described in the previous chapters is, in one sense, too neat.'[32] Is their argument that there is a 'straightforward' or 'direct' correspondence between the social relations of schooling and work too simple? In their chapter on the origins of mass public education they make the revealing remark that 'no very simple or mechanistic relationship between economic structure and educational development is likely to fit the historical evidence . . . political factors have intervened between economic structures and educational outcomes in complex and sometimes, apparently, contradictory, ways.'[33] I would want to argue that in the theoretical chapters a direct straightforward notion of correspondence between the social relations of economic life (or work) and the social relations of schooling is assumed, and that the analysis is simplistic compared with the rich complexity of inter-related factors in the historical chapters. Moreover, their thesis of the reproduction of social relations through the reproduction of consciousness is too mechanistic: they write, for example: 'Different levels of education feed workers into different levels within the occupational structure'.[34] And they argue that in schools attended by pupils of different social classes there are different socialization patterns. Now, they might well be right in general — but it could be argued against them that there are many progressive primary schools, for example, which emphasize the internalization of norms, rather than rule-following and close supervision as one might expect from their thesis. In some schools, at any rate, it is difficult to teach docility. In brief, I am not entirely convinced that all that the educational system does is directly to produce pupils to be slotted into the system. Bowles and Gintis forget the heterogeneity of education and tend to conceive of it as a monolithic category.

The Mechanisms of Educational Change

We come, at last, to the question: What, according to Bowles and Gintis, are the mechanisms of educational change? They suggest that 'the economic and educational systems possess fairly distinct and independent internal dynamics of reproduction and development.' The economic system is incessantly changing; the educational system, however, is less dynamic:[35]

> The independent internal dynamics of the two systems present the ever-present possibility of a significant mismatch arising between economy and education . . . Thus, the relatively static educational system periodically falls out of correspondence with the social relations of production and becomes a force antithetical to capitalist development. This disjunction between an economic dynamic which extends the wage-labor system and incessantly alters the organization of work and the class structure on the one hand, and the educational system which tends to stabilize it in a given form on the other, is, we believe, an essential aspect of the process of educational change.

They argue that the moving force behind educational change is the contradictory nature of capital accumulation and the reproduction of the capitalist order. But, in their brief description of the process of educational change, they do not identify the mechanisms whereby economic interests are translated into educational programmes. And though they are constantly asserting that a correspondence exists between the social relations of production and the social relations of education, they do not show how or why there are significant 'mismatches'. In other words, they give no account of how the relatively static educational system can periodically fall out of correspondence with the social relations of production. In their book the main argument is that changes in the structure of production have preceded parallel changes in schooling, and that this establishes a strong *prima facie* case for the causal importance of economic structure as a major determinate of educational structure: 'every major transformation of the educational system and ideology has been precipitated by a shift in the structure of production, in the class composition of the work force, and in the identity of oppressed groups.'[36] In their view the sources of repression lie outside the school system; they stress the priority of economic causation. But they do not address the precise nature of the relationships, the articulations (the amount of relative autonomy, etc.), between the economic and educational systems, and the other systems in the totality.

Moreover, because of their reliance on a functional correspondence they sometimes make simplistic analyses. For example, writing of disjunctions and mismatches they state, 'the relatively static educational system periodically falls out of correspondence with the social relations of production and becomes a force antithetical to capitalist development.' But why antithetical? They immediately assume that a mismatch must necessarily be opposed to capitalist development, and do not perceive that it could be a part of a more complex, dialectical system of different relationships amongst a whole ensemble of relations – which they do not consider. In a totality each dimension, the economic, political social and cultural, are closely interwoven. And, with the increasing complexity of civil society and its interpenetration with the State, the attempt to abstract and isolate particular elements – such as the social relations of production and the social relations of schooling – from the larger whole becomes more difficult.

In conclusion, the important points I wish to stress are these: the political economy of education that has been developed by Bowles and Gintis has been deliberately designed at one macro-level, but there are other concepts at different levels to which they give insufficient attention. Their stress, for example, on wage-labour means that they tend to overlook the split between mental and manual labour. I have argued that their notion of the direct correspondence between relations of work and relations of schooling is too mechanistic. Of course reproduction does take place, but it should not be thought of in a reductionist way. There is reproduction of the whole system but not necessarily all at once; it occurs at different levels and in different forms, such as language, culture and politics. In the political economy of Bowles and Gintis the mediations are missing, a series of connections at many levels, which we need to explore. The study of Gramsci, Althusser, Mao Tse-tung and other Marxists is important for this reason. This neglect by empiricists such as Bowles and Gintis amounts almost to an hostility towards theory.

As we have seen, they stress the notion of 'hidden' curriculum but make no mention of the formal curriculum — what students are supposed to be taught. The implication of this is that the content of education does not matter at all! Or, to put it another way, socialization is done only through the forms of schooling and not its content. As Bowles and Gintis believe that education is a reflection of the contradictions of the *economic* system, there is little place for superstructural elements. They underestimate the pervasiveness of ideology in its many guises, the complex ways an entire system of attitudes, beliefs, morality, values, are supportive of the established order and the class interests that dominate it. Bourgeois hegemonic values and behaviour patterns extend throughout every sphere of civil society, not only in the schools, the family and the workplace, but in all aspects of political, cultural and social life, and become interwoven into the structural and ideological totality of capitalism. Bowles and Gintis have stressed functional reproduction, but have not extended our knowledge of the articulations between different parts of this totality. This work has yet to be done. This brings us to the main question: How do we make a socialist society? They themselves admit: 'Indeed, we have no firm, strongly held, overall, and intellectually coherent answer to the central issue.'[37] If this is the case, how, then, do Bowles and Gintis propose 'getting there'?

They argue that a liberated educational system can emerge only from a socialist movement that abolishes the private ownership of essential productive resources and takes control over the production process itself. A workers' democracy is advocated in which individuals have the right and obligation to structure their work-lives through direct participatory control. The struggle to liberate education and the struggle to democratize economic life are inextricably related. But institutional change can only be the culmination of the co-ordinated activity of social classes. It is admitted that there is a lack of unified consciousness – a fragmentation facilitated by racial, sexual and socio-economic antagonisms. This problem can be overcome only by offering an alternative in which the disparate objectives of different groups are simultaneously met. Though Bowles and Gintis believe that the over-riding objective must be the ultimate dismantling of the capitalist system, they recognize that the preparatory phase of a revolutionary movement involves working in, and through, existing capitalist institutions – 'the long march through the institutions'. As for the form of socialism, this will be determined by practical activity more than by abstract theorizing.

Though I support their commitment to the transformation of the capitalist economy, I have already argued that their programme does not flow out of their work, and perhaps, given their methodology and ontology, cannot follow from it. Lacking a theory of consciousness and inter-subjectivity, of ideology and counter-hegemony, the 'strategy' of Bowles and Gintis gives the impression of being 'tacked on'.

The guidelines towards a socialist strategy for education that Bowles and Gintis offer are these. It is suggested that revolutionary educators should press for the democratization of schools and colleges by working towards a system of participatory power – where work processes are self initiated and controlled by the workers themselves. They should attempt to undermine the correspondence between the social relations of education and the social relations of production in capitalist economic life – that is, to undermine the capacity of the system to perpetuate inequality. Moreover, radicals should create a unified class-consciousness by seeking to unify diverse groups, to form alliances between students, teachers, workers' organizations. We must fight for egalitarian educational practices which reduce the power of the schools to fragment the labour force. The development of the vision of a socialist alternative requires a revolutionary transformation to aid the daily struggles of the working people. Socialism is not an event. It is a process. The aim of such a movement is not a mere re-orientation of political power but a transformation of social life.

Chapter 12

Summary
and Conclusions

Why is this, the last chapter, so hard to write? I feel that one of the problems in writing a summary is that the author is involved in telling the reader (retrospectively) that the text should have been read 'this' way. A conclusion is difficult for similar reasons – one is supposed to draw all the various contradictory strands together, to give a sense of 'coherence' and completeness to something essentially unfinished. But I must try – if only to see what the conclusion is.

Let me begin with *a* summary. In the first part of the book I gave an account of the 'new' phenomenological sociology of education and tried to portray something of the intellectual excitement that it engendered.

It could be said that the dominant assumptions in the 1950s and 1960s were that education was a social 'good', and that there should be an efficient use of human resources. It was hoped that the emphasis on efficiency would lead to an increase in investment from which benefits were expected to accrue. This was the 'human capital' theory in which the worker embodied capital in his body and work. The main founders of the sociology of education in Britain should be seen in this context. Some of the 'traditional' sociologists of education, such as Halsey, Floud and Douglas were, of course, concerned with equal opportunity and justice, but their stress on educational opportunity for all was related to this theory of economic growth. Education was conceived by them as the means to social mobility. But if we now see social mobility as an ideology, what were the assumptions underlying their views? These sociologists of education thought of working-class 'success' in terms of upward social mobility.[1] De-streaming and comprehensivization were strategic means of increasing equality of opportunity but they did not challenge the *status quo*. That society should be based on private property and the division of labour remained unquestioned assumptions; it is for this reason that I would call them reformist.[2] It is not surprising that the class structure was not transformed. We can now more clearly see some of the key features of the 'traditional' sociology of education. It was a social science which spoke to administrators and policy-makers who commissioned research on the underprivileged. As there was an increase in government influence, which led to a decrease in the autonomy of sociologists of education, their work increasingly came to be used for correctionalist purposes. It is possible to argue that in the political conflict of interest between government and social science, the latter was involved in a process of incorporation and assimilation by the State.

Similarly, most changes in education can be seen as representing changing ways of consolidating the existing pattern of domination. Whenever there is a movement for a radical alteration in the educational system or for its abolition, the cry is heard that the system is basically sound, that it only needs minor reforms. Measures such as de-streaming, comprehensivization, mixed-ability teaching, progressive or 'learner-centred' education have been gradually adapted and changed. It is well known how, when the system is in acute danger, the rhetoric of the attackers is co-opted for limited change. The original critiques become displaced and distorted in the process as they become incorporated into the capitalist State.

I have stressed the point that the methodology of the 'traditional' sociologists of education was positivist. Positivism believes in a passive model of Man which, allied to a behaviouristic psychology and its emphasis on explanation and prediction, enables it to be used for social control.

A positivist methodology leads to numerical assessment and quantification becoming fetishized. Only that which can be measured is thought of as interesting and real.

After the period when functionalist sociology was pervasive, there followed a time in which there was a predominance of symbolic interactionist work. These studies expressed humanistic sympathy with 'the little guy who made out' against the coercive rules of total institutions – an expression, perhaps, of a 'liberal anarchism'. But symbolic interaction is only one strand in interpretive social science; another important one is phenomenological sociology. This stance, adopted by the 'new' sociology of education, was based largely on the social phenomenology of Alfred Schutz, and was also influenced, at a later date, by some elements of the work of Merleau-Ponty. The new sociology utilized work from ethnography and anthropology in order to question our assumptions, and to show that other possibilities of learning and living together are possible. The 'new' sociologists criticized some of the liberal philosophers for their elitist assumptions and the 'hidden' political nature of their work, and a bitter controversy ensued. I believe that in this debate questions of knowledge came to be highlighted because the political thrust of the new sociologists towards egalitarianism was not explicit enough. However, the importance of the new sociologists of education, writers such as Geoff Esland, Nell Keddie and Michael F.D. Young, is that they introduced the question of *meaning*. The perceptions of the actor, the pupil, the native, the deviant, which had previously been ignored by positivists, were again given credence. Writers of the 'new' sociology raised this question at three levels.

1   Meaning at the level of schoolteachers: that is, how they perceive their classrooms and how they can transform their consciousness, and so de-reify felt constraints.

2   Meaning at the level of the pupils. I am referring to the sense pupils make of what is presented to them, and the ways in which they are restrained from theorizing and from being 'the authors of their worlds'.

3   Meaning at the level of school subjects, the curriculum. This refers to the mediation between teachers and pupils; how school-knowledge is selected, by whom, and for what purpose?

The 'new' sociology of education emphasized the power of consciousness of teachers in the classroom to overcome coercive situations and to alter educational contexts. This form of philosophical idealism has been termed 'possibilitarianism'. Expressed most clearly in the work of Maxine Greene, it assumes a vast potential for change and a naive optimism. An important feature of the new sociology of education was its use of anthropological material which was a weapon in the debates about cultural deprivation, the relativity of knowledge, the nature of rationality – the possibility of alternative ways of teaching and living, of forms of life. One such debate was about whether members of other (sub) cultures, such as working-class children, could be characterized as having a 'deficit' or being different. Phenomenological sociologists of education supported the case for difference, the implication of which was enormous – it was an accusation that the schools were a predominantly middle-class institution, and that as it assumed that its values and tests were 'natural' and right, it defined working-class children as inferior. The 'new' sociology of education, in this way, valuably focused on various aspects of the curriculum, which had previously been a neglected area.

The 'new' sociologists of education were not alone, however, in their dissatisfaction with current notions of 'education'. Critiques of schooling were also being made by Illich, Postman, Reimer, and others. Illich became a cult figure and his ideas were sympathetically received by those who knew that as there was no likelihood of his ideas being realized there was no danger in adopting his views. Social change, according to Illich, was going to be brought about by a change in personal consciousness. His most serious weakness was that he did not consider the complex inter-relations between schooling and politico-economic factors. In spite of these shortcomings the thrust of the de-schoolers was to make problematic the prevailing assumption that education was a social 'good'.

Recently the 'new' sociologists of education have reviewed their work and have acknowledged certain weaknesses. Quite rightly the emphasis on meaning came to be seen as inadequate. This is because consciousness and theoretical de-reification are only *part* of the story. Moreover, the new sociology of education failed to take its own assumptions of cultural relativism seriously. It raised many problems dealing with classroom practice which could not be resolved because schools were not seen as part of a social whole, a totality. It was unhistorical and uncritical of its own framework, which had many of the weaknesses that are characteristic of interpretive social science, such as philosophical idealism and relativist epistemology. Moreover, theories such as symbolic interaction, phenomenological sociology, ethnomethodology, have implications for political practice that are fundamentally conservative. The main shortcomings of phenomenology have been aptly summarized by Richard Lichtman, and apply also to the 'new' sociology of education:[3]

> But the view is inadequate as it stands. It is overly subjective and voluntarist, lacks an awareness of historical concreteness, is naive in its account of mutual typification and ultimately abandons the sense of human beings in struggle with an alien reality which they both master and to which they are subordinate. It is a view which tends to dissolve the concept of ideology or false consciousness and leaves us often against its will, without defense against the present inhuman reality.

Though the new sociology of education argued that we should study the social organizations of knowledge this was, ironically, what was excluded from the discussion. As I argued earlier, one of the consequences of adopting the phenomenological framework was that concepts with which to analyse power were not available, and therefore questions as to how education is organized by the State, its relationship to authority and domination were not analysed.[4] This was the reason so many of the debates were ultimately self-defeating; education was seen in a philosophically idealist way, as something apart from the economy, the mode of production. As 'society' was a reification, the notion that the State may consist of complex structures at different levels was not recognized.[5] A phenomenological sociology of education was then inadequate as a lever for social change; our analysis of education was such that we could never transcend the logic of prevailing structure. There was a need to have a form of explanation and understanding that integrated a moral commitment with an awareness of political action, of praxis.

After a reappraisal of the new phenomenological sociology of education, I provided an introduction to Marxism and attempted to analyse alienation and schooling. I then suggested that Marxism, too, can be idealist — and neglect structural elements.[6] The chapters that followed represented a move away from 'humanist Marxism', which tends to concentrate on an ideological conception of society, discussing it largely in terms of knowledge and ideas, towards an analysis of economic and political structures.[7] I moved on to consider the work of American historians of the rise of the corporate liberal State, and the 'political economist of education'. The work of the historians, Clarence Karier for example, is important because of the research into the origins of mass schooling, the functions it serves and its connections with the liberal State. The question of education is central to our understanding of society and yet very little historical research has been done. We know little about the origins of education, for example, and its connection with the economic basis of society, its mode of production. The precise relationship between mass schooling and the rapid transformation of agrarian to industrial monopoly capitalism is something that has yet to be demonstrated. In what ways, in this period of momentous change, did public schooling become a means of controlling the working class? Why have the hopes of the early pioneers, who believed that schools would have a liberating effect, not been fulfilled?

It was argued that any understanding of the complex inter-relationships between education and the economy must be based on an analysis of the nature of work and of monopoly capitalism in the twentieth century. A chapter on how the capitalist mode of production operates in contemporary society was included. From this account certain parallels can be drawn that reinforce the thesis of the political economists of education. Many features from the factory system, that resemble the time and motion of 'Taylorism', have been introduced into the schools. There has been a systematic fragmentation of different sectors of education, and then *within* each sector. A parallel process in industry is the increasing division of labour.[8] There is the increase of competition, in 'pacing' the rate of expected learning. And, as the period of formal schooling has increased in terms of years, its content has gradually been trivialized. Again, this reflects a parallel process that has been taking place in industry: de-skilling. I have suggested that these features are encouraged in schools because they sustain hierarchies. These are some of the mechanisms of social control by capital. The new interest in modes of production and re-production is also expressed in the penultimate chapter, which dealt with the political economy of Bowles and Gintis.[9] In spite of some reservations, I broadly agreed with their thesis that the experiences of the workplace are first formed in the school, and that there are linkages between family and school to the occupational structure.[10] This is why any discussion of the nature of schooling and the persistent legitimacy of its methods has to take account of the ways in which they are pervaded by economic structures.

Conclusion

Now, it might be felt by some readers that the two parts of this book represent a 'break' or disjunction; that the phenomenological and Marxist viewpoints on education are completely different and, therefore, incommensurable. But I see this re-orientation not as a break but as a continuity – as a different part of the same journey. Life changes, and the way we look at the world changes with it. After all, the differences between a Marxist phenomenology and a phenomenological, or humanistic, Marxism are difficult to define. For me there are many similarities in both perspectives. I have argued throughout this book that in our society there are the following divisions. There is a division between so-called 'experts' and lay people. In the section on work I wrote that there is a division between conception (the role of management) and execution (the role of labour), which is Taylorism. There are also rigid divisions between subjects, and between the arts and the sciences. In these and other divisions, one element is always placed higher than the other, and so hierarchies come into being. The 'expert', the mental worker, the manager, is granted deference. Capitalism brings about and encourages this segmentation and fragmentation.

Let me now, briefly, recall some of the similarities. The struggle to overcome the gulf between experts and laymen, intellectuals and masses, mental and physical forms of activity is a feature of both phenomenological and Marxist approaches. The 'new' sociology of education opposed

elitism and wanted to break down hierarchies. This phenomenological approach lacked an adequate analysis of the
problem; a Marxist viewpoint, however, does provide a
method through the concept of the division of labour. I
mentioned the egalitarianism of the 'new' sociology and,
as an expression of it, the belief that all human beings are
theorists. This idea that we are all philosophers and intellectuals is also a Marxist notion, expounded, for example, in
Gramsci's work. Similarly, I used to write of coercion, but
is this not a less precise term for alienation? And again, in
both perspectives, the concept of de-reification is essential.
The transformation of consciousness is vital in Marxism, too,
and is an inseparable part of structural change. The necessity
of *practical* de-reification has made me more aware of the
importance of praxis. I believe that we can combat the
division of labour in our everyday lives. Being aware of these
'splits', such as those of mental and physical labour, we
should try and overcome all hierarchical distinctions where-
ever they appear.

My main purpose has been to show how alienation is
manifested in different aspects of school life; how inequality
and injustice come about and are sustained. I have written
about schooling, and selected aspects of anthropology,
philosophy and political economy, as I believe they are
closely interwoven in a *totality*. The struggle to change one
is bound up with the struggle to change all the *ensemble* of
social relations. Seeing the educational world as one of
alienation, my starting-point is a consideration of the ways
in which sociology of education can become a mechanism
for transforming social reality. And so praxis is my other
underlying theme, the relationship between theory and
practice. There is an urgent need to explore the possibilities
of transforming the repressive social order. Ultimately, a
socialist revolution will not come mechanically from a
breakdown of the capitalist economy, but will have to be
built by purposive human actors. This was precisely what
was forgotten during the time of the Second International,
when a positivist form of Marxism, based on economism,
became dominant. This type of vulgar Marxism, because of
its stress on laws, was a scientism. The 'new' sociology of
education, having once rejected positivism, continues to

repudiate it whenever it appears in Marxism. Deterministic Marxism is rejected because it transfers political initiative and responsibility from self-conscious human beings to structural entities. This is why consciousness is so important. Of course, the phenomenological concept of consciousness was found to be inadequate because it was individualistic. It has now to be reformulated in terms of a collective, a *class*-consciousness, if it is to become an active force and intervene to transform structures. In our attempt to understand economic and political structures we should not, then, neglect consciousness. You may think that here and elsewhere in the book the debates have centred around such dichotomies such as idealism *v.* materialism, voluntarism *v.* determinism. My argument is that a revolutionary theory will have to transcend these polarities. We need a conception of revolutionary praxis that transcends the classical dichotomy of idealism and materialism. We require a conception of knowledge, of consciousness, as both an expression of the material world, and a creative transforming agent. In other words, a dialectical conception of the relationship between consciousness and structures; a theory in which human activity is shaped by social structures, but is also the creator of new forms that challenge and overcome those same structures. This should be manifest in the sociology of education that we now construct.

Please correct me if I am wrong.

Notes

These notes are unusual in that they are intended to be read. They contain carefully organized *suggestions for further reading*. The bibliographical notes have been constructed as a guide for readers who may wish to study other texts concurrently with this one. If a discussion group was formed it could plan its own course centred on these readings.

1 The Injunctions of the New Approach

[1] The change from the traditional to the 'new' sociology of education can be most clearly seen by comparing a book such as Olive Banks, *The Sociology of Education*, Batsford, 1968, with some of the work prepared by Geoff Esland for the Open University. See, for example, *The Construction of Reality* (1971) and *Language and Reality* (1973), The Open University Press. They are excellent introductions to symbolic interaction and phenomenological perspectives. Also recommended is B.R. Cosin *et al.* (eds), *School and Society*, 2nd ed., Routledge & Kegan Paul, 1977. In it the articles by Becker, Blumer, Schutz, Berger and Cicourel represent some of the many different strands within what can be called the 'interpretive' model of social science.

[2] What I term the 'traditional' sociology of education was based on the positivist model of social science. Drawing largely on structural functionalism, it stressed the point of view of the scientific observer and used educator's categories. Talcott Parsons's paper, 'The School Class as a Social System: Some of its Functions in American Society' is typical of this approach. It is in A.H. Halsey, Jean Floud and C.P. Anderson's *Education, Economy and Society*, Free Press, 1961. J.B.W. Douglas, *The Home and the School*, Panther, 1969, also belongs to this period. Halsey, and others who founded the sociology of education in this country, argued for destreaming,

comprehensivization, equality for the working-class child. But 'success' for the working-class child was thought of in terms only of upward social mobility. Now, would one want to call this success? Undoubtedly they did question, but only within the parameters of a capitalist society. These sociologists of education can perhaps now be seen as liberal reformist. For an argument along similar lines see the paper by Dann Finn, Neil Grant and Richard Johnson, 'Social Democracy, Education and the Crisis', in *On Ideology*, Working Papers in Cultural Studies, no. 10, University of Birmingham, 1977, pp. 162–70.

3 Michael F.D. Young (ed.), *Knowledge and Control*, Collier-Macmillan, 1971, p. 5.

4 Generally problems, ideas and institutions are taken as given and their consequences seen as self-evident facts of nature. In an interesting paper, L. Dexter asks us to imagine a society which stresses grace and style in movement as we stress intellectual skill. He suggests that grace being taken as a matter of course, there would be discrimination against clumsy people – but this would not be an inherent necessity. In our society we discriminate against the mentally deficient because they are stupid, and not because the stupidity is relevant to the task, claim or situation. See 'On the Politics and Sociology of Stupidity in Our Society', in L. Becker (ed.), *The Other Side, Perspectives on Deviance*, Free Press, 1964, p. 37. In a similar way we can begin to question our notions of childhood by a work such as P. Aries, *Centuries of Childhood*, Penguin, 1973. Or education and rationality by the works of C. Castaneda, for example, *The Teachings of Don Juan: A Yaqui Way of Knowledge*, Penguin, 1970. In this way we can come to realize that intelligence, childhood, education and rationality are not facticities like those in the natural world, but are *social constructs*.

5 One of the clearest introductions to these notions is in David Silverman's *The Theory of Organisation*, Heinemann, 1970, chapter 6. This chapter, 'The Action Frame of Reference', also appears in K. Thompson and J. Tunstall (eds), *Sociological Perspectives: Selected Readings*, Penguin, 1971. See also T.P. Wilson, 'Normative and Interpretive Paradigms in Sociology', in Jack D. Douglas (ed.), *Understanding Everyday Life*, Routledge & Kegan Paul, 1971. The reader can then turn to Paul Filmer *et al.*, *New Directions in Sociological Theory*, Collier-Macmillan, 1972. This book contains an excellent bibliography.

6 I believe my reading of Sartre expresses *the spirit* of optimism and challenge of the new phenomenological sociology of education. It was in fact mainly influenced by the work of Alfred Schutz, whose writings can be seen as an attempt to popularize the work of his

master Husserl, to bring it down to earth, and synthesize it with Weber's 'verstehen' sociology. See, for example, Helmut Wagner (ed.), *Alfred Schutz, On Phenomenology and Social Relations*, University of Chicago Press, 1970. An important essay by Schutz, 'The Problem of Rationality in the Social World', is in D. Emmet and A. MacIntyre (eds), *Sociological Theory and Philosophical Analysis*, Macmillan, 1970. Schutz's essays are analyses of the structure of the social world; it is largely on his work that ethnomethodology is based. In the ethnomethodological model persons are treated as reality constructors. Persons construct social structures without being aware of this work; they create situations and rules, and so at once create themselves and their social realities. I recommend Hugh Mehan and Houston Wood, *The Reality of Ethnomethodology*, Wiley, 1975.

2 The Use of Anthropological Studies

[1] It is often assumed that concepts expressed in the native's language are translatable into the anthropologist's language without distortion. Anthropologists can influence the consciousness of their subjects by asking them to make explicit what they normally take for granted. An excellent introduction to these ideas is Michael Cole *et al.*, *The Cultural Context of Learning and Thinking*, Methuen, 1971.

[2] The view that other cultures are not necessarily deficient but different is clearly expressed in Nell Keddie (ed.), *Tinker Tailor . . . The Myth of Cultural Deprivation*, Penguin, 1973. Anthropological studies, such as those in the above book, were used by the 'new' sociologists of education to criticize the dominant view of cultural deprivation. This was, briefly, that there was something wrong with working-class kids (the social pathology view) and that they must learn to speak standard English/the elaborated code, and be initiated into 'mainstream' culture. In studying the debate on cultural deprivation the following are essential: Nell Keddie (course consultant), *Sorting Them Out, Social Differentiation II*, Unit 10, Open University Press, 1972. In A. Cashdan *et al.* (eds), *Language in Education*, Routledge & Kegan Paul, 1972, there are these important articles: S. Baratz and J. Baratz, 'Early Childhood Intervention: the social science base of institutional racism'; W. Labov, 'The Logic of Nonstandard English'; B. Bernstein, 'Education cannot Compensate for Society'. In B.R. Cosin *et al.* (eds), *School and Society*, 2nd ed., Routledge & Kegan Paul, 1977, see the articles: R.V. Dumont and M.L. Wax, 'Cherokee School Society and the Intercultural Classroom', and A. Platt, 'The Rise of the Child-Saving Movement'.

Notes

³ Thomas Gladwin, *East is a Big Bird; Navigation and Logic on Puluwat Atoll*, Harvard University Press, 1970. On psychologists such as Bruner, Guilford, Hobb, Piaget and their work on intelligence and intellectual processes, Gladwin comments: 'Their work immediately strikes an anthropologist as culture bound. Their starting point is our familiar symbolic logic and relational abstract thinking. They do not have before them a range of other possible basic approaches to thinking, learning, and problem solving. . . . Anthropologists stoutly defend the equality of all men. . . .' See T. Gladwin, 'Culture and Logical Process', in N. Keddie (ed.), *Tinker Tailor . . .*, p. 119. I think such work demonstrates that asking questions of other cultures sometimes means that we may be able to ask new questions of our own society.

⁴ Robin Horton's work challenges that of Lévy-Bruhl, who believed that primitive culture implied primitive thought. Horton contends that there is considerable similarity between the thought patterns of African and western peoples. He believes that all people try to understand their world by constructing explanatory theories, and that there are analogies between traditional African belief systems and western so-called scientific beliefs. In both there is a quest for unity underlying apparent diversity. Both theories place events in a causal context wider than provided by common-sense. For example, in the absence of antibiotics, etc., in Africa the traditional healers' efforts to remedy the stress-producing disturbances in the patients' social life was very relevant. In the west the success of the germ-theory has prevented us from fully exploring the extent of psycho-somatic illness. See Robin Horton, 'African Traditional Thought and Western Science', in Michael Young (ed.), *Knowledge and Control*, Collier-Macmillan, 1971. This paper also appears in Bryan R. Wilson (ed.), *Rationality*, Basil Blackwell, 1970, and is discussed in it by Lukes, Beattie and others.

⁵ Harold Conklin, 'Hanunoo Colour Categories', in Dell Hymes (ed.), *Language in Culture and Society*, Harper & Row, 1964. Charles Frake, 'The Diagnosis of Disease among the Subanun', is in N. Keddie (ed.), *Tinker, Tailor . . . .*

⁶ A well-known study of 'passing' and 'management devices' is H. Garfinkel, 'Passing and the managed achievement of sex status in an "intersexed" person', in *Studies in Ethnomethodology*, Prentice-Hall, 1967. It deals with a person who was recognized by everyone as a boy, and who at the age of seventeen decided to become a female. 'Agnes' had to learn to act and feel like a woman. As she had male genitals she was unable to fulfill the things expected of her by males, yet she wanted to present herself as a sexually attractive female. She was continually engaged in the work of 'passing', and

197

had to live up to standards of conduct, appearance, skills and feeling
while simultaneously learning what these standards were. The study
is an examination of the relationship between routine, trust and
rationality, and Garfinkel argues that Agnes was a practical metho-
dologist: 'she was self-consciously equipped to teach normals how
normals make sexuality happen in commonplace settings as an
obvious, familiar, recognisable, natural' (ibid., p. 180).

7 Routledge & Kegan Paul, 1958. The leading opponent of Winch's
relativism is Ernest Gellner. In Bryan Wilson (ed.), *Rationality*, it
is interesting to read Winch's 'Understanding a Primitive Society',
followed by Gellner's 'Concepts and Society'. I discuss this issue
further in chapter 6. Only a few selected aspects of anthropology
important for 'interpretive' sociology of education have been discussed above. The following references will enable students to
follow currents that I have not been able to mention. See, for
example, Mary Douglas, *Purity and Danger*, Penguin, 1970. In
Natural Symbols, Penguin, 1973, pp. 41–58, she applies Bernstein's
approach to the analysis of ritual. See also C.R. Badcock, *Lévi-
Strauss, Structuralism and Sociological Theory*, Hutchinson, 1975;
Michael Lane, *Structuralism; A Reader*, Cape, 1970; Miriam Glucks-
mann, 'The Structuralism of Lévi-Strauss and Althusser', in John
Rex (ed.), *Approaches to Sociology*, Routledge & Kegan Paul, 1974.

3 The Adoption of a Phenomenological Model of Man

1 Mary Warnock, *Existentialism*, Oxford University Press, 1970,
contains essays on these philosophers. Extracts from these philosophers appear in an anthology edited by Joseph Kockelmans,
Phenomenology, Anchor Books, 1967.

2 A useful introduction to Heidegger and some of these ideas is
William Barrett, *Irrational Man: A Study in Existential Philosophy*,
Heinemann, 1958.

3 I am thinking particularly of Habermas. For useful introductions
to his work, see David Frisby, 'The Frankfurt School: Critical
Theory and Positivism', in John Rex (ed.), *Approaches to Sociology*,
Routledge & Kegan Paul, 1974; the Introduction by Thomas Mc-
Carthy to Jurgen Habermas, *Legitimation Crisis*, Heinemann, 1976;
also Theodor W. Adorno *et al.*, *The Positivist Dispute in German
Sociology*, Heinemann Educational Books, 1976. See also Paul
Connerton (ed.), *Critical Sociology*, Penguin, 1976.

4 The attempt to integrate phenomenology and Marxism has a long
tradition; see, for example, Fred Dallmayr's article 'Phenomenology
and Marxism', in George Psathas (ed.), *Phenomenological Sociology*,

198

Wiley, 1973. It is an exegesis of writers such as Lukács, Merleau-Ponty, Piccone and, of course, Sartre. See Sartre's *Search for a Method*, Vintage Books, 1963. I also recommend Pietro Chiodi, *Sartre and Marxism*, Harvester Press, 1976.

5 An essay that discusses this is Thomas P. Wilson, 'Normative and Interpretive Paradigms in Sociology', in Jack D. Douglas (ed.), *Understanding Everyday Life*, Routledge & Kegan Paul, 1971.

6 See, for example, the essay 'Existentialism', in E. San Juan (ed.), *Georg Lukács' Marxism and Human Liberation*, Dell, 1973. Theodor W. Adorno, *The Jargon of Authenticity*, Routledge & Kegan Paul, 1973, is a critique of German existentialism.

7 See Geoff Whitty, 'Sociology and the Problem of Radical Educational Change', in Michael Flude and John Ahier (eds), *Educability, Schools and Ideology*, Croom Helm, 1974, p. 115.

8 *On the Beginning of Social Inquiry*, Routledge & Kegan Paul, 1974, p. 2.

9 See, for example, Maxine Greene, *Teacher as Stranger: Educational Philosophy for the Modern Age*, Wadsworth, 1973, p. 149.

10 Recently Zygmunt Bauman has argued that the phenomenological programme, if scrupulously observed, can generate no sociology. 'The critique of sociology, currently undertaken ostensibly under the auspices of phenomenology, emanates, in actual fact, from a different source – that of existentialist philosophy. . . . The guiding motif of existentialist philosophy is provided by the search for the authentic, undistorted nature of man, rather than the undistorted knowledge man can acquire' (*Towards a Critical Sociology*, Routledge & Kegan Paul, 1976, pp. 2–53). This upholds my view of the importance of Sartre. For a study of the work of Sartre and of its relevance for contemporary sociology see Ian Craib, *Existentialism and Sociology*, Cambridge University Press, 1976.

4 The Rejection of the Liberal Philosophy of Education

1 R.S. Peters, *Ethics and Education*, Allen & Unwin, 1966; P.H. Hirst and R.S. Peters, *The Logic of Education*, Routledge & Kegan Paul, 1970; Paul H. Hirst, *Knowledge and the Curriculum*, Routledge & Kegan Paul, 1974. In Hirst's collection of papers see the review of Philip H. Phenix's *Realms of Meaning* (McGraw-Hill, 1964), pp. 54–68. Although Hirst is critical of Phenix, Maxine Greene places him with Hirst and Peters in the same 'Anglo-American' tradition.

2 R.S. Peters, 'Education as Initiation', in R.D. Archambault (ed.), *Philosophical Analysis and Education*, Routledge & Kegan Paul, 1965, p. 110.

3   Paul H. Hirst, 'Liberal Education and the Nature of Knowledge', in R.D. Archambault (ed.), op. cit., p. 125.

4   For the view that socialization must be understood as an inter-action process which involves the child as *an active partner*, see Hans P. Dreitzel (ed.), *Childhood and Socialization*, Recent Sociology, no. 5, Collier-Macmillan, 1973, especially the papers by Robert MacKay, 'Conceptions of Children and Models', and John O'Neill, 'Embodiment and Child Development'.

5   Paul H. Hirst, 'Liberal Education and the Nature of Knowledge', pp. 128–31.

6   Richard Pring, 'Knowledge out of Control', in *Education for Teaching*, no. 89, autumn 1972, pp. 19–28.

7   This is the main thesis of Hanna Pitkin, *Wittgenstein and Justice*, University of California Press, 1972.

8   Some of these criticisms are discussed more fully in David Adelstein, 'The Philosophy of Education, or the Wisdom and Wit of R.S. Peters', in Trevor Pateman (ed.), *Counter Course*, Penguin, 1972; Keith Paton, *The Great Brain Robbery* (obtainable from 102, Newcastle Street, Silverdale, Staffs.).

9   I admit the difficulty of holding such a position on hierarchies and values. On the one hand there is the acceptance of a phenomeno-logical relativism which enjoins a refusal to make hierarchical dis-tinctions, and yet we live in a world where we are forced to make some decisions. Nevertheless, the presuppositions I mention were the basis of some stimulating work. The value of teacher-research was stressed by John Bartholomew, 'The Teacher as Researcher', in *Hard Cheese*, no. 1, January 1973. That actors' categories are more adequate than those of 'scientific' observers is the view of most interpretive sociologists. The refusal to make a distinction between lay and professional theorizing, in the construction of accounts of the social world, is a feature of the work of Garfinkel and other ethnomethodologists. Important books include Roy Turner (ed.), *Ethnomethodology*, Penguin, 1974; Jack D. Douglas (ed.), *Understanding Everyday Life*, Routledge & Kegan Paul, 1971; Harold Garfinkel, *Studies in Ethnomethodology*, Prentice-Hall, 1968.

10   See the following three books by Freire: *Pedagogy of the Oppressed*, Penguin, 1972; *Cultural Action for Freedom*, Penguin, 1972; *Education for Cultural Consciousness*, Sheed & Ward, 1974.

11   Maxine Greene, 'Curriculum and Consciousness', *Teachers College Record*, 73, December 1971; see also her 'Defying Determinism', *Teachers College Record*, 74, December 1972.

12   See, for example, M.F.D. Young *et al.* (eds), *Worlds Apart: Readings for a Sociology of Education*, Collier-Macmillan, 1976. This collec-

tion, besides drawing on anthropology, contains writings on literature, philosophy, and sociology.

13 Karl Marx, *The German Ideology* (ed. C. J. Arthur), Lawrence & Wishart, 1970, p. 64.

14 These features of ideology are drawn from the account by Henri Lefebvre, *The Sociology of Marx*, Penguin, 1972, ch. 2. See also Alan Swingewood, *Marx and Modern Social Theory*, Macmillan, 1975, pp. 58–86. Things are seldom quite so simple; we know little about the forms and processes of ideology. Indeed, there is at present no wholly satisfactory theory of ideology. For the theoretical contributions of Lukács, Gramsci, Althusser and Nicos Poulantzas to this 'region' see *On Ideology*, Working Papers in Cultural Studies, no. 10, 1977.

5 The Importance of Classroom Studies

1 This is urged, for example, by John Seeley, 'The Making and Taking of Problems: Towards an Ethical Stance', in Jack D. Douglas (ed.), *The Relevance of Sociology*, Appleton-Century-Crofts, *1970*.

2 See, for example, Jerome Manis and Bernard Meltzer (eds), *Symbolic Interaction*, Allyn & Bacon, 1972, especially the essays by Becker, Blumer, Goffman and Garfinkel; Howard S. Becker, *Sociological Work*, Allen Lane, 1971.

3 Alfred Schutz, *The Phenomenology of the Social World*, Heinemann, 1972; Schutz and Thomas Luckmann, *The Structures of the Life World*, Heinemann, 1974.

4 For a useful introduction see Roger Dale, 'Phenomenological perspectives and the Sociology of the School', in Michael Flude and John Ahier (eds), *Educability, Schools and Ideology*, Croom Helm, 1974.

5 'Social-Class Variations in the Teacher-Pupil Relationship', in B.R. Cosin *et al.* (eds), *School and Society*, 2nd ed., Routledge & Kegan Paul, 1977. See also, in this book, Robert Dumont and Murray Wax's study, 'Cherokee School Society and the Intercultural Classroom'.

6 'Student Social Class and Teacher Expectations: the Self-Fulfilling Prophecy in Ghetto Education', *Harvard Educational Review*, 40, 1970, pp. 411–51.

7 Routledge & Kegan Paul, 1967; see also Colin Lacey, *Hightown Grammar: the School as a Social System*, Manchester University Press, 1970.

8 On labelling, see Howard Becker, 'On Labeling Outsiders', in Earl

Rubington and Martin Weinberg (eds), *Deviance: the Interactionist Perspective*, Macmillan, 1968; Edwin Schur, *Labeling Deviant Behavior*, Harper & Row, 1971.

9   On increasing bureaucratization, see A.V. Cicourel and J. Kitsuse, 'The Social Organisation of the High School and Deviant Adolescent Careers', in *School and Society*, 2nd ed., p. 114.

10   Aaron V. Cicourel and John Kitsuse, *The Educational Decision-Makers*, Bobbs-Merril, 1963, p. 147.

11   'Delinquents in Schools: a Test for the Legitimacy of Authority', in *School and Society*, 2nd ed., p. 34. A useful discussion of Werthman is in David Hargreaves, S.K. Hester and F.J. Mellor, *Deviance in Classrooms*, Routledge & Kegan Paul, 1975, p. 19.

12   Douglas Barnes *et al.*, 'Language in the Secondary Classroom', in *Language, the Learner and the School*, Penguin, 1969.

13   For an excellent discussion of these issues see Maurice Roche, *Phenomenology, Language and the Social Sciences*, Routledge & Kegan Paul, 1973, pp. 227–35.

14   See Carol Warren and John Johnson, 'A Critique of Labeling Theory from the Phenomenological Perspective', in Robert Scott and Jack D. Douglas (eds), *Theoretical Perspectives on Deviance*, Basic Books, 1972.

15   Nell Keddie, 'Classroom Knowledge', in Michael F.D. Young (ed.), *Knowledge and Control*, Collier-Macmillan, 1971.

16   Ibid., p. 155.

17   Ibid., p. 148.

18   Routledge & Kegan Paul, 1975.

19   Ibid., p. 227.

20   Ethnographic research on social interaction in schools is now flourishing; see Martyn Hammersley and Peter Woods (eds), *The Process of Schooling: A Sociological Reader*, Routledge & Kegan Paul, 1976.

21   For an opposing view see Bill Williamson 'Continuities and Discontinuities in the Sociology of Education', in M. Flude and J. Ahier (eds), op. cit., p. 10.

22   An example of a (possible) difficulty is 'indefinite triangulation'. A.V. Cicourel uses this expression to suggest 'that every procedure that seems to "lock in" evidence, thus to claim a level of adequacy, can itself be subjected to the same sort of analysis that will in turn produce yet another indefinite arrangement of new particulars or a rearrangement of previously established particulars in "authoritative", "final", "formal" accounts' (*Cognitive Sociology*, Penguin, 1973, p.124).

6 Some Problems in Phenomenological Sociology

1 For a discussion of these theoretical and methodological problems see, for example, D. Emmet and A. MacIntyre (eds), *Sociological Theory and Philosophical Analysis*, Macmillan, 1970, especially the papers by Schutz and Gellner; Alan Ryan, *The Philosophy of the Social Sciences*, Macmillan, 1970; Aaron V. Cicourel, *Method and Measurement in Sociology*, Free Press, 1964; Paul Filmer *et al.*, *New Directions in Sociological Theory*, Collier-Macmillan, 1972, especially chapter 5 on Theory, Methodology and Conceptualization.

2 Bryan Wilson (ed.), *Rationality*, Basil Blackwell, 1970, has excellent papers on these matters.

3 For a stimulating analysis of ideology and language see Trevor Pateman, *Language, Truth and Politics* (published by Jean Stroud and Trevor Pateman, 1975), particularly chapter 4. Repressive Discourse. Pateman makes a distinction between an oppressive relationship where there is an element of disguise of either the status of the message, or of the social relationship. The Marxist theory of ideology often dissolves into the theory of truth: 'If the critical concept of "ideology" arises from a preoccupation with truth or logic, that of "mystification" arises directly from concern with freedom. The repressive forms of discourse reduce a person's freedom in so far as they reduce the possibility of rational appraisal of either social institutions or utterances or both. Hence, the possibility of rational action is curtailed and there is scarcely a definition of freedom which does not make that possibility a component of freedom. Ideology produces misunderstanding of the world; mystification produces apathy fragmentation and disorientation' (p. 51).

4 As Michael Phillipson remarks, 'Sociological theories are indexical accounts by sociologists of the social world and, like anybody else's accounts, they are glosses of the experiences which comprise that world. In this sense they carry no special privileged status being more "objective" or nearer the "truth" than the accounts of anybody else'. See Paul Filmer *et al.*, op. cit., p. 107.

5 Some of these criticisms of phenomenological sociology and ethnomethodology are made by Hans P. Dreitzel, *Patterns of Communicative Behavior*, Recent Sociology, no. 2, Collier-Macmillan, 1970, p. xvi.

6 See, for example, Paul Filmer *et al.*, op. cit.: 'In contrast, a given social world would necessarily cease to exist if human recognition were withdrawn from it, since it has no existence apart from such recognition. In this sense society is real (has objective facticity because its members define it as real)' (p. 19). 'Social order is the accomplishment of members' describing and accounting practices

Notes

and has no existence independent of them' (p. 21).

[7] See 'A Revolution of Sociology?', *Sociology*, 7, 1973, pp. 449–62.

[8] Karl Popper, *Objective Knowledge: An Evolutionary Approach*, Oxford University Press, 1972. Though Popper has made some criticisms of positivism, he is in the positivist camp; for a critique of his views I recommend Theodor W. Adorno *et al.*, *The Positivist Dispute in German Sociology*, Heinemann Educational Books, 1976; also Karel Williams, 'Facing Reality', *Economy and Society*, 4 (3), August 1975.

[9] C. Wright Mills, *Power, Politics and People* (Collected essays, ed. Irving Horowitz), Oxford University Press, 1967, p. 428. An article critical of Mill's position, to which I have not referred in the text, is J. Rytina and C. Loomis, 'Marxist Dialectic and Pragmatism: Power and Knowledge', *American Sociological Review*, 35(2), 1970.

[10] See chapter 2, n. 7.

[11] Ernest Gellner, 'The New Idealism', in Anthony Giddens (ed.), *Positivism and Sociology*, Heinemann Educational Books, 1974.

[12] A useful article on sociological theory and truth (with relativist implications) is Peter McHugh, 'On the Failure of Positivism', in Jack D. Douglas (ed.), *Understanding Everyday Life*, Routledge & Kegan Paul, 1971.

[13] This point is from Stanley Rosen, *Nihilism*, Yale University Press, 1970. He argues that the conception of 'reason' has become detached from its traditional affiliation with the conception of 'good'.

[14] For a useful attempt to inquire into the concepts of theory and practice in different traditions, see Richard J. Bernstein, *Praxis and Action*, Duckworth, 1972. He argues that Marxism, Dewey's pragmatism and existentialism can be understood only as it emerges out of, and violently reacts to, Hegelianism.

[15] The all-pervasive power of reification is one of the main themes of Georg Lukács, *History and Class Consciousness*, Merlin, 1971. See the chapter, 'Reification and the Consciousness of the Proletariat'.

[16] John Horton, 'The Fetishism of sociology', in David Colfax and Jack Roach (eds), *Radical Sociology*, Basic Books, 1971, p. 271. Another influential essay in the book is Richard Lichtman, 'Social Reality and Consciousness', a criticism of Mead, Husserl, Schutz and others, whom he terms 'social idealists'. An example of philosophical idealism, deriving partly from the phenomenology of Heidegger, is Chris Jenks (ed.), *Rationality, Education and the Social Organization of Knowledge*, Routledge & Kegan Paul, 1977, which includes papers by Nell Keddie on 'Education as a Social Construct', Chris Jenks's critique of Paul H. Hirst, the liberal philosopher of education, and Michael F.D. Young's paper on the problems of relativity and commitment, 'Taking Sides against the Probable'.

7 Towards a Radical Reappraisal

1 See, for example, the essay by Herbert Marcuse in Anthony Giddens (ed.), *Positivism and Sociology*, Heinemann, 1974; Theodor Adorno *et al.*, *The Positivist Dispute in German Sociology*, Heinemann, 1976.

2 Brian Fay, *Social Theory and Political Practice*, Allen & Unwin, 1974. This is a good introduction to the work of the critical theorists of the Frankfurt School. I believe that Fay's main weakness is that the main object of criticism becomes positivism, science, technological society. He becomes forgetful of capitalism and the need for an organized working class.

3 'For most modern thinkers, relativism is a problem: for Winch and Wittgenstein, it is a solution' (Gellner, 'The New Idealism', in Giddens, ed., op. cit.). Michael F.D. Young's response to the problem of relativism is entitled 'Taking Sides against the Probable: Problems of Relativism and Commitment in Teaching and the Sociology of Knowledge', and appears in *Educational Review*, 25 (3), June 1973. The paper was influenced by a reading of Merleau-Ponty's *Humanism and Terror*, Beacon Press, 1969, and *Sense and Non-Sense*, Northwestern University Press, 1964.

4 A clear introduction is David McLellan, *The Thought of Karl Marx*, Macmillan, 1971.

5 I referred to some aspects of their work in chapter 5, in the section entitled 'Ideology in the Classroom: Progressivism'.

6 It could be argued that, for example, Peter Berger and Thomas Luckmann, *The Social Construction of Reality*, Penguin, 1967, have *not* neglected the dialectical process involving both subjective human activity and an objective social structure, that they are aware that men produce society and are produced by it. The work is largely based on the combination of the theoretical positions of Weber and Durkheim. See also the paper 'Reification and the Sociological Critique of Consciousness' by P. Berger and S. Pullberg, *New Left Review*, 35, 1966. In their book they refer to Schutz only in an early section; moreover, their reading of Schutz seems to be very deterministic. But they are not Marxists either; they doubt that a de-reified world is really possible. Theirs is fundamentally an ahistorical, apolitical stance which can only describe the reified construction of bourgeois reality.

7 Karl Marx, *Economic and Philosophic Manuscripts of 1844* (ed. Dirk Struik), Lawrence & Wishart, 1973, p. 229.

8 For a discussion of these matters see John Bartholomew, 'Sustaining Hierarchy through Teaching and Research', in M. Flude and J. Ahier (eds), *Educability, Schools and Ideology*, Croom Helm, 1974. Bartholomew argues that it is a feature of research and teaching

that neither is organized in such a way that its 'subjects' have an opportunity to ask about the relevance of what is being done to them.

8 An Introduction to Marxism

[1] Dawe suggests that there are two sociologies: The sociology of social systems is concerned with order; this doctrine holds that individuals cannot create and maintain order and therefore constraint is necessary for society to exist. Society must define social meanings of its members for them. Constraint becomes total through internalization and society is self-generating and self-maintaining. The sociology of social action is concerned with the problem of how human beings can regain control over essentially man made institutions and historical situations. The emphasis is on man, who realizes his full potential only when freed from external constraint. In this view the social system is *not* ontologically and methodologically prior to the participants; society is the creation of its members. For this argument, that sociology has developed on the basis of the conflict between order and control, see Alan Dawe, 'The Two Sociologies', in K. Thompson and J. Tunstall (eds), *Sociological Perspectives*, Penguin, 1971. Those wishing to study the 'order' approach may find the following texts useful: R.A. Nisbet, *The Sociological Tradition*, Heinemann, 1966; A. Giddens, *Emile Durkheim: Selected Writings*, Cambridge University Press, 1972; A. Giddens, *Capitalism and Modern Social Theory*, an analysis of the writings of Marx, Durkheim and Max Weber, Cambridge University Press, 1971; S. Lukes, *Emile Durkheim*, Penguin, 1973.

[2] *Ideology and the Development of Sociological Theory*, Prentice-Hall, 1968, pp. 83–108.

[3] Hegel denied the reality of what the senses perceive. He believed that the senses do perceive something – but this is only appearance, not the truth. And so he concluded that only logical concepts worked up by the mind have any reality. This became 'The Mind', outside and independent of anyone's head. It then governed the development of the world and then gradually unfolded itself through the centuries. Hegel gathered together in a systematic way a history of dialectics from many parts of the world and developed his own system of logic on dialectical principles. The first problem is that of grasping a thing that is in motion. The dialectic therefore has movements; this refers to what, in a system, would be called an element or factor. Another problem is to grasp the *whole*; for this one has to move from surface to essence. On the surface there is the appearance

of rest and harmony, of one-sided, immediate unity. Beneath the surface there is a process of conflict, of raging contradiction. At a certain point there is an abrupt, leap-like inversion or overthrow in which the previous is negated, the underlying contradiction is suspended and the whole is transformed into its opposite, with identities and contradictions of a different order and on a higher level. This method – how to grasp wholes as contradictions – is the greatest of the lessons Marx learned from Hegel. Marx, of course, criticized Hegel's method, and stripped off 'the mystical shell from the rational core', but he utilized the same basic structure of the argument. On this, and on the difference between Hegel's dialectic and Marx's, see the Foreword by Martin Nicolaus to Marx's *Grundrisse*, Penguin, 1973, pp. 26–40.

4   George Lichtheim, *Marxism*, Routledge & Kegan Paul, 1961, p. 8.
5   The two differences between Marx and Feuerbach that I wish to stress here are: first, Marx, unlike Feuerbach, fully recognized the significance of the Hegelian dialectic. He realized that it was to be the basis of any dialectic – but only after its mystical form had been cast off. Second, their views on nature differed. Feuerbach seemed to believe in a pure nature, an object of intuition rather than a production of social activity or practice. But for Marx, Nature could not be separated from Man, nor Man from Nature. Nature did not exist 'in itself' without human mediation. Nature that was unworked remained of potential value, awaiting realization. Technology disclosed Man's mode of dealing with Nature.
6   Karl Marx, *Economic and Philosophic Manuscripts of 1844*, Lawrence & Wishart, 1973 (quoted in David McLellan, *The Thought of Karl Marx*, Macmillan, 1971, p. 107).
7   Quoted in ibid., p. 112.
8   In his early work Marx portrayed labour as a process of progressive humanization of nature, a process which coincided with the naturalization of man. Later, he took the view that the struggle of Man with Nature could be transformed but not abolished. Marx wrote of how men incorporate their own essential forces into natural objects which have undergone human labour. Through the same process, natural things gain a new social quality as use-values. Use-values are combinations of two elements: the stuff of nature and the labour which shapes it, the labour transforming the 'in-itself' of nature into a 'for-us'. For Marx the supersession of alienation takes place not in philosophy but in socialism. But even then men will always have to work. Work, the creator of use-values, is a necessary condition. See Alfred Schmidt, *The Concept of Nature in Marx*, New Left Books, 1971, p. 71.
9   There is a clear introduction to some of his ideas in Avineri, *The*

Notes

Social and Political Thought of Karl Marx, pp. 124–8.

10 Karl Marx, *Early Writings* (ed. Lucio Colletti), Penguin, 1975, p. 422.

11 *The Social and Political Thought of Karl Marx*, Cambridge University Press, 1968, p. 142. In these sections I am much indebted to Avineri's work.

12 Marx was very critical throughout his life of the Left Hegelians because many of them believed in idealist philosophy. That is to say, they left out material production and the impact of the natural sciences in their interpretation of history. They spent their time musing on abstract utopias. Marx wrote very little about the future as he did not want to falsify the picture of a new society by transferring to it categories taken from the old. Nevertheless, from what he did write, it can be said that he looked forward to two main phases: the first lower phase of communist society would inevitably bear the 'birth-marks' of the old society, but this would lead to a second higher phase where social equality would mean not that all were treated alike, but that the richness and diversity of individuals could develop. For Marx, which desires would disappear and which would appear in a society free from commodity fetishism were questions which could not be decided abstractly. Social practice will determine how these things, and relations between human beings, will be shaped in a situation freed from economic compulsion. Thus the development of the *forces* of production was never an end in itself for Marx; what really matters is that there should be a radical change in the *relations* of production.

13 Idealist philosophy, in its Kantian form, had shown that the intuitively given world of experience was not something ultimate, but rather the result of the shaping and unifying activities of the subject. In German thought the idealist trend continued from Kant to Hegel, and then came Feuerbach, whose materialism was the abstract antithesis to Hegel's absolute idealism. Marx's main objection to Feuerbach and previous materialists was that they viewed Nature as a fixed datum, and knowledge as the mirror which reflected it. Marx argued that consciousness was not a fixed datum, that moments of knowledge change as men enter into new productive relationships with each other and with physical nature. The practical mastery over Nature is the basis for the development of the capacity of thought. Consciousness, then, is something springing from history, and subject to historical change. Man's relation to Nature is neither fixed nor theoretical but practical and transforming. Thus the rigid dualism of idealism and materialism can be overcome by the concept *practice*. Social life is essentially practical. Thought that is isolated from practice, thought that is not directed towards the accomplishment of practical tasks, is merely whimsical — or scholastic. The resolution of

theoretical contradictions is possible only through practical means.

14 Engels was a strict materialist, believing that 'everything material is real, and everything real is material'. He emphasized that natural science was the expression, the instrument, of the progress of the forces of production, and believed that he could abstract fundamental dialectic laws – this was, significantly, something Marx did not attempt to do. In a very sympathetic reading of Engels, Bertell Ollman discusses these laws, the transformation of quantity to quality, the mutual penetration of polar opposites, the development through contradiction. See his *Alienation*, Cambridge University Press, 1971, pp. 52–61. I wish to argue that Engels was undialectical and positivist for the following reasons. Engels did not regard Man and Nature as being united primarily through historical practice, but believed that Man appeared only as a product of evolution. Man was a passive reflection of the processes of Nature, not a productive force. Whereas Marx saw Nature and history as being interwoven, Engels believed that the method of materialist dialectic had two different areas of application. (In a similar way, a rigid distinction was made between dialectical and historical materialism by Stalin, who insisted that the former had to do only with Nature, the latter only with society.) In the Engels version, the moments of the dialectic thus come to be divorced from the concrete historical situation. They shrink down into the three hypostatized 'fundamental laws' mentioned above. For Marx, however, the relationship between Man and Nature is dialectical; men are consciously-acting subjects transforming nature. Men change their own nature as they progressively deprive Nature of its strangeness and externality, as they mediate Nature through themselves and make it work for their own purposes.

9 Alienation and Schooling

1 Bertell Ollman, *Alienation: Marx's Conception of Man in Capitalist Society*, Cambridge University Press, 1971; 2nd ed., 1977.

2 By extracting the 'rational kernel within the mystical shell' of Hegel's thought, Marx developed a materialistic dialectic. Marx argued that history was *not* the product of a *sui generis* 'Mind', as Hegel believed, but of a human 'head' anchored in real history, both driven and limited by changing social-economic modes of existence. That is to say, Marx adopted Hegel's method but rejected his system. Or, to be more precise, he criticized Hegel, and stripped away 'the mystical shell from the rational care' – and yet utilized the same basic structure of argument. For example, Hegel begins his *Logic*

with the most general abstraction, the most elementary reality, pure indeterminate 'being', and then shows that pure being is *identical* (with its opposite) to 'nothing'. Marx, in the Introduction to the *Grundrisse*, proceeds similarly; he begins with material production in a society and then proceeds to the opposite, consumption, without which production cannot be conceived. See Marx, *Grundrisse*, Penguin, 1973, p. 32.

3   Thinking relationally is another way of conceiving the category of totality, the notion that parts or elements can have meaning only in terms of the whole. It is difficult to think relationally because a totality is never immobile but in a constant state of tension, between parts and whole, structure and consciousness, economy and culture. Also to be considered are the effects of the growth of the division of (mental) labour. Much work needs to be done in this area. Ollman discusses the objections raised by his critics in the Appendix to his book, pp. 256–62.

4   Karl Marx, *Economic and Philosophic Manuscripts of 1844*, Lawrence & Wishart, 1973, p. 136.

5   Even among Marxists there is considerable debate about the nature of dialectic. See, for example, *Radical Philosophy*, 14, summer 1976, which contains articles by Richard Norman and Sean Sayers, and a bibliography on dialectic. See also Ollman, op. cit., pp. 52–69.

6   'I am *social* because I am active as a *man*. Not only is the material of my activity given to me as a social product (as is even the language in which the thinker is active): my own existence *is* social activity, and therefore that which I make of myself I make of myself for society and with the consciousness of myself as a social being. . . Above all we must avoid postulating "Society" again as an abstraction vis-a-vis the individual. The individual *is the social being*' (See Marx, *Economic and Philosophic Manuscripts of 1844*, p. 137).

7   Marx was able to develop his categories of economics out of private property and alienated labour; see *Economic and Philosophic Manuscripts*. . . The short chapter of fourteen pages, 'Estranged Labour', is the basis of most writings on alienation. Other important essays are on private property and the power of money, and there is a critique of Hegel's 'Phenomenology'. Marx argues that, for Hegel, mind is the true essence of Man (that religion, wealth, etc., are only spiritual entities). If, for Hegel, Man is mind, then alienation is alienation of self-consciousness. Hegel thus never gets out of his world of ideas. As Marx saw it, Hegel recognized only abstract labour, the labour of thinking and knowing. Hegel's alienation is transcended only in the mental process and he fails to see that transcendence must have its roots in human practice. Marx thus placed labour and alienation in the real world in which we

live, and makes the abstract concept historically concrete.

8 The basic difference between objectification and alienation is this: *objectification* is the process by which a human will is transferred by a human activity onto a material, resulting in an object that embodies that will and activity. This process operates in all ages and forms of society. *Alienation*, however, refers to the specific mode of objectification in which the wage-worker operates within capitalist society only; when he is quite unconscious of himself and his doings. The term must not be subjectified or psychologized. It is *not* a state or a condition of mind, but a relation of property. See the paper by Martin Nicolaus in Paul Walton and Stuart Hall (eds), *Situating Marx*, Chaucer Pub. Co., 1972. This book is a valuable introduction to a study of Marx's *Grundrisse*.

9 'As individuals express their life, so they are. What they are, therefore, coincides with their production, both with *what* they produce and with *how* they produce' (*The German Ideology*, ed. C.J. Arthur, Lawrence & Wishart, 1970).

10 These themes are discussed in two books by Hilary and Steven Rose (eds): *The Radicalisation of Science*, Macmillan, 1976, and *The Political Economy of Science*, Macmillan, 1976. See also Alfred Sohn-Rethel, 'Science as Alienated Consciousness', in *Radical Science Journal*, nos. 2/3, 1975, obtainable from Radical Science Journal, 9 Poland Street, London W1V 3DG. In this context the work of the Critical Theorists of the Frankfurt School is important. Criticisms of ideologies as instrumental rationality and technicism which reinforce a positivist culture can be found in the work of Jurgen Habermas; see the essays 'Technology and Science in Ideology' in *Toward a Rational Society*, Heinemann, 1971, and 'On Theory and Praxis in our Scientific Civilization', in *Theory and Practice*, Heinemann, 1974.

11 Ivan Illich, *Deschooling Society*, Penguin, 1973, especially ch. 3: Everett Reimer, *School is Dead*, Penguin, 1971; N. Postman and C. Weingartner, *Teaching as a Subversive Activity*, Penguin, 1971. A useful reader is Ian Lister (ed.), *Deschooling: A Reader*, Cambridge University Press, 1974, which contains an extensive bibliography. For a criticism of de-schooling from a Marxist perspective see the paper in it by Herbert Gintis, 'Towards a Political Economy of Education', pp. 24–33.

12 Gintis makes this point. He regards Illich's analysis (but not his description) as simplistic, and his programme a diversion from the complex political demands of revolutionary reconstruction. Gintis argues that the main function of schooling is not necessarily the reproduction of the social relations of consumption, but, through the 'hidden curriculum', the reproduction of the social relations

of *production*. The system of education is concerned with supplying a properly socialized and stratified labour force. Illich glorifies the small-scale entrepreneurial enterprise, 'non-addictive' human institutions, 'individual' liberation, but all this is based on an affirmation of a 'laissez-faire' model of capitalism. He accepts the basic economic institutions which structure decision-making power, and, ultimately, rejects political action. Gintis sees Illich's views as an affirmation of a utilitarian individualistic conception of humanity. His suggestion is that we should first understand the core economic institutions and their operation, the way they produce the outcomes of alienating work, fragmented community, environmental destruction, commodity fetishism, and other estranged cultural forms, and then consider how we might overcome them through political action. Praxis is indeed one of my main concerns in this book — practice so often becomes a kind of external appendage to theory. But the question that confronts us is: If men must prove the truth of their thinking in practice, in praxis, what then are the necessary checks? Perhaps the truth or falsity of a particular theory is established not within conceptual thought but through experiment. This criterion of practice — certainly not a form of pragmatism — can never confirm or refute any human idea completely. These problems will be discussed in the chapters that follow.

13 Marx writes that the need for *money* is the true need produced by the economic system. You must make everything that is yours saleable, that is, useful. It is use that determines a thing's value . . . it is money, which appears as a means, that constitutes true power. Similarly the need for qualifications, for certification, may be seen as the need produced by the modern education system. See Marx's essays 'The Meaning of Human Requirements' and 'The Power of Money in Bourgeois Society' in *Economic and Philosophic Manuscripts* . . .

14 Some of the features involved in the processes of educational assessment, grading, are referred to in Howard Becker *et al.*, *Making the Grade*, Wiley, 1968; A. Cicourel and J. Kitsuse, *The Educational Decision-Makers*, Bobbs-Merrill, 1963; Nell Keddie, 'Classroom Knowledge', in Michael F.D. Young (ed.), *Knowledge and Control*, Collier-Macmillan, 1971. Keddie remarks (p. 144): 'Like the pupils who are categorized in terms of ability, knowledge is categorized in terms of its supposed hierarchical nature.' One consequence of this is the way categories of analysis are made available to or withheld from pupils.

15 Basil Bernstein, 'On the Classification and Framing of Educational Knowledge', in M.F.D. Young (ed.), *Knowledge and Control*, p. 56; also in Bernstein, *Class, Codes and Control*, vol. 1, 2nd ed., Routledge

& Kegan Paul, 1974, p. 213. He comments that even the pacing of knowledge, the rate of expected learning, is class based, as it is connected with middle-class socialization. The pacing of knowledge resonates with Marx's notion that all economics is the economics of time. His labour theory of value defines value as socially necessary labour time. Commodities have values because they absorb the productive time of society. For an important paper on cultural deprivation see Bernstein, 'Education Cannot Compensate for Society', in B.R. Cosin *et al.* (eds), *School and Society*, 2nd ed., Routledge & Kegan Paul, 1977, p. 65.

16 Considerable work on the origins of 'the testing movement' has been done by American historians. Edgar Gumbert and Joel Spring, for example, have argued that the development of IQ tests were socially biased from the beginning, both in terms of the way they were validated and in terms of the presuppositions the test constructor had of society. The measurement of intelligence reflected the social values of the testers. The movement's fundamental premises were that all men were not born equal, nor was it possible to make them equal. It followed that only the most intelligent should rule. Democracy thus came to be redefined as that form of organization which allowed freedom to men of ability to attain power. The testing movement, then, was based on the fatalistic presupposition that little could be done through education to eradicate social and racial barriers. Education could, however, help in the making of an efficient social machine — it could properly classify children according to their future social positions. The fact that classification paralleled class and racial lines did not bother the testers. Both Edward Thorndike and Lewis Terman had these elitist ideas; their conception of intelligence (as the ability to solve technological and scientific problems) fitted nicely the 'efficient society' model. 'Intelligence' was seen as the ability to function in modern corporate forms of activity such as the army, the factory and the school (see Gumbert and Spring, *The Super-school and the Superstate: American Education in the Twentieth Century*, Wiley, 1974). Besides analysing the assumptions of the testing movement, and how the process of classifying and channelling students towards a specific social role in a 'efficient' society became one of the major social purposes of the school, the authors also discuss youth and the custodial role of the school, de-schooling and the changing needs of corporate capitalism. The most comprehensive critique of the heritability of IQ is Leon Kamin, *The Science and Politics of IQ*, Penguin, 1977. But I do not wish to give the impression that the origins of education have been researched only in America. For a history of British education see, for example, Brian Simon, *Studies*

in the History of Education, 3 vols, Lawrence & Wishart, 1960.
17 See 'Response to my Critics', in the second edition of Ollman's *Alienation*, pp. 272–3.

10 Current Developments: The Primacy of the Mode of Production

1 Louis Althusser, *For Marx*, Penguin, 1969, p. 35; Althusser and Etienne Balibar, *Reading Capital*, New Left Books, 1970, p. 17.
2 Louis Althusser, *Lenin and Philosophy and Other Essays*, New Left Books, 1971. It also appears in B.R. Cosin (ed.), *Education: Structure and Society*, Penguin Books, 1972.
3 For Althusser the role that human individuals play in history as *individuals* is that of the embodiments of the process, not as its subjects. This does not mean that he denies the role of political organization or activity. Althusser stresses that there is no such thing as the individual as such, but that each mode of production produces its own mode of individuality. For the connection of this concept of history as a process without a subject, and the theory of ideology, see Alex Callinicos, *Althusser's Marxism*, Pluto Press, 1976, p. 66.
4 'The pragmatic liberal philosophy of Dewey and Hook operationalized within a bureaucratic structure, in effect, turned every moral question into a tactical survival problem. Pragmatism, as a philosophy, was admirably suited to facilitating a growing bureaucratic state ... American pragmatic liberalism, when stripped of its restraining humanitarian ethic and reduced to a cold, hard operationalism, came dangerously close to a Fascist perspective on thought and action' (Clarence Karier, *Shaping the American Educational State*, Free Press, 1975, p. 82–3).
5 C.J. Karier, P. Violas and J. Spring, *Roots of Crisis*, Rand McNally, 1973, p. 99.
6 Ibid., p. 123.
7 Ibid., p. 4.
8 Ibid., p. 5.
9 Routledge & Kegan Paul, 1976.
10 Braverman's book is an outstanding contribution to a much neglected area: the labour process. He remarks: 'there is no continuing body of work in the Marxist tradition dealing with the capitalist mode of production in the manner in which Marx treated it in the first volume of *Capital*' (*Labour and Monopoly Capitalism*, Monthly Review Press, 1974, p. 9).
11 *Scientific Management*, New York and London, 1947.

12 Braverman, op. cit., p. 439. Other useful books on work include Huw Beynon, *Working for Ford*, Penguin, 1973; *The Labour Process and Class Strategies*, Conference of Socialist Economists Pamphlet no. 1 (obtainable from Department of Economics, Birkbeck College, 7–15 Gresse Street, London W1P 1PA); André Gortz (ed.), *Essays on the Division of Labour*, Harvester Press, 1976. An essay by Gortz, 'Technical Intelligence and the Capitalist Division of Labour', appears in Michael F.D. Young and Geoff Whitty (eds), *Society, State and Schooling*, Falmer Press, 1977.

11 The Political Economy of Education: Schooling in Capitalist Society

1 Note the change between 1971 and 1977 in the contents of the 'Schooling and Society' Course at the Open University. In the original course, most of the material was based on symbolic interactionist and phenomenological perspectives. Perhaps the key work of such an approach was P.L. Berger and T. Luckmann, *The Social Construction of Reality*, Penguin, 1967. We now have a new approach which draws heavily upon political economy; see, for example, Roger Dale, Geoff Esland and Madeleine MacDonald (eds), *Schooling and Capitalism*, Routledge & Kegan Paul, 1976.
2 *Schooling in Capitalist America*, Routledge & Kegan Paul, 1976, p. 151.
3 Ibid., p. 222.
4 Ibid., p. 224.
5 Ibid., p. 255.
6 Gintis made a radical critique of Ivan Illich's *Deschooling Society* as early as 1972 (see ch. 9, nn. 11 and 12 of this book). Gintis's article, 'Towards a Political Economy of Education' appears in Ian Lister (ed.), *Deschooling: A Reader*, Cambridge University Press, 1974, and also in *Schooling and Capitalism*, pp. 8–20.
7 Op. cit., p. 275.
8 Ibid., p. 55.
9 For an excellent introduction which relates Gramsci's thought to that of Luxemburg, Lukács and Lenin, see Carl Boggs, *Gramsci's Marxism*, Pluto Press, 1976.
10 Op. cit., p. 35.
11 Ibid., p. 119.
12 Ibid., p. 70.
13 Ibid., p. 135.
14 Ibid., p. 214.
15 For an extensive critique of statistics see the following: Aaron V.

Cicourel, *Method and Measurement*, Free Press, 1964: Jack D. Douglas, *The Social Meanings of Suicide*, Princeton University Press, 1967. See also David Triesman, 'The Radical Use of Official Data', in Nigel Armistead (ed.), *Reconstructing Social Psychology*, Penguin, 1974; Barry Hindess, *The Use of Official Statistics in Sociology*, Macmillan, 1973.

[16] Op. cit., p. 302.
[17] Ibid., p. 42.
[18] Ibid., p. 196.
[19] Ibid., p. 21.
[20] Ibid., p. 143.
[21] Ibid., p. 71.
[22] Ibid., p. 277.
[23] Ibid., p. 104.
[24] Ibid., p. 265.
[25] Ibid., p. 266.
[26] I draw this term from Zygmunt Bauman, *Towards a Critical Sociology*, Routledge & Kegan Paul, 1976. 'Durksonianism' is his term for positivism, the science of unfreedom.
[27] Op. cit. p. 47.
[28] Ibid., p. 130.
[29] Ibid., p. 127, my emphasis.
[30] Ibid., p. 128.
[31] Ibid., p. 130.
[32] Ibid., p. 151.
[33] Ibid., p. 179.
[34] Ibid., p. 132.
[35] Ibid., p. 236.
[36] Ibid., p. 253.
[37] Ibid., p. 282.

12 Summary and Conclusions

[1] These sociologists were shaped by the meritocratic tradition, and their sociological perspective led them to an empiricist view of class. That is to say, they understood class not as a dynamic relationship, but as a number of variables correlated with income. In the 1950s and 1960s the validity of grammar schools and streaming were largely unquestioned. The achievement of these sociologists of education was that they undermined these presuppositions (symbolized by the '11 plus' IQ test), and initiated the campaign for comprehensive schools. They held the view that working-class children had certain deficiencies and that their language and culture must be compensated.

Notes

But the policies of comprehensive and compensatory education failed to eradicate the inequalities in our society. Inequality cannot be abolished through education; the determinants of inequality lie elsewhere. See Christopher Jenks, *Inequality*, Peregrine, 1975.

2 It has been argued, recently, that particular agencies constructed a coalition in post-war Britain. In the 1960s these agencies acquired a hegemony over educational policy. The three elements in the alliance were the Labour Party, sociologists of education (academics who were often outside the party) and teachers within their professional organizations. It is characteristic of the Labour Party that it believes in the sanctity of Parliament, and the notion that the State is neutral. These untheorized assumptions influence its policies. It is not surprising that the party adopted a Fabian, piecemeal, social-engineering model. See Dan Finn, Neil Grant and Richard Johnson, 'Social Democracy, Education and the Crisis', in *On Ideology*, Working Papers in Cultural Studies, no. 10, 1977. Considerable work needs to be done along these lines on the ideology of educational systems and their particular histories.

3 'Social Reality and Consciousness', in J.D. Colfax and J.L. Roach (eds), *Radical Sociology*, Basic Books, 1971, p. 161.

4 We still have no adequate concept of the State. In contrast to Bowles and Gintis, who say little about the class struggle and ignore the State, Nicos Poulantzas is developing a theory of class and State, and of the inter-relationship between social formations, during a period of growing hegemony of US capital in Europe. For the relation between classes and the State, questions concerning hegemony and the dominant ideology, see Poulantzas, *Political Power and Social Classes*, New Left Books, 1973. For the notion of the educational system as an ideological State apparatus reproducing the cardinal distinction between mental and manual labour, see his *Classes in Contemporary Capitalism*, New Left Books, 1975.

5 I am thinking of Althusser, who suggests that every society is constituted by levels, groups of practices. The infrastructure, or economic base, consists of the means of production, the productive forces, and the relations of production. The superstructure consists of the State and its institutions (the repressive and ideological State apparatuses), and ideology. The superstructure has 'relative autonomy' in its relation to the base, and acts reciprocally on it. There is not just one contradiction (between labour and capital); in the structural totality there is the possibility of a multiplicity of contradictions which may be related to each other in complex ways. A situation like the 1917 Revolution, then, depended on an accumulation of contradictions that fused. Focus is thus taken away from the economy

217

as the sole location of contradiction, as there may be other contradictions internal to particular levels of the social formation. For
sympathetic introductions to Althusser's project see Robin Black-
burn and Gareth Stedman Jones, 'Louis Althusser and the Struggle
for Marxism', in Dick Howard and Karl Klare (eds), *The Unknown
Dimension*, Basic Books, 1972, which contains excellent studies of
European Marxists since Lenin. See also Goran Therborn, *Science,
Class and Society*, New Left Books, 1976, pp. 50–60.

6 One of the problems when we study ideas is: How does one prevent
the study of ideology (which can be a *critique* of idealism) from
itself becoming idealism? At present there is no wholly satisfactory
theory of ideology. Althusser, for example, has constructed a new
theory of ideology. He regards it as a set of illusory representations
of reality expressing the imaginary relationship of men to their
conditions of existence, and inherent in their immediate experience.
Ideology is the unconscious medium of lived experience, a lived
medium of delusion. It is permanent and immutable because its
function, in all human societies, is to bind people together. Ideology,
the ensemble of false beliefs and errors, constitutes individuals as
imaginary 'subjects' of society, so as to assure their real subjection
to the social order as blind supports. In every period of history,
ideology adapts people to the objective positions allocated them by
the dominant mode of production. Because it gives vital social
cohesion, 'historical materialism cannot conceive that even a communist society could ever do without ideology' (L. Althusser, *For
Marx*, Penguin, 1969, p. 232). To what extent is this Althusserian
approach to ideology in conceptual opposition to the more familiar
Marxist notion? See P.Q. Hirst, *Problems and Advances in the Theory
of Ideology*, Communist University of Cambridge Pamphlet, 1975;
P.Q. Hirst, 'Althusser's Theory of Ideology', *Economy and Society*,
5(4), November 1976. It appears that Barry Hindess and Paul Q.
Hirst now reject class analysis. They argue that the economic,
political and cultural phenomena are completely autonomous; that
the relations between them are contingent and not amenable to class
analysis. For critical readings of several important theorists of
ideology such as Lukács, Gramsci, Althusser and Poulantzas, see
On Ideology, Working Papers in Cultural Studies, no. 10, 1977.

7 The best-known theoretical anti-humanist (which has nothing to
do with humanitarianism) is Althusser. His highly significant contributions have encountered heavy criticism. Criticisms of Althusser
can be found in Perry Anderson, *Considerations on Western Marxism*,
New Left Books, 1977. Critical texts by Norman Geras and André
Glucksman appear in *Western Marxism: A Critical Reader*, New Left
Books, 1977. See also Michael Erben and Denis Gleeson, 'Education

as Reproduction' in Michael F. D. Young and Geoff Whitty (eds), *Society, State and Schooling*, Falmer Press, 1977. It should be noted that Althusser is rigorously critical of his own work – as is shown by *Essays in Self-Criticism*, New Left Books, 1976.

8 See, for example, Alfred Sohn-Rethel, 'Mental and Manual Labour in Marxism', in Paul Walton and Stuart Hall (eds), *Situating Marx*, Chaucer Pub. Co., 1972; 'Intellectual and Manual Labour', in *Radical Philosophy*, 6, winter 1973.

9 We need to know more about how capitalist societies reproduce themselves. In a short book like this I have had to be selective and have omitted such important theories of social reproduction as those of Bernstein and Bourdieu. See, for example, the paper 'Class and Pedagogies: Visible and Invisible', in Basil Bernstein, *Class, Codes and Control*, vol. 3, Routledge & Kegan Paul, 1975; Pierre Bourdieu and Jean-Claude Passeron, *Reproduction: In Education, Society and Culture*, Sage Publications, 1977. Another book that deals with how social formations tend to reproduce themselves, different modes of domination, and a theory of symbolic power, is Pierre Bourdieu, *Outline of a Theory of Practice*, Cambridge University Press, 1977. An essay by Bourdieu on symbolic power can be found in Denis Gleeson (ed.), *Identity and Structure: Issues in the Sociology of Education*, Nafferton Books, Nafferton, Driffield, 1977.

10 According to Bowles and Gintis, the education system mirrors the economy. While they believe in a theory of correspondence, which results in a crude reductionism, I argue that there *is* some autonomy between the agents of capital and the requirements of the labour market. What we need to know is: what, precisely, are the articulations between the family, schooling, industry and the State? I want to suggest that is is now necessary to focus on those aspects of Marxist theory which are underdeveloped in the work of Bowles and Gintis. There is a necessity for theorization in the 'regions' of ideology, reproduction, class and State.

Index

221

Index